Signature Tastes
of
SAN ANTONIO

SMOKE ALARM

MEDIA

To Jennifer, who is the embodiment of what every Texas girl should aspire to be. You can take the girl out of Texas, but you can't take Texas out of the girl.

To the restaurants, for making these incredible recipes available, and constantly improving them so that we can do a second edition.

Welcome to San Antonio photography from Wikipedia

To others unnamed, because my memory is as short as my hair.

gnaturetastes.com and on Facebook: Smok

Layout by Steven W. Siler

Photography by Rosalie Anne Fradella and team, except where noted

Library of Congress Control Number: 2010914234

Siler, Steven W.

Signature Tastes of San Antonio: Favorite Recipes from our Local Kitchens

ISBN 978-1-927458-09-9

1. Restaurants Texas-San Antonio-Guidebooks. 2. Cookery-Texas-San Antonio

Printed in the United States of America

This book is dedicated to the emergency responders...

From the first frantic call to 9-1-1
To the comforting hands at the E.D.
You give your time...

away from spouses,
away from friends,
away from children,
And yes, even from meals...

To assure all of us:

"Tonight, I will make it better for you
no matter what,
I will watch over you..."

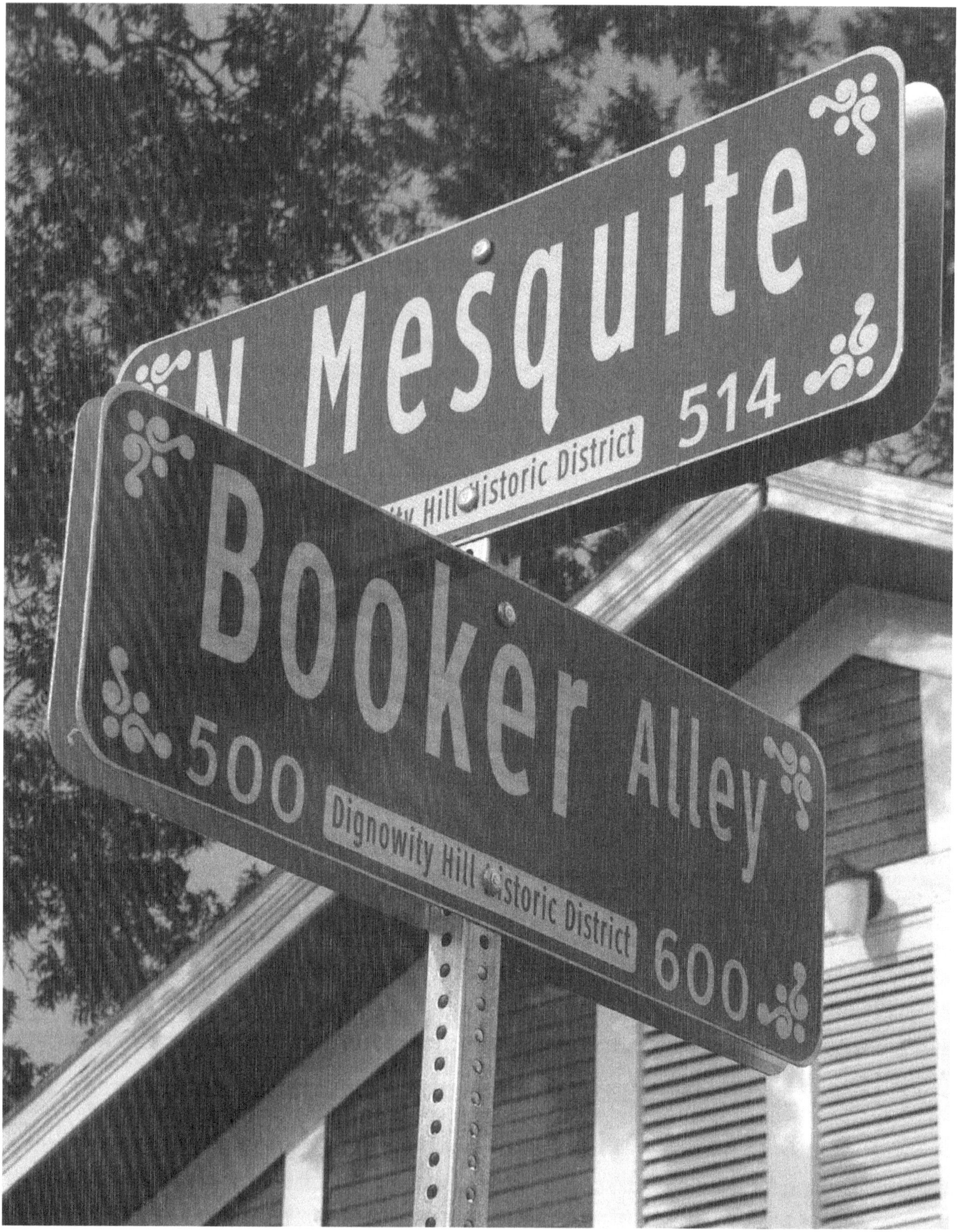
N Mesquite
514
Booker Alley
500
Dignowity Hill
600

I have always wondered if anyone really reads the Table of Contents. Now since this is a cookbook, I should have organized everything under its proper heading, like soups, pasta, desserts and the like. This is not just a cookbook as much as a Culinary Postcard; a celebration of the city itself...about the eateries, fine dining, casual dining, bars, drive -ins, and of course, the people.

Signature Tastes of SAN ANTONIO

Welcome to San Antonio: The River City..7

The Eateries...

Signature Tastes of SAN ANTONIO

There have been many ideas of what Texas is, what it should become, and we are not all in agreement. But I'd like to ask each of you what it is you value so highly that you are willing to fight and possibly die for. We will call that Texas

William Travis, **The Alamo**

Welcome to San Antonio! The fastest-growing of the largest cities in the United States in the past decade, San Antonio is home to 1.3 million people, making it both

the second most populous city in Texas and the seventh most populous city in the whole country. In addition to its residents, at least 26 million tourists visit each year, drawn by the many popular attractions, including the downtown area's River Walk, SeaWorld, a theme park for special-needs children called Morgan's

WELCOME TO SAN ANTONIO
STACEY BREITBERG, EDITOR-AT-LARGE

Wonderland, and, of course, the Alamo. The Alamo is actually the entire state's top tourist attraction, and is so widely visited that San Antonio is often referred to as "Alamo City".

Originally, the area around the San Antonio River Valley was inhabited by Native Americans who called it "Yanaguana" – "refreshing waters". Then, in 1691, a group of Spanish explorers and missionaries arrived at the river and its Native settlement, which they called San Antonio in honor of St. Anthony of Padua, whose

feast day is on June 13th, the day they had arrived. The following couple of decades saw the beginnings of Spanish settlement in the area, and in the spring of 1718 the Mission San Antonio de Valero – the Mission later known as the Alamo – was founded, along with the establishment of what eventually became the most impor-

tant town in Spanish Texas, Presidio San Antonio de Béjar. The following winter, a proposal was made to the king of Spain to move 400 families from the Canary Islands, Galicia, or Havana to the province of Texas. The proposal was approved, and by the summer of 1730 25 families had reached Cuba and 10 more had gotten as far as Veracruz when orders to stop arrived from Spain. Those already in Veracruz, however, continued, led by Juan Leal Goraz, and arrived in the Presidio San Antonio de Valero in March of 1731, by which time marriages had increased their numbers to a total of 56 people. That party of immigrants formed the first regularly organized civil government in Texas, and to this day some of the oldest families in San Antonio can trace their lineage back to those Canary Islanders. San Antonio continued to grow, becoming the largest Spanish settlement in Texas. After the

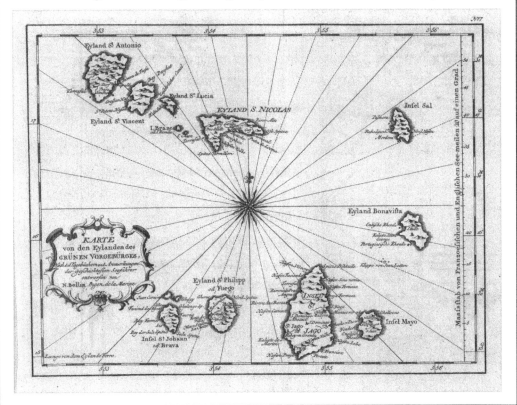

WELCOME TO SAN ANTONIO
STACEY BREITBERG, EDITOR-AT-LARGE

abolishment of the Mexican Constitution of 1824, a series of battles and widespread violence throughout many Mexican states began, and in the next ten years the Texian Army was successful in forcing Mexican soldiers out of the settlements east of San Antonio and then, in 1835, recaptured San Antonio itself from the command of Santa Anna's brother-in-law, General Martin Perfecto de Cos. However, the following spring, Santa Anna himself

marched on San Antonio, while a volunteer force led by James C. Neill occupied the then-deserted mission. William Barrett Travel and James Bowie then took over the

defense of the mission, and were leading its defense during the Battle of the Alamo, which took place from February 23rd – March 6th, 1836. The Texians were outnumbered, and ultimately defeated and killed, which led to them being seen as martyrs for the cause of Texas freedom; "Remember the Alamo" became the rallying cry for the Texian Army, and they eventually defeated Santa Anna's army. Finally, almost a decade later in 1845, the United States annexed Texas, including it as a state in the Union, which led to the Mexican-American War; the war devastated San Antonio and reduced its population by nearly two-thirds, leav-

Signature Tastes of SAN ANTONIO

ing only 800 inhabitants by its end. The city bounced back quickly, however, and by 1860 and the start of the Civil War, the population had grown to nearly 15,000.

Post-Civil War, San Antonio was a prosperous center of the cattle industry, and although it was still very much a frontier city, it developed a reputation as being exotic and beautiful, culturally mixed and strange in ways similar to New Orleans. In 1877 the railroad reached the city, taking it out of the frontier and into American society, and by the early 1900s the downtown streets were widened to accommodate

street cars, modern traffic, and modern city life – growth which also unfortunately destroyed many historic buildings. Today, the city is a huge, prosperous metropolis. Much of its economy

WELCOME TO SAN ANTONIO

STACEY BREITBERG, EDITOR-AT-LARGE

stems from the financial services industry, government, health care, and – of course – tourism; the defense industry is also a huge part of the city, which is home to one of

the largest military concentrations in the country. In addition to its historic sites and large tourist attractions, the city hosts one of the largest annual rodeos in the country, and is home to beautiful public parks, fine museums – including the McNay Art Museum, which was Texas' first museum of modern art – as well as offering plenty of traditional folklorico

and flamenco music during a variety of outdoor festivals and fiesta nights. San Antonio is also famous for its food – besides being the birthplace of Fritos and Cheetos, the

city claims to be the originator of chili, first introducing it at their "San Antonio Chili Stand" at the 1893 Columbian Exposition in Chicago. Today, not only can you still find a wide variety of chili when you visit, you'll also find some of the best Tex-Mex cuisine in the country. Mexican restaurants are also well represented – not to mention inexpensive -- with

more choices than you can count. While you might expect tamales, tacos, and fajitas, you might not expect traditional German fare – the Germanic influence in the city is, *however, undeniable, giving you the chance to sample hearty potato salads, a variety of wursts and sausages, and all Germanic specialties in between, including delicious locally-microbrewed beers. You'll also find plenty of traditional Texas barbecue, especially juicy, pit-smoked brisket. Thanks to San Antonio's*

military bases, Asian cuisine is also strongly represented among the city's restaurants, with excellent Thai, Korean, Vietnamese, and Japanese meals to satisfy your cravings. Food trucks are also making an entrance, with a citywide Food Truck Pilot Program that was rolled out this year; currently, a wide array of food trucks can be found in various city parks and public centers throughout the week, on a rotating schedule. If a leisurely afternoon visit to an outdoor market is your thing, then The Market Square is a must-visit. Comprised of three markets: a Farmers Market, El Mercado – the largest Mexican market outside of Mexico -- and Produce Row; it has a little bit of everything, from fresh vegetables for your kitchen to crafts and gifts to a delicious meal. Large, well-attended farmers markets can also be found almost every day of the week in various locations throughout the city. To finish off your day, you can

even sample a glass or two of some excellent, locally-brewed bourbons and whiskies, from a variety of local distilleries. Whether you come for chili and authentic tacos, a history lesson, or any of the other fine foods and attractions on offer, you're certain to find something to love in San Antonio.

WELCOME TO SAN ANTONIO
STACEY BREITBERG, EDITOR-AT-LARGE

RECIPES
& RESTAURANTS

Hunan Salmon

20nine Restaurant & Wine Bar specializes in wine country cuisine, using only the finest ingredients. Executive Chef Scott Boone has created an eclectic cuisine to achieve flavorful wine pairings. The menu selections include duck, salmon, pork, and steak entrees. Our European sized portions enable our guests to save room for dessert. Changing the menu seasonally allows Chef Stefan to showcase seasonal fruits, vegetables, and meats.

Signature Tastes of SAN ANTONIO

2 tbsp. soy sauce
1 tbsp. Chinese oyster sauce
2 tsp. oriental chili paste
2 tsp. tomato paste
1 C. clam juice
3 tbsp. cornstarch
¼ tsp. sugar
1 lb. salmon filet, boned, skinned, cubed
2 tbsp. chili powder
¼ C. peanut oil
½ lemon, for juice
2 scallions, chopped
2 cloves garlic, minced
1 in. ginger root minced
½ C. pumpkin seeds, toasted
4 C. hot cooked rice

1. In a bowl, whisk together the soy sauce, oyster sauce, chili paste, tomato paste, clam juice, 2 tsp. of the cornstarch, the sugar, and lemon juice. Set aside.

2. Toss the salmon in the remaining cornstarch mixed with the chili powder. Heat a large wok until smoking. Add the peanut oil and gently stir fry the salmon, in 2 batches, until its surface is lightly browned and crisp, about 2 minutes. Remove the salmon with a slotted spoon to a strainer or colander to drain. Pour off all but a thin film of the oil.

3. Add the scallions, garlic and ginger root and stir fry 10 seconds. Return the salmon, add the reserved liquid and simmer until lightly thickened. Toss in the pumpkin seeds. Serve over rice. Makes 4 servings.

2ONINE RESTAURANT AND WINE BAR
255 E BASSE RD STE 940 SAN ANTONIO, TX

"If more of us valued food and cheer above hoarded gold, it would be a much merrier world."
J.R.R. Tolkien

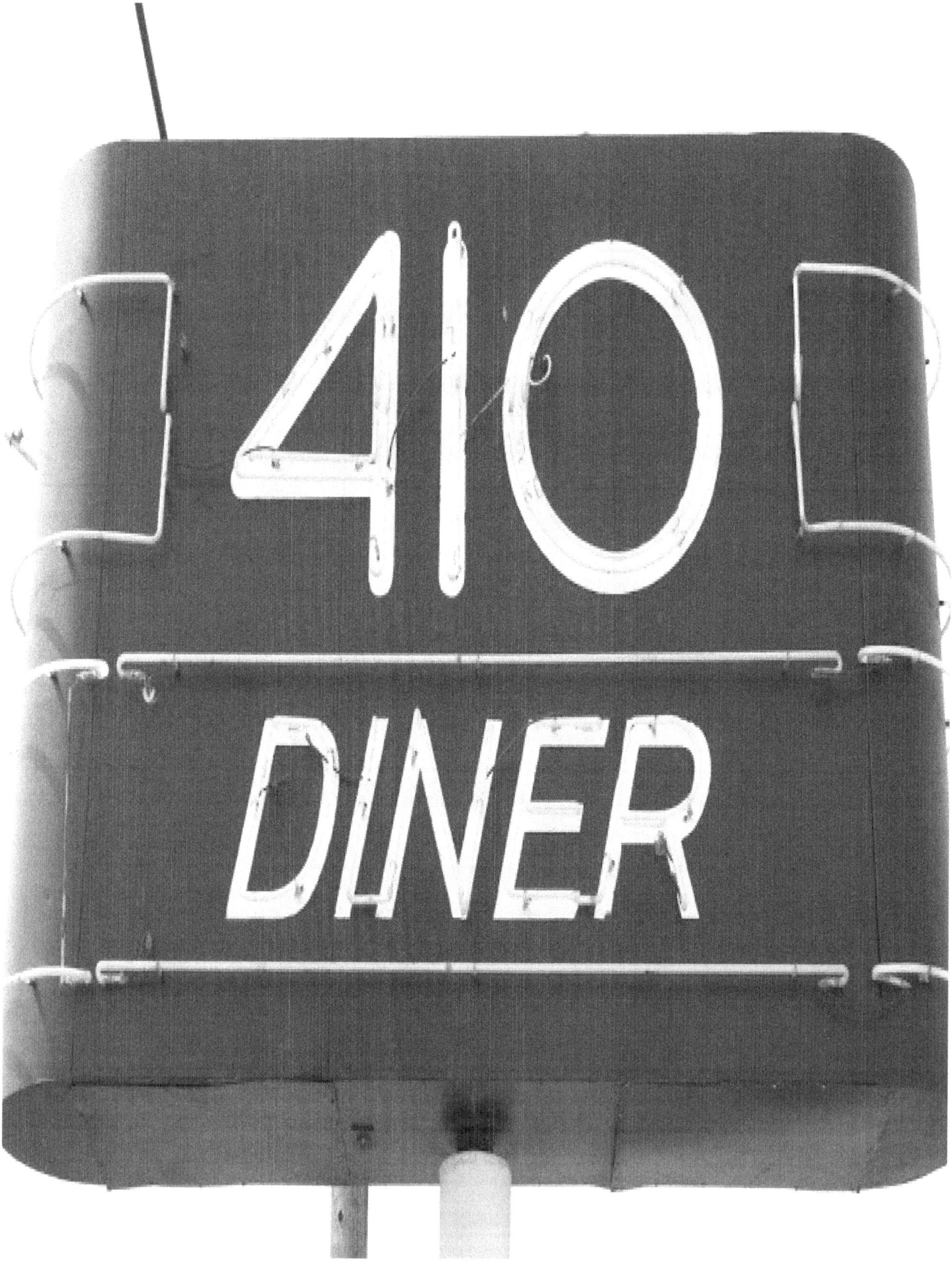
410
DINER

Signature Tastes of SAN ANTONIO

Our menu features fresh catfish and shrimp, several prime steaks and amazing pork chops prepared fresh daily. We also offer creative chicken and fresh fish dishes, as well as tasty vegetable selections. All prepared with keen attention to perfect preparation. All of our menu items are prepared fresh daily following our own homemade recipes.

4 skinless, boneless chicken breasts
1 tsp. olive oil
½ tsp. onion powder
1 pinch salt
1 pinch ground black pepper
2 avocados - peeled, pitted and sliced
2 ripe tomatoes, sliced
1 (8 oz.) package Monterey Jack cheese, cut into 10 slices

1. Preheat oven to 350 degrees F (175 degrees C).

2. Warm oil in skillet and add chicken and onion. Cook 15 minutes or until chicken is browned and just about done. Add salt and pepper to taste.

3. Place chicken on cookie sheet and top each breast with 1 to 2 slices of tomato and 2 to 3 slices of cheese.

4. Place in oven for 10 to 15 minutes, until cheese melts. Remove from oven, add 2 to 3 slices of avocado on top of each breast, and serve immediately.

8315 BROADWAY SAN ANTONIO, TX
410 DINER

"Business is never so healthy as when, like a chicken, it must do a certain amount of scratching around for what it gets."
Henry Ford

19

VEGGIE SPINACH QUESADILLAS

With a blend of contemporary and cool style wrapped in wall to wall windows that create a perfect view of the beautiful Alamo, the 1909 Bar and Bistro offers the perfect ambiance for any occasion. Located inside of the luxurious Hotel Indigo at the Alamo inside of the historical Gibbs Building at the corner of Houston St and Alamo Plaza, the 1909 Bar and Bistro offers a vast menu sure to tantalize the most critical of taste buds.

4 C. fresh baby spinach
4 green onions, chopped
1 small tomato, chopped
2 tbsp. lemon juice
1 tsp. ground cumin
¼ tsp. garlic powder
1 C. (4 oz) shredded
reduced-fat Monterey
Jack cheese or Mexican
cheese blend
¼ C. reduced-fat ricotta
cheese
6 flour tortillas (6 in.)
¼ C. fat-free sour cream

1. In a large nonstick skillet, cook the spinach, onions, tomato, lemon juice, cumin and garlic powder over medium heat until spinach is wilted. Remove from the heat; stir in cheeses.

2. Divide spinach mixture evenly among three tortillas. Top with remaining tortillas. Cook in a large skillet coated with cooking spray over low heat for 1-2 minutes on each side or until heated through.

3. Cut each quesadilla into four wedges. Serve with sour cream. Yield: 6 servings.

105 N. ALAMO PLAZA, IN THE HOTEL INDIGO, SAN ANTONIO, TX

1909 BAR & BISTRO

"Without civilization, we would not turn into animals, but vegetables."
Mason Cooley

CHICKEN FRIED BREAST

Signature Taste of SAN ANTONIO

A San Antonio institution for 73 years, Earl Abel's offers an extensive breakfast menu including homemade biscuits, omelets and freshly-squeezed orange juice. The lunch and dinner menu includes seafood, steaks, chicken fried steaks and many other traditional comfort foods, all prepared fresh daily. And you cannot leave the restaurant without one of their many baked desserts. As Earl Abel himself said, "Eat Here and Diet Home."

2 tbsp. light soy sauce
2 tbsp. sweet chilli sauce
2 tbsp. oyster sauce
2 tbsp. peanut oil
600g chicken breast fillets, trimmed, thinly sliced
1 brown onion, cut into thin wedges
2 garlic cloves, crushed
2 eggs, lightly beaten
3 C. cold cooked rice
1 C. Thai basil leaves
4 green onions, sliced diagonally
¼ C. fried shallots

1. Combine soy sauce, sweet chilli sauce and oyster sauce in a small bowl. Set aside. Heat a wok over high heat until hot. Add 3 teaspoons oil and swirl to coat. Add half the chicken and stir-fry for 2 minutes or until browned. Transfer to a plate. Repeat with oil and remaining chicken.

2. Add remaining 2 teaspoons oil and onion to wok. Stir-fry for 2 to 3 minutes or until golden. Add garlic and stir-fry for 30 seconds. Add egg and rice. Stir-fry for 2 to 3 minutes or until egg is well combined with rice.

3. Return chicken to wok. Add soy sauce mixture, basil and green onions. Stir-fry for 1 to 2 minutes or until well combined. Spoon into bowls. Sprinkle with fried shallots and serve.

17605 INTERSTATE 35 N SCHERTZ, TX

ABEL'S DINER

"I make a good fried chicken."
Norah Jones

23

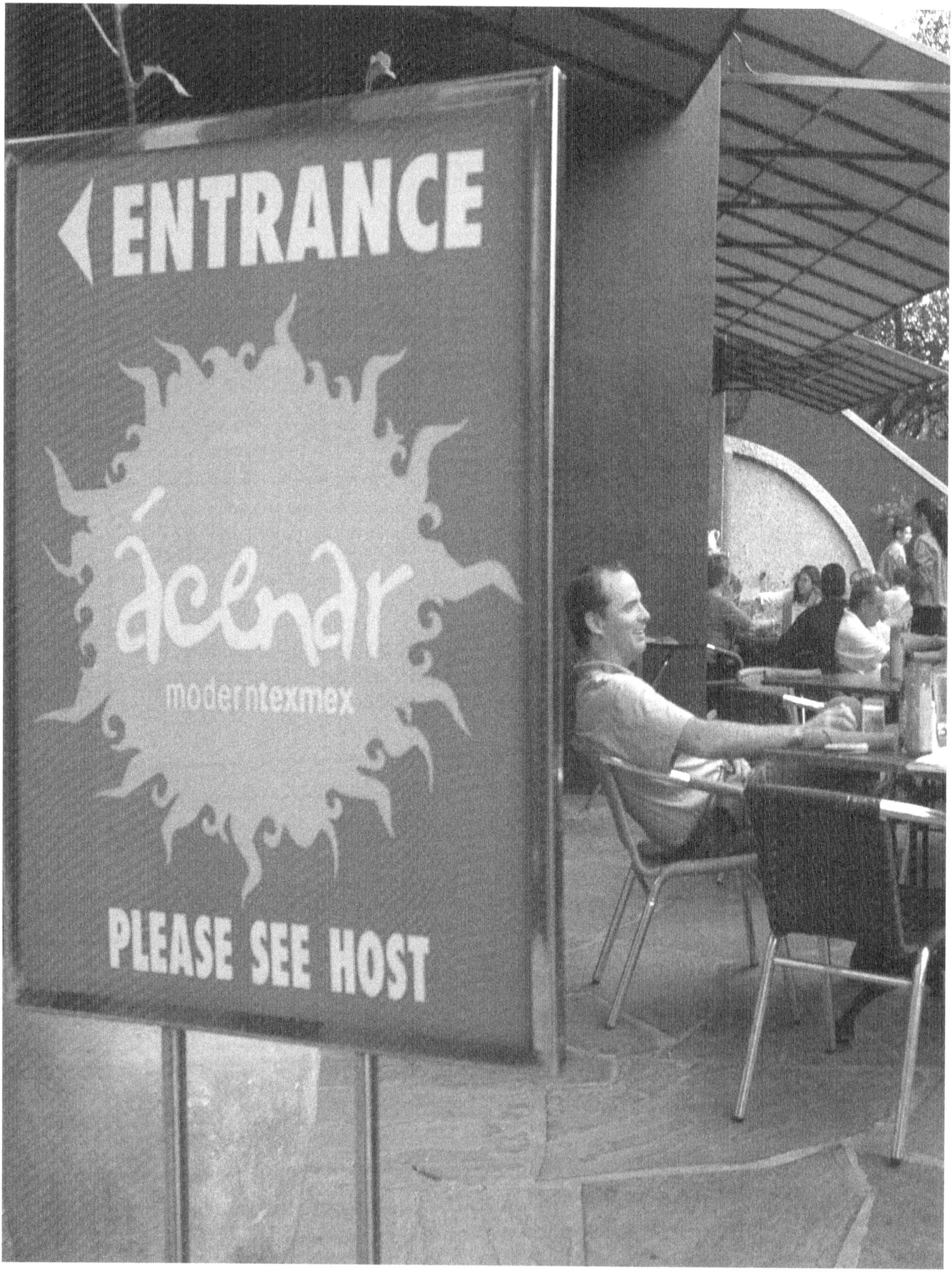
ENTRANCE
moderntexmex
PLEASE SEE HOST

CRAB TING TACOS

Lisa Wong (of Rosario's fame) launches the most innovative contemporary Mexican restaurant and bar on San Antonio's River Walk. Patrons will enjoy Texas regional Mexican dishes along with tantalizing tastes inspired by the history and heritage of Mexico and Texas. The combination of years of experience in the preparation of quality food "with the right Sazon and artistic panache" that Lisa brings to the table, is the talk of the town. Ácenar features indoor and outdoor patio dining for lunch and dinner... or if you're in the mood for socializing over extraordinary cocktails, join your friends and colleagues at the Houston street level bar, Átomar!

Signature Tastes of SAN ANTONIO

4 roma tomatoes, halved, seeded, and sliced
1 large garlic clove, minced
2 large jalapeño chiles, halved, seeded, and sliced, divided
½ C. fresh cilantro leaves, divided
3 tbsp. fresh lime juice
kosher salt and freshly ground black pepper
1 tsp. olive oil
½ C. chopped onion
8 oz. shelled cooked crab
8 taco shells or tortillas
1 C. iceberg lettuce, thinly sliced
1 C. shredded jack or cheddar cheese
1 avocado, thinly sliced
¼ C. chopped green onion

1. Preheat oven to 350°.

2. Put tomatoes, garlic, half of the jalapeño, ¼ cup cilantro, and the lime juice in a food processor and pulse a few times to chop.

3. Add salt and pepper to taste. Set salsa aside. In a large skillet, heat oil over medium heat. Sauté onion and remaining jalapeño until soft, 4 minutes.

4. Add crab and cook just until crab is warm, about 2 minutes. Put taco shells or tortillas on a baking pan and warm in oven, about 3 minutes. Arrange on a platter and fill with crab mixture, dividing evenly.

5. Top crab with lettuce, cheese, and avocado.

6. Sprinkle tacos with green onion and remaining ¼ cup cilantro. Serve immediately, with salsa on the side or on top.

146 E HOUSTON ST, SAN ANTONIO, TX

ÁCENAR

"After a good dinner one can forgive anybody, even one's own relatives."
Oscar Wilde

MUSHROOM BURGER

Signature Tastes of SAN ANTONIO

We are known for our Texas-Style Burgers and Beer and for being one of the best places to eat in San Antonio, TX! Although the staple side with great hamburgers is generally French Fries, we think you should pick the perfect accompaniment for your meal. Sides include classic French fries, tator tots, onion rings, chili cheese fries, or bacon cheese fries. We've thought about your little dillos, too. Our burgers and cheeseburgers become miniaturized to a ⅓ pound for smaller hands. Gooey grilled cheese sandwiches are an option for the small one as well.

2 tbsp. vegetable oil
1 onion, diced
1 clove garlic, minced
3 green onions, diced
½ tsp. cumin
¾ C. diced fresh mushrooms
1 15-oz can pinto beans
1 tsp. parsley
salt and pepper to taste
oil for frying

1. Sautee the onions and garlic in olive oil for 3 to 5 minutes, until onions are soft. Add the green onions, cumin and mushrooms and cook for another 5 minutes, until mushrooms are cooked. Set aside.

2. Mash the beans with a fork or a potato masher, or process in a food processor until well mashed.

3. Add the mushrooms to the beans and add parsley, salt and pepper. Stir until well combined.

4. Shape the mixture into patties. Heat about two tablespoons of olive oil and cook each patty until the veggie burgers are done, about 3 minutes on each side.

1423 McCullough Avenue, San Antonio, TX

ARMADILLO'S

"I would rather be having a burger and beers with my mates but I can't do that when I know I've got to dance."
Michael Flatley

Asia Kitchen

The Art of
Exceptional
Thai Cuisine

Tord Mun Pla (Fish Cake)

Our customers who travel to Thailand come back to us because our food is "better than the original". Our chef Sally has created her own recipes that blend delectable Oriental flavors into unique dishes that will astound your taste buds. You must try her signature dishes -- Pad Thai and Thai salads --to really experience the taste of Thai.

8 oz. fish paste
½ egg (beaten)
2 tbsp. Thai red curry paste (Mae Ploy brand or Maesri brand)
5 snake beans/long beans (thinly sliced)
5 kaffir lime leaves (cut into fine thin strips)

1. In a small bowl, mix all the ingredients above to form a smooth fish paste. Make sure the red curry paste is well blended with the rest of the ingredients.

2. Heat up a pot of oil. Wet your hands and pick up the fish paste (about the size of a ping pong ball). Use your fingers and palms to flatten it and make it into a patty.

3. Drop it into the cooking oil and fry till golden brown. Repeat the same for the rest of the fish paste. Alternatively, you can prepare all the fish aste first and then deep fry all of them at once.

4. Serve the fish cakes hot with Thai sweet chili sauce and sliced fresh cucumber. (Please refer to my Thai Fried Chicken recipe and find out how I dressed up store-bought Thai chili sauce.)

1739 SW Loop 410, San Antonio, TX

Asia Kitchen

"Part of the secret of success in life is to eat what you like and let the food fight it out inside."
Mark Twain

TOSTONES WITH MOJO

Selected Azuca Nuevo Latino on the recommendation of a friend for our office Holiday luncheon. The atmosphere was great - decorated with unusual and beautiful blown glass creations from a neighboring business. The staff was very courteous and helpful and the waiters kept everyone's glass full throughout the meal. The menu featured a wide variety of interesting item, from safe items to the exotic, and was a nice change from the usual Tex-Mex fare served throughout San Antonio, Texas.

Signature Tastes of **SAN ANTONIO**

6 fresh garlic cloves, minced
1 tbsp. fresh lemon juice
¾ C. extra virgin olive oil
1 tsp. salt
⅛ tsp. freshly ground pepper
4 green plantain, peeled and sliced into six-eight pcs.
½ qt. canola oil
salt

1. In a non-reactive mixing bowl, prepare the garlic mojo by blending the garlic, lemon juice, olive oil, salt and pepper. Set aside.

2. In a deep fryer or a medium size pot, heat the canola oil until the temperature reaches 325°F. Deep-fry the plantains until lightly golden, or until a wooden skewer can be easily inserted through them, about 3 minutes. With a slotted spoon, remove them from the oil and place them on paper towels to drain.

3. While they are still warm, pick up one plantain at a time, place it between two pieces of foil or in a tostonera and mash it until flat. Repeat with the remaining plantain pieces. (Tostones may be made up to this point, cooled, and kept tightly covered in a plastic container for up to a week in the freezer.)

4. To serve, bring the temperature of the deep fryer or medium size pot back to 350°F. Deep-fry the plantains until they reach a golden color and are crispy, about 1 minute.

5. Using a slotted spoon, remove the plantains from the oil and place them on a paper towel-lined sheet pan to drain. Sprinkle with salt. Keep warm.

6. Arrange in a serving platter and serve with the garlic Mojo.

AZUCASABOR LATINO
713 S ALAMO ST, SAN ANTONIO, TX

"I am not a glutton - I am an explorer of food"
Erma Bombeck

31

RANCHERO

Welcome To San Antonio's place for New York style Bagels & Breads! At Bagel Factory our goal is to bring you a New York style bagel made and baked fresh right here in San Antonio. Locally owned and operated, we serve bagels, breakfast and lunch sandwiches all day long.

1¼ C. hot water
½ lb. tomatillo (husked and quartered)
8 chilies (anaheim, roasted peeled stem and seeds removed)
1 yellow onion (chopped)
2½ garlic cloves (peeled minced)
1 tsp. dried oregano
salt
pepper
4 corn tortilla (cut to fit ramekins)
4 eggs
15 oz. chili beans (ranch style)
½ C. cheddar cheese (grated longhorn)

1. Prepare the sauce ahead of time by placing the ingredients in Vita-Mix along with 1 cup of water; quickly increase speed to high; allow to run for 4 to 5 minutes or until steam escapes from opening; adjust with salt and pepper to taste.
2. If you do not have a Vita-Mix and are using a standard blender, place the tomatillos, garlic and onion in medium skillet along with enough oil to coat the bottom; sauté until onion and garlic are soft; approximately 5 minutes.
3. Add the hot water and additional spices, simmer for 20 to 30 minutes; pour cooked ingredients into blender container and process until smooth; adjust salt and pepper to taste.
4. Pour the sauce into a quart jar and refrigerate until ready to use.
5. For the huevos rancheros, preheat oven to 350 degrees.
6. Lightly spray individual ramekins with non-stick cooking spray and place on a cookie sheet. The ramekins I used measured 5 inches across and 1 inch deep.
7. Place a cut tortilla in the bottom of each dish, top with egg in center.
8. Sprinkle ¼ of the canned beans around each casserole leaving the yolk exposed.
9. Pour the 1-1½ cups tomatillo sauce over the beans, again leaving yolk exposed; top with grated cheese.
10. Place in pre-heated oven and bake for 15 minutes; lightly cover each with foil and bake an additional 5 minutes or until yolk is slightly runny and white is set.
11. Top with additional grated cheese if desired. Enjoy!

BAGEL FACTORY
15909 SAN PEDRO AVE, #115 SAN ANTONIO, TX

Signature Tastes of SAN ANTONIO

This is every cook's opinion: no savory dish without an onion, but lest your kissing should be spoiled, your onions must be fully boiled.
Jonathan Swift

32

BANGKOK 54 THAI CUISINE
2515 NACOGDOCHES RD, SAN ANTONIO, TX

Signature Tastes of SAN ANTONIO

Bangkok 54 Thai Cuisine brings our family's tradition of exceptional food and warm, friendly service to San Antonio. Each selection is prepared fresh when you order, using our family's recipes with that special touch of authentic Thai home cooking. You will experience the culinary excitement of exotic flavors for which Thai food is justifiably famous, served in the our comfortable dining room which reflects the delicate beauty and friendly charm of Thailand.

24 small mussels
1 tbsp. table salt
¾ lb. medium (51 to
60 per lb.) fresh shrimp,
peeled and deveined
½ lb. cleaned squid, bodies
sliced crosswise into ¼-inch
rings and tentacles cut in
half if large
½ lb. sea scallops or bay
scallops
¼ lb. fresh or pasteurized
jumbo lump crabmeat

For the Dressing:
6 tbsp. fresh lime juice (from
2 limes)
4½ tbsp. fish sauce
1½ tbsp. granulated sugar
2 tsp. finely chopped un-
seeded fresh hot green chiles
(like serrano or jalapeño)
2 tsp. finely chopped garlic
(2 medium cloves)

For the Salad:
2 C. bite-size pcs. of Boston
lettuce, rinsed and spun dry
(1 large head)
3 tbsp. thinly sliced shallot
(1 large)
⅓ C. thinly sliced scallions
(4 to 5, white and green
parts)
¼ C. coarsely chopped fresh
cilantro
¼ C. coarsely chopped fresh
mint
½ C. sliced English
cucumber (halve cucumber
lengthwise and slice into
¼-in.-thick half-moons)
½ C. halved cherry or grape
tomatoes

Cook the Seafood:
1. Scrub the mussels well under running water and pull off any "beards". Discard any mussels that don't close tightly when tapped on the counter. Put closed mussels in a medium saucepan.
2. Add about ½ cup water, just enough to cover the bottom of the pan by about ¼ inch. Cover and set over high heat. Bring to a rolling boil and cook until the shells have opened, 1 to 2 minutes. Remove from the heat, transfer to a plate, and let stand until cool enough to handle. Discard any unopened ones.
3. Remove the cooked mussels from their shells and put in a medium bowl; discard the shells and cooking liquid.
4. To cook the remaining seafood, bring a 3-qt. saucepan of water to a rolling boil over high heat. Add the salt and let the water return to a boil. Pour the shrimp into the boiling water and cook until the largest one is pink on the outside, opaque on the inside, and just cooked through, about 2 minutes.
5. The water may not return to the boil before they are done. Scoop them out with a slotted spoon and drop into the bowl with the mussels.
6. After the water returns to a rolling boil, add the squid and cook just until they become firm and the rings turn bright white, about 1 minute. Scoop them out and drop them into the bowl along with the shrimp and mussels.
7. When the water returns to a rolling boil, cook the scallops until just cooked through and no longer translucent inside, 1 to 2 minutes for bay scallops, 2 to 3 minutes for sea scallops.
8. Scoop them out and drop into the bowl as well (if using sea scallops, you may want to halve or quarter them first).
9. Add the lump crabmeat chunks to the bowl of seafood. Set the seafood aside on the counter while you prepare the dressing and other ingredients for the salad.

Make the Dressing:
1. In a medium-large bowl, combine the lime juice, fish sauce, sugar, chiles, and garlic. Stir to dissolve the sugar and combine everything well. Set aside.

Assemble the Salad:
1. Arrange the lettuce on a large serving platter or on individual serving plates as a bed for the seafood.
2. Transfer the cooked seafood to the bowl containing the lime-juice dressing. Add the shallots and use your hands or a wooden spoon to gently toss everything well. Add the scallions, cilantro, and mint and mix well again.
3. Scoop the seafood onto the platter or serving plates with a slotted spoon. Toss the cucumber and tomato in the dressing remaining in the bowl and scatter around the seafood.
4. Drizzle any remaining dressing from the bowl over the salad, especially over any lettuce not covered by the seafood. Serve immediately.

"There is one thing more exasperating than a wife who can cook and won't, and that's a wife who can't cook and will."
Robert Frost

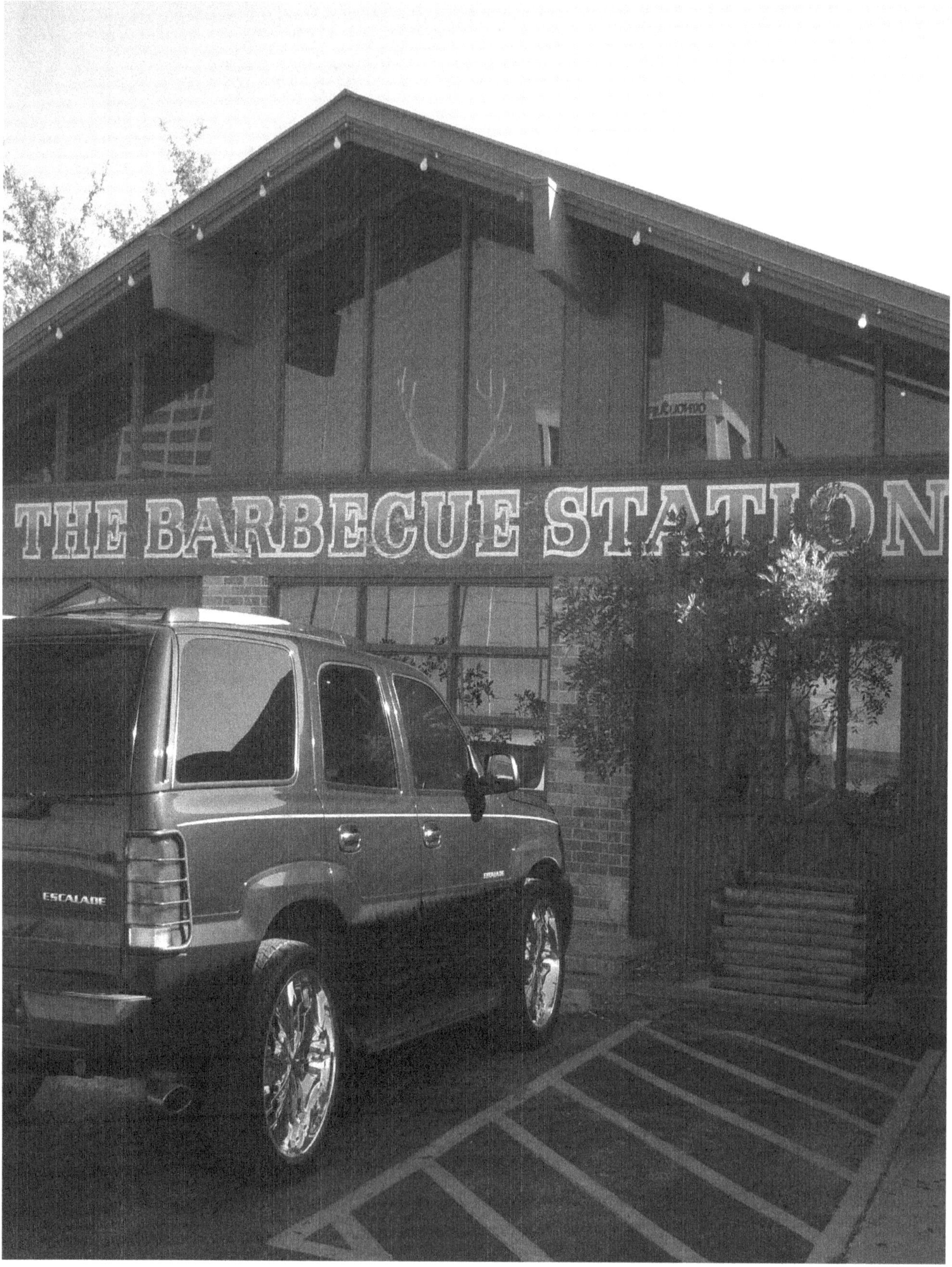
THE BARBECUE STATION
ESCALADE

CHOPPED BEEF SANDWICH

In 1992 the Peacock family bought an old Exxon station with one purpose in mind – to create in San Antonio the same great barbecue that can be found in some of the small towns across Texas. The result is the best barbecue in all of South Texas. At the Barbecue Station you will find all the traditional meats and side dishes. What you won't find are fancy tablecloths and all the non-barbecue items found in so many of the chain BBQ restaurants. If what you're looking for is authentic 100% wood smoked barbecue where all the sides are made fresh daily from scratch, then the Barbecue Station is your place.

2 green onions, quartered
¾ lb. beef, cooked, cut into ¾-in. cubes
⅓ C. mayonnaise
2 tbsp. sweet pickle relish
1 tbsp. lemon juice
½ tsp. dry mustard
¼ tsp. salt
a few rolls or bread

1. In an electric blender's container finely chop the onions and add the beef.

2. Cut the beef in the blender just until finely chopped, for three 1-second pulses.

3. In a bowl add the rest of the ingredients with the onion and beef and mix nicely.

4. Cut the bread rolls into half spread the beef mixture and serve with a salad or French fries.

BARBECUE STATION
1610 NE LOOP 410, SAN ANTONIO, TX

"I love sandwiches. Let's face it, life is better between two pieces of bread."
Jeff Mauro, a.k.a. The Sandwich King

CHARCOAL BROILED CHICKEN BREAST

Great steaks, chicken, and lamb!! They make their own salad dressings and bread, that are all so very good. Everytime we have visitors in town we make sure we take them!! They just added a brand new handicap accessible restroom too.

1 chicken breast (skin and bones removed)
¼ C. soy sauce
¼ C. white wine
1 tsp. dry mustard
¼ C. melted butter (must be real)
1 tsp. tarragon

1. Mix the ingredients together (except chicken).

2. Pour over chicken for three or more hours.

3. Broil over charcoal for 10 minutes (that's right unless the breasts are extra thick) or until tender and juicy, basting with sauce often.

BARN DOOR RESTAURANT
8400 N NEW BRAUNFELS AVE, SAN ANTONIO, TX

"Different types of chicken come at different price points. Filets are going to be more expensive. If it's bone-in and skin-on it's going to be less expensive."
Sandra Lee

Signature Tastes of SAN ANTONIO

On Friday May 19th 2000 we opened for business and ended up selling out of just about everything we had. The business was supposed to be just me and my mother, but after that huge response we knew it was alot bigger than just the two of us and we have been growing ever since. It all started with my mother, volunteer nieces, and me…and my dad on the weekends. Since 2002 we have been winning critical acclaim for our pizza, wings, and just being the best all around neighborhood joint.

¼ C. warm water
(100 to 110 degrees)
1 tsp. active dry yeast
1 tsp. white sugar
4 C. bread flour
2 tbsp. Italian style seasoning
1 tsp. salt (divided)
1¼ C. beer (flat)
1 tbsp. olive oil
2 tbsp. olive oil
⅓ C. onion (chopped)
2 tbsp. chopped garlic
28 oz. roma tomatoes (with juice)
12 oz. tomato paste
1 tbsp. fresh basil (chopped)
1 tbsp. fresh parsley (chopped)
1 tsp. fresh oregano (chopped)
½ tsp. black pepper

1. In a small bowl, dissolve yeast and sugar in warm water. Let stand until creamy, about 10 minutes.
2. In a food processor, combine flour, Italian seasoning and salt. Pulse until mixed. Add yeast mixture, flat beer and oil. Pulse until a ball is formed. Scrape dough out onto a lightly floured surface, and knead for several minutes until dough is smooth and elastic.
3. Allow dough to rest for 2 to 3 minutes. Divide dough in half, and shape into balls. Place dough balls in separate bowls, and cover with plastic wrap. Allow to rise at room temperature for about 1 hour, then store in the refrigerate overnight.

To make the sauce:
1. Heat olive oil in a saucepan over medium heat. Sauté onions until tender. Stir in garlic, and cook for 1 minute. Crush tomatoes into saucepan.
2. Add tomato paste, basil, parsley and oregano. Simmer for 10 minutes.

2048 S WW WHITE RD, SAN ANTONIO, TX

BIG LOU'S PIZZA

"There's no better feeling in the world than a warm pizza box on your lap."
Kevin James

BIGA
ON THE
BANKS
RESTAURANT
& BAR

CHEESE LASAGNA

Bruce Auden's award-winning Biga on the Banks is located in a spectacular setting in downtown San Antonio's modern International Center. Overlooking a romantic tree-canopied bend in the river, the historic and the new find common ground in Biga's dynamic re-emergence with ultra contemporary cuisine propelling San Antonio's recent ascent to a new level of River Walk dining. Gourmet Magazine named Biga one of the five best restaurants in Texas.

Sauce:
2 large egg yolks, lightly beaten
1 C. whole milk
2½ tbsp. sugar
1 tsp. vanilla extract
dash of salt

Soufflé:
cooking spray
1 tbsp. sugar
3 large egg yolks, lightly beaten
3 tbsp. all-purpose flour
⅔ C. 2% reduced-fat milk
¼ C. sugar
1 tbsp. butter
3 tbsp. Grand Marnier (orange-flavored liqueur)
2 tsp. vanilla extract
5 large egg whites
½ tsp. cream of tartar
⅛ tsp. salt
2 tbsp. sugar

1. To prepare sauce, place 2 egg yolks in a medium bowl. Combine whole milk and 2½ tablespoons sugar in a small, heavy saucepan over medium heat; heat to 180° or until tiny bubbles form around edge (do not boil).
2. Gradually add hot milk mixture to 2 egg yolks, stirring constantly with a whisk. Return mixture to pan; cook over medium heat until thick and bubbly (about 3 minutes), stirring constantly. Remove from heat. Stir in 1 teaspoon vanilla and dash of salt. Pour into a glass bowl; cover and chill.
3. Preheat oven to 375°.
4. To prepare soufflé, coat a 1½-quart soufflé dish with cooking spray; sprinkle with 1 tablespoon sugar.
5. Place 3 egg yolks in a medium bowl; set aside. Place flour in a small, heavy saucepan; gradually add 2% milk, stirring with a whisk. Stir in ¼ cup sugar; add butter. Cook over medium heat until thick (about 5 minutes), stirring constantly. Gradually add hot milk mixture to 3 egg yolks, stirring constantly with a whisk.
6. Return mixture to pan; cook over medium heat until thick and bubbly (about 3 minutes), stirring constantly. Stir in liqueur and 2 teaspoons vanilla; cook 1 minute, stirring constantly. Remove from heat.
7. Place egg whites, cream of tartar, and ⅛ teaspoon salt in a large bowl; beat with a mixer at high speed until soft peaks form. Gradually add 2 tablespoons sugar, 1 tablespoon at a time, beating until stiff peaks form. Gently stir one-fourth of egg white mixture into milk mixture; gently fold in remaining egg white mixture.
8. Spoon into prepared soufflé dish. Place soufflé dish in a 9-inch square baking pan; add hot water to pan to a depth of 1 inch. Bake at 375° for 30 minutes or until puffy and set. Spoon about 3 tablespoons sauce over each serving. Serve immediately.

BIGA ON THE BANKS
203 S St Marys St., San Antonio, TX

"Lasagna: the world's most perfect food!"
Garfield (Jim Davis)

41

BIN 555

RESTAURANT& WINE BAR

SANGRIA

Signature Tastes of SAN ANTONIO

Jason Dady, Executive Chef/Owner of Bin 555, offers Modern American cuisine with small plate offerings as well as a entrees and chef market menu coupled with contemporary ambiance, an intimate bar and large patio make Bin 555 Restaurant & Wine Bar one of the most innovative restaurants in San Antonio. Jake Dady, General Manager/Owner of Bin 555, joined with his brother Jason in opening The Lodge Restaurant.

1 bottle of red wine (Cabernet Sauvignon, Merlot, Rioja reds, Zinfandel, Shiraz)
1 lemon cut into wedges
1 orange cut into wedges
2 tbsp. sugar
1 shot brandy
2 C. ginger ale or club soda

1. Pour wine in the pitcher and squeeze the juice wedges from the lemon and orange into the wine. Toss in the fruit wedges (leaving out seeds if possible) and add sugar and brandy.

2. Chill overnight. Add ginger ale or club soda just before serving.

3. If you'd like to serve right away, use chilled red wine and serve over lots of ice.

BIN 555 RESTAURANT AND WINE BAR

555 W BITTERS RD, SAN ANTONIO, TX

Everything I eat has been proved by some doctor or other to be a deadly poison, and everything I don't eat has been proved to be indispensable for life. But I go marching on.
George Bernard Shaw

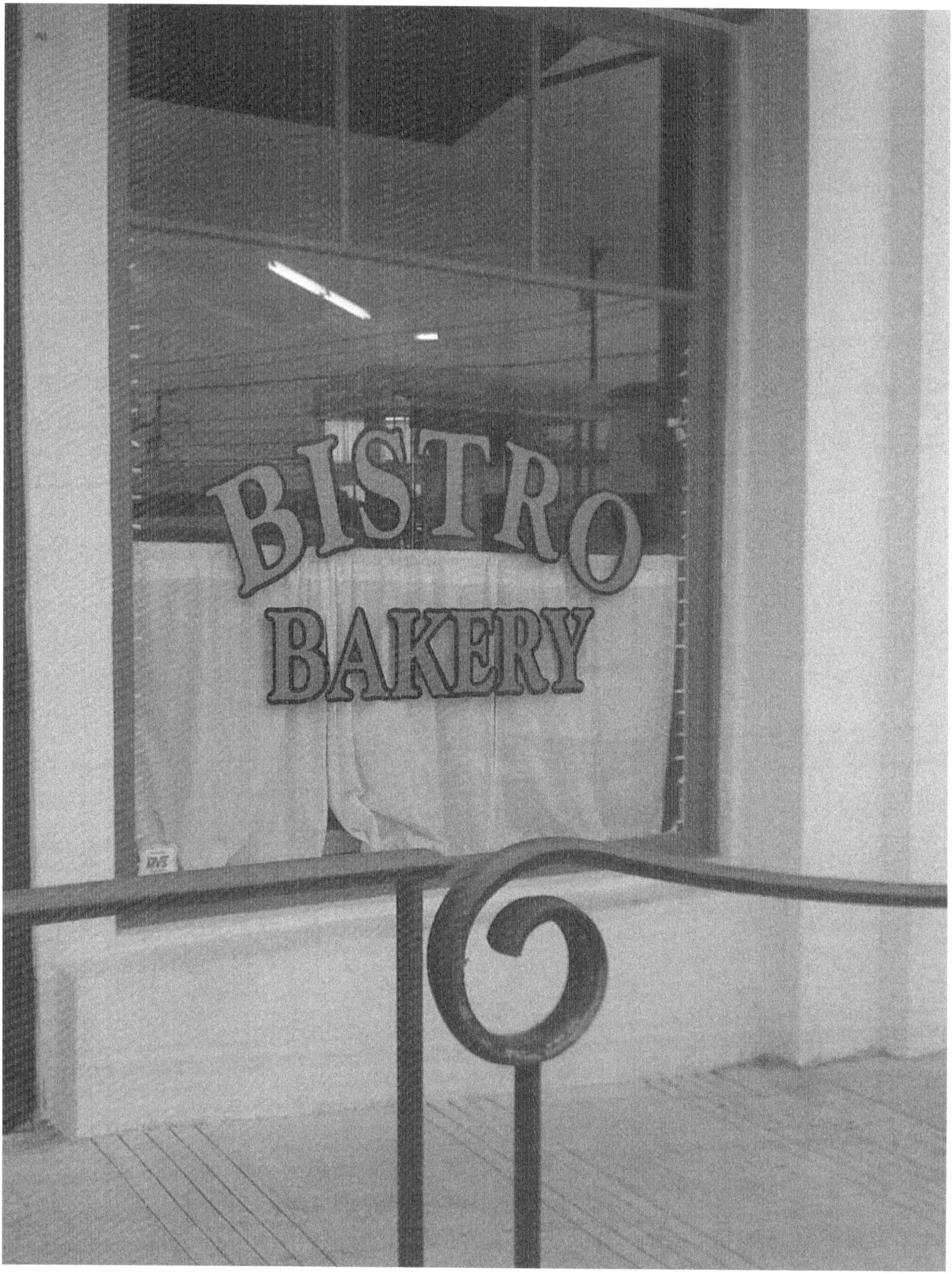
BISTRO
BAKERY

Welcome to Bistro Bakery, specializing in authentic French pastries, gourmet light lunches, and tantalizing sandwiches. We have a variety of sweet rolls, croissants, tarts, baguettes, breads, quiches and coffee. The bakery also offers some takeout entrees. For example, on Tuesday, lobster terrine, duck pâté, beef Wellington, crab and shrimp quiche, chicken mushroom vol-au-vent and small pizzas were available.

Signature Tastes of SAN ANTONIO

1 (12 in.) hoagie rolls (or the bread of your choice)
1 tbsp. olive oil
2 oz. Italian dressing
2 slices provolone cheese
4 slices deli ham
8 slices genoa salami
8 slices deli pepperoni
4 slices tomatoes
2 pepperoncini peppers (chopped)

1. Cut roll open.

2. Brush outside of roll with olive oil.

3. Brush both sides of inside with italian dressing.

4. Cut cheese in half, add the 4 halves to the bread.

5. Add the remaining ingredients in order listed.

6. Cut in half.

7. Grill in your panini press or George Foreman grill. Enjoy.

4300 McCullough Ave., San Antonio, TX

BISTRO BAKERY

"He who distinguishes the true savor of his food can never be a glutton; he who does not cannot be otherwise."
Henry David Thoreau

Portobello Mushroom and Brie Fondue

Signature Tastes of SAN ANTONIO

Bistro Vatel endures as San Antonio's favorite French culinary destination, and has been hailed as an oasis of intimate, unpretentious dining replete with a four-star menu that rivals the best menus of France's elegant, countryside haunts. Chef Damien Watel, who has built a small empire of authentic European eateries around the metro area, continues to actively direct the menu - a tempting and delicious document that changes daily with the city's only prix-fixe menu.

1 sheet puff pastry, thawed
8 oz. mushrooms, cleaned and trimmed
1 tbsp. olive oil
¼ tsp. salt
⅛ tsp. ground black pepper
¾ tsp. chopped fresh thyme
⅓ C. onion confit
¾ tsp. balsamic vinegar
4 oz. Brie, thinly sliced

1. Preheat an oven to 400F. Line 12 standard muffin tins or 24 tartlet molds with the puff pastry. Prick the bottom of the tartlets with a fork and weight them down with pie weights, dried beans, or uncooked rice. Bake the pastry for 8 to 12 minutes, until it puffs and becomes a very light, golden brown.

2. Cool them on a wire rack and set them aside.

3. Raise the oven heat to 425F. Toss the mushrooms with the olive oil and arrange them in a single layer on a baking sheet. Roast the mushrooms for 35 minutes, turning once, until they are deep brown.

4. Transfer them to a cutting board and chop them coarsely. Toss the mushrooms with the salt and pepper and set them aside.

5. In a small saucepan, bring the thyme and onion confit to just steaming and remove it from the heat. Stir the roasted mushrooms and balsamic vinegar into the onion confit.

6. Divide the mushroom mixture between the prepared pastry shells and top the pastries with the sliced Brie.

7. Broil the pastries for 3 to 5 minutes, until the Brie melts and becomes bubbly. Serve the mushroom tartlets hot or at room temperature.

218 E Olmos Dr., San Antonio, TX

BISTRO VATEL

"Recipe: A series of step-by-step instructions for preparing ingredients you forgot to buy, in utensils you don't own, to make a dish the dog wouldn't eat."
Author Unknown

TUSCAN CHICKEN IN LIMONE

It was 1978 when two guys who had a great recipe for deep dish pizza opened the first BJ's in Santa Ana, California. The pizza was an immediate hit and, as years went by; new BJ's restaurants were opened in beach cities along Southern California's coastline. In 1996, with seven restaurants in operation from San Diego to Los Angeles, the first BJ's brewery began production in our new restaurant in Brea, California. The introduction of fine handcrafted beer was welcomed by guests and the newly renamed BJ's Restaurant & Brewery concept was launched. New menu items and new beers have been added through the years as the BJ's brand has expanded across the U.S.

Signature Tastes of SAN ANTONIO

4 boneless skinless chicken breast halves
¼ tsp. salt
⅛ tsp. fresh ground pepper
2 tbsp. flour
1 tbsp. butter
1 tbsp. olive oil
½ C. white wine
½ C. chicken broth (or water and bullion cube)
¼ C. fresh parsley, chopped
1 large egg, well beaten
¼ C. fresh lemon juice, freshly squeezed

1. Flatten each chicken breast by pounding gently with a flat meat mallet (Hint - pound chicken inside a Ziploc bag - no mess!). Sprinkle flattened breasts with salt and pepper. Then dredge chicken in flour; shake off excess.
2. Heat butter and oil over HIGH heat; just before butter starts to brown, add the chicken pieces and saute quickly to brown, about 3 minutes. Flip and brown other side (3 more minutes). It doesn't need to be totally cooked through because it will cook more in the sauce later.
3. Remove chicken to platter but leave all browned bits in the skillet.
4. Add wine to browned bits in skillet and boil to reduce wine by almost half (about 3 minutes). Add chicken broth and bring to a boil.
5. In a small bowl, whisk together egg and lemon juice. Stir egg/lemon mixture into simmering wine and broth, whisking constantly until sauce is smooth and a little thickened (about 2 minutes). It will thicken more when you put in the chicken breasts which have a flour coating.
6. Add chicken and any juices back into the sauce; allow to simmer about 5 minutes until chicken is cooked through, turning chicken once. Add chopped parsley.
7. Place chicken on platter and pour sauce over top; garnish with lemon slices and additional parsley sprigs.

BJ'S RESTAURANT & BREWHOUSE
22410 US HWY 281 N, SAN ANTONIO, TX

"I find myself eating different kinds of chicken each and every day, even if it's by surprise."
Ludacris

THIN APPLE CRISPY TART

180 g puff pastry, thinly rolled into a circle 30cm in diameter
30 g butter, cut into cubes
4 Granny Smith apples, peeled
2 tbsp. sugar
2 tbsp. apricot jam
2 Granny Smith apples, peeled and diced
½ tsp. cinnamon powder
85 g sugar
1 wide saucepan
1 wooden spoon
1 baking tray
1 cutting board
1 knife
1 brush
1 small saucepan
1 spoon

1. Place a wide saucepan on a medium heat and put in the diced apples and with the sugar. Heat and stir until they start to break down. You can mash them with the back of the spoon to help them along.

2. Keep stirring until most of the liquid has evaporated. Then turn off the heat and put in the cinnamon powder.

3. Continue to stir and mash the apple mixture for about a minute more, then set aside.

4. Preheat the oven to 230°C, 450°F or gas mark 8.

5. Take one of the peeled apples and cut off the sides without cutting into the core, which you can then discard. Cut the apple pieces into thin wedges and repeat this with the rest of the apples.

"This special feeling towards fruit, its glory and abundance, is I would say universal.... We respond to strawberry fields or cherry orchards with a delight that a cabbage patch or even an elegant vegetable garden cannot provoke."
Jane Grigson

SHRIMP SAAG

Bombay Hall Cuisine Indian Restaurant here at San Antonio, Texas. Here at Bombay Hall we bring you delectable, fresh, healthy, home-style authentic Indian cuisine, served in a beautiful, calm atmosphere. It is our wish that your dining experience be nourishing & enjoyable for both your body and spirit. What makes our food unique is the care we put into choosing the ingredients, how we cook the food, and the fact that we prepare most of it from scratch, like you would at home. Bombay Hall ambiance is perfect for intimate gatherings or large parties with a party room available for up to 80 people.

Signature Tastes of SAN ANTONIO

1½ lb. shrimp; large, peeled
24 oz. spinach; fresh, finely chopped
1 onion; finely chopped
2 tsp. ginger; minced
½ tsp. cumin seeds
½ tsp. coriander seeds; ground
½ tsp. turmeric
¼ tsp. cinnamon; ground
¼ tsp. cardamom; ground
1 pinch cloves; ground
1 C. clam broth; or fish stock
24 oz. spinach; finely chopped
pinch salt
pinch black pepper

1. Heat the oil in a sauté pan. Add the ginger, cumin seeds, ground coriander, cinnamon, cardamom, and cloves. When they start to pop, add the onions, ginger, garlic, and turmeric. Cook until soft, but don't brown.

2. Add the clam broth (or fish stock) and bring to a boil. Stir in the spinach and cook for 10-15 minutes, or until the spinach is soft and mushy. Add more broth (or stock) if the mixture dries out too much.

3. Add the shrimp and simmer for 1 - 2 minutes, or until cooked.

4. Season with a pinch of salt and pepper to taste, and garnish with cilantro if you would like.

8783 WURBACH RD., SAN ANTONIO, TX

BOMBAY HALL

"But when the time comes that a man has had his dinner, then the true man comes to the surface."
Mark Twain

BOUDRO'S FAMOUS GUACAMOLE

Boudro's is an experience to savor, embracing all the flavor of our regional heritage with a distinctive menu of Texas and southwestern specialties. Relax in the cool, comfortable interior or take a sidewalk table right on San Antonio' renowned Riverwalk. Then it's time for the best food on the River, from smoked shrimp enchiladas and blackened prime rib to seafood straight from the Gulf. Boudro's is the ideal spot for intimate lunches or dinners as well as large parties and convention groups. We can accommodate you inside or on one of our special river barges, catered exactly to your taste.

juice of ¼ of an orange *juice of ½ a lime* *1 avocado seeded and scooped out of skin* *2 tbsp. roasted and charred Roma tomatoes diced* *1 serrano pepper roasted seeded and diced* *1 tbsp. medium dice red onions* *1 tsp. chopped cilantro* *coarse ground salt to taste (sea salt is better)*	**1.** Squeeze juices into bowl. **2.** Add avocado and coarsely chop. **3.** Add onions, roasted tomato, serrano and cilantro fold into avocado mixture. **4.** Add salt (more is better). Result should be crudely chopped not mashed. That's it.

BOUDRO'S ON THE RIVERWALK

421 E COMMERCE ST., SAN ANTONIO, TX

"To the old saying that man built the house but woman made of it a 'home' might be added the modern supplement that woman accepted cooking as a chore but man has made of it a recreation."
Emily Post

BOURBON STREET SEAFOOD KITCHEN

24165 IH 10 WEST SUITE 433 SAN ANTONIO, TX

Signature Tastes of **SAN ANTONIO**

Welcome to Bourbon Street Seafood Kitchen Restaurant... a place for an exquisite New Orleans cuisine in the heart of San Antonio, Texas. Voted as one of the best restaurants in San Antonio, we are sure that you will have a great dining experience. At Bourbon Street Seafood Kitchen, it's our goal to provide you with a great place for parties and informal get-together's, evenings out with the family or a delicious change of taste from fast-food lunches. All served with a smile.

2 tsp. shortening
1 C. onion, finely chopped
1 C. green pepper, finely chopped
1 C. celery, finely chopped
4 garlic cloves, minced
1 chicken, cut into pieces
2 lb. chorizo sausage (or a good reliable hot sausage you know of) or 2 lb. andouille sausages (or a good reliable hot sausage you know of)
3 c. fresh ripe tomatoes, chopped or 2 (14½ oz.) cans diced tomatoes
2 ½ C. chicken stock
2 tsp. thyme
½ tsp. oregano
1 tsp. parsley
1 tsp. cayenne (what ever your taste buds can handle) or 1 tsp. chili powder (what ever your taste buds can handle)
1½ tsp. salt
1 tsp. black pepper
6 C. cooked long-grain rice
cayenne (to offer at table) or Tabasco sauce (to offer at table)

1. Melt shortening in a large/huge saucepan over medium heat.

2. Cook chicken pieces until brown on all sides and cooked about half way through, around 20 minutes or so.

3. Remove and add onion, green pepper, celery and garlic.

4. Cook slowly stirring now and again until onions are tender.

5. Add sausage and cook 10 min more.

6. Return chicken and add all remaining ingredients EXCEPT rice and stir together well.

7. Cover and simmer for 30 min stirring now and again.

8. Remove cover and continue to cook until broth cooks down a bit-you don't want it too thick as the rice will soak up the juice.

9. Serve up the rice in bowls and ladle the Jambalaya on top, and offer more cayenne or Tabasco at the table.

"I do adore food. If I have any vice it's eating. If I was told I could only eat one food for the rest of my life, I could put up with sausage and mash forever."
Colin Bake

PENNE MEDITERRANEAN

Signature Tastes of SAN ANTONIO

1 oz. blended oil
2 oz. cremini mush-
rooms, sliced
½ tsp. garlic, chopped
1 tbsp. basil, julienned
1 tbsp. sundried
tomatoes
1 tbsp. caramelized
onions
3 oz. vegetable stock
1 tbsp. feta cheese,
crumbled
2 tbsp. herb butter
salt and pepper totaste
7 oz. barilla plus penne
pasta, cooked
1 oz. spinach
1 tbsp. feta cheese
1 tsp. pinenuts

1. Heat oil in pan. Add mushrooms, garlic, basil, sun-dried tomatoes and onions, then sauté. Add vegetable stock, Feta and herb butter. Season with salt and pepper. Reheat pasta in hot water, drain and add to pan with spinach. Stir to combine. Place in a bowl. Garnish with Feta and pinenuts.

Herb Butter:
1. Mix ingredients (butter, garlic, herbs, kosher salt, black pepper) well until smooth.

15900 LA CANTERA PARKWAY, SAN ANTONIO, TX

BRIO TUSCAN GRILLE

"Great restaurants are, of course, nothing but mouth-brothels. There is no point in going to them if one intends to keep one's belt buckled."
Frederic Raphael

FRENCH ONION SOUP

Signature Tastes of SAN ANTONIO

CAFE BISTRO AT NORDSTROM'S/LA CANTERA

15900 LA CANTERA PKY., SAN ANTONIO, TX

Ingredients:

6 large red or yellow onions, peeled and thinly sliced.
Olive oil
¼ tsp. of sugar
2 cloves garlic, minced
8 C. of beef stock, chicken stock, or a combination of the two (traditionally the soup is made with beef stock)
½ C. of dry vermouth or dry white wine
1 bay leaf
¼ tsp. of dry thyme
salt and pepper
8 slices of toasted French bread
1½ C. of grated Swiss Gruyere with a little grated Parmesan cheese

1. In a large saucepan, sauté the onions in the olive oil on medium high heat until well browned, but not burned, about 30-40 minutes (or longer). Add the sugar about 10 minutes into the process to help with the carmelization.

2. Add garlic and sauté for 1 minute. Add the stock, vermouth or wine, bay leaf, and thyme. Cover partially and simmer until the flavors are well blended, about 30 minutes. Season to taste with salt and pepper. Discard the bay leaf.

3. To serve you can either use individual oven-proof soup bowls or one large casserole dish. Ladle the soup into the bowls or casserole dish. Cover with the toast and sprinkle with cheese. Put into the broiler for 10 minutes at 350 degrees F, or until the cheese bubbles and is slightly browned. Serve immediately.

"Soup is just a way of screwing you out of a meal."
Jay Leno

BREADED CHICKEN TENDERS

Signature Tastes of SAN ANTONIO

6 boneless skinless chicken breast halves (sliced into strips)
1 egg (beaten)
1 C. buttermilk
1½ tsp. garlic powder
1 C. all-purpose flour
1 C. seasoned breadcrumbs
1 tsp. salt
1 tsp. baking powder
oil (for deep frying)

Honey Mustard Sauce:
¼ C. mayonnaise
1 tbsp. prepared mustard
1 tbsp. honey
½ tbsp. lemon juice

1. To make honey mustard sauce, in a bowl whisk together mayonnaise, mustard, honey, and lemon juice. Store covered in the refrigerator until needed. In a large bowl (or resealable plastic bag) add the chicken strips. In a small bowl combine egg, buttermilk, and garlic powder. Pour the mixture over the chicken strips. Cover and refrigerate for 2 to 4 hours.

2. In a large plastic bag mix together flour, breadcrumbs, salt, and baking powder. Drain the chicken of the buttermilk mixture and discard the buttermilk mixture. Place chicken in the bag with breadcrumbs, seal and shake tossing to coat.

3. Heat oil in a deep fryer to 375 degrees. Deep fry chicken tenders in batches until golden brown and the juices run clear (the internal temperature of the chicken needs to have reached 165 degrees). Drain on paper towels. (Makes 6 Servings)

CANDY'S OLD FASHION BUGERS

117 S FLORES ST., SAN ANTONIO, TX

"As for those grapefruit and buttermilk diets, I'll take roast chicken and dumplings."
Hattie McDaniel

SHRIMP AND GRITS

Signature Tastes of SAN ANTONIO

This building was built by Ernie Schrivener and a couple of helpers in the late 30's. Ernie's father, a frugal English-born builder, had saved broken bricks from the many homes he had built in the then young suburban neighborhood of Alamo Heights. When Ernie returned home from college to work with his dad, his first project was to build this building from what would have been rubble to most. Well, George persisted and Cappy's was opened in 1977. It took George two years to convince City Hall and me that revitalization was economical and necessary.

¼ C. Canadian bacon, diced
2 tsp. olive oil
1 onion, diced
½ green bell pepper, seeded and diced
1 dozen large shrimp, peeled and de-veined, with tails on
3 garlic cloves, minced
1 (14½-oz.) can petite-cut diced tomatoes
¼ C. dry white wine
1 tsp. hot sauce
¾ tsp. salt
¼ C. fat-free half-and-half
3 C. water
¾ C. uncooked quick-cooking grits
1 tbsp. chopped fresh chives

1. Add bacon to a nonstick skillet and sauté over medium heat until crisp. Transfer the bacon to a plate; set aside. Add the oil to the skillet and set over medium heat. Add the onion and bell pepper, and cook, stirring occasionally, until the vegetables are tender, about 8 minutes.

2. Add the shrimp and garlic to the skillet and cook, stirring, until the shrimp being to turn pink, about 1 – 2 minutes. Transfer the shrimp to a bowl; set aside. Add the tomatoes, wine, hot sauce, and ½ teaspoon salt; bring to a boil, stirring constantly to scrape the browned bits from the bottom of the pan.

3. Reduce the heat and simmer, uncovered, until the flavors are blended and the sauce begins to thicken, about 6 – 8 minutes. Return the bacon and shrimp to the skillet. Stir in the half-and-half; heat through.

4. Meanwhile, bring the water to a boil in a medium saucepan. Slowly whisk in the grits, and the remaining ¼ teaspoon salt. Reduce the heat, and simmer, covered, until thickened, about 5 minutes. Remove from the heat. Serve the shrimp mixture over the grits. Sprinkle with the chives.

5011 BROADWAY ST., SAN ANTONIO, TX

CAPPY'S

"A recipe has no soul. You, as the cook, must bring soul to the recipe."
Thomas Keller

coffee, juice & neighborhood bar

5003

NUTELLA CREPES

Signature Tastes of SAN ANTONIO

1¼ C. milk
2 eggs
1 tbsp. butter, melted, or canola oil
¾ C. all-purpose flour
1 tsp. sugar
pinch salt
extra oil, butter or nonstick spray for cooking with

1. Pulse the milk, eggs and butter in a blender until foamy or whisk until well blended; add the remaining ingredients and pulse or whisk until smooth. Let the batter sit for half an hour.

2. When ready to cook, preheat a large skillet or griddle and brush it with butter or oil or spray it with nonstick spray. Pour about a quarter cup onto the skillet and tilt it around so that it runs into a circle. Cook until the top loses its gloss, which should only take a minute or two, then flip.

3. The bottom should be golden. Cook the other side for about 30 seconds and then slide out onto a plate. Keep warm in a 250F oven or serve right away spread with butter, sugar and cinnamon, jam or Nutella, and folded or rolled up. Makes about 12 crepes.

5003 BROADWAY ST., SAN ANTONIO, TX

CAPPYCCINO'S

"One cannot think well, love well, sleep well, if one has not dined well."
Virginia Woolf

ARROZ CON LECHE

The food is very flavorful with a nice presentation - all at a very reasonable price. Cascabel's seems to serve authentic Mexican food - the menu is written somewhat Spanglish, but you can figure it out. The service was good and the patio area is quite nice when weather is cool enough - the inside dining atmosphere good too.

2¼ C. water
1½ C. short grain rice
1 (¼ inch x 3 inch) strip lime peel
½ C. water
1 cinnamon stick
2 tbsp. anise seed, crushed
1 (12 oz.) can evaporated milk
1 (14 oz.) can condensed milk
1 tbsp. vanilla extract
¼ tsp. salt
¾ C. raisins (optional)

1. Combine 2¼ cups of water, rice, and lime peel in a saucepan. Bring to a boil over medium-high heat, then reduce heat to medium-low, cover, and simmer for 20 minutes until the rice is tender.

2. While the rice is cooking, combine ½ cup of water, the cinnamon stick, and anise in another saucepan over medium-high heat. Bring mixture to a low boil for 3 minutes, then remove saucepan from stove. Strain flavored water into a bowl and set aside, discarding cinnamon stick and anise pieces.

3. After rice has simmered for 20 minutes, carefully remove the lime peel with a slotted spoon, and over low heat, gradually stir evaporated milk and condensed milk into the rice. Mix in the cinnamon and anise-flavored water, vanilla, and salt. Add raisins, if desired. Continue to stir until the mixture thickens, about 7 to 10 minutes.

4. If the pudding is too watery after 10 minutes, turn up heat to medium-low and stir continuously. When pudding reaches desired consistency, remove from heat and pour into individual dishes, or a large bowl. Store in the refrigerator until ready to serve.

CASCABEL MEXICAN PATIO
1000 S SAINT MARYS ST., SAN ANTONIO, TX

"I'll bet what motivated the British to colonize so much of the world is that they were just looking for a decent meal."
Martha Harrison

Catalano's Pizzeria's specialties are pizza, pasta, calzone, stromboli, salads, subs and peanut butter n jelly pizza. This is a bring your own beer and wine establishment, we have frosted mugs and wine glasses for your drinking pleasure. It was established in 2002. We will try to make your dining experience something you will tell your friends about . We are a kid friendly and family orientated restaurant.

2 prepared pizza doughs
2 packages of spinach (10 oz. each)
1 medium-large onion, finely chopped
5 cloves of garlic, finely chopped
1 C. ricotta cheese
½ C. parmesan cheese, grated
½ C. mozzarella, shredded
about 8-10 slices of deli ham, cut into long strips
salt & pepper to taste
approximately 4 tbsp. olive oil
dashes of living the gourmet dry herb rub

Homemade Marinara Sauce:
29 oz. can of crushed tomatoes
5 cloves of garlic – chopped
1 yellow onion – sliced
healthy handful of fresh basil
dashes of fresh ground black pepper
pinch of sugar
dashes of sea salt
dashes of oregano
drizzles of olive oil

1. In a large skillet on medium low heat, drizzle about 2 tablespoons of olive oil.

2. Add onion and sauté until tender and golden. Then add garlic and spinach, sautéing until large clumps are broken up. Add the dashes of salt and pepper.

3. Transfer to a medium bowl and let cool. Once cool enough, stir in ricotta, parmesan, mozzarella, and ham.

4. Preheat oven to 350 degrees.

5. Prepare 2 cookie sheets by lining them with parchment paper and sprinkling the paper with cornmeal. Set aside.

CATALANO'S PIZZERIA
102 N MAIN ST., CIBOLO, TX

"Salt is born of the purest of parents: the sun and the sea."
Pythagoras

CARNE GUISADA TACO

Chacho's is part fast food restaurant and part casual dining restaurant, with a very large variety of freshly prepared food with the best ingredients at low prices. This is a combination that has proved immensely popular. Our food is prepared with care by knowledgeable food people. It is more Mom's home cooking than fancy gourmet cooking. We purchase the best ingredients which also makes a big difference.

Signature Tastes of SAN ANTONIO

2 lb. beef stew meat
salt & pepper
2 tbsp. vegetable oil or olive oil
1 carton H-E-B pico de gallo
1 tbsp. minced garlic in oil
2 tsp. chili powder
1 tsp. each: ground cumin and leaf oregano
⅓ C. flour
1 carton (16 oz.) H-E-B low-sodium chicken broth
1 can (10.5 oz.) diced tomatoes with green chilies
2 bay leaves
tortillas + toppings (cheddar cheese, cilantro, green onions, lime wedges and avocados)

1. Season beef with salt and pepper. Heat 1 tablespoon oil in a large skillet over medium-high heat. Cook beef in 2 separate batches about 5 minutes each, or until well-browned.

2. Transfer beef to a 5 or 6-quart pot (may use slow cooker). Add remaining oil to same skillet; cook pico de gallo and garlic 3 minutes. Add seasonings and flour; stir and cook 2 or 3 minutes to combine.

3. Add broth to skillet slowly, stirring constantly. Bring to a boil; simmer 2 or 3 minutes to thicken slightly. Add to beef mixture, along with diced tomatoes and bay leaves. Cover; bring to a boil.

4. Simmer 1½ hours or until beef is tender (6 hours for slow cooker). Serve in tortillas with desired toppings.

7870 CALLAGHAN RD., SAN ANTONIO, TX

CHACHO'S

"In general I love to eat anything. I enjoy anything that is well prepared, a good spaghetti, lasagna, taco, steak, sushi, refried beans."
Martin Yan

Chama, meaning "flame" in Portuguese, is the essence of the authentic, Brazilian steakhouse. This "flame" also describes the "passion" the gauchos, Brazilian cowboys, have for their culture and tradition. This heritage spans back centuries as European immigrants migrated to Southern Brazil. In the vast plains and fertile lands, region known as Pampas, the gauchos tend to large herds of cattle as they roam and graze through Southern Brazil. At the end of the day, they gather around the churassco, the fire pit or grill, to eat and share stories.

Signature Taste of SAN ANTONIO

1 (12-oz.) good-quality
ribeye steak
2 tsp. kosher salt
1 tsp. fresh black pepper
1 tsp. olive oil
1 tsp. sea salt

1. Season ribeye with salt and pepper on both sides. Heat a medium cast-iron skillet over high heat and add the olive oil. When oil begins to smoke slightly gently lay the ribeye into the hot skillet and press down gently with the back of a spatula to ensure it is laying flat in the pan.

2. For medium rare cook each side about 4 to 5 minutes.

3. Transfer to a plate and let the steak rest for 5 minutes. Serve sliced or not with sea salt sprinkled on top.

18318 Sonterra Place, San Antonio, TX

Chama Gaúcha

"Opening a family-style restaurant with comfort food like mac 'n' cheese, ribs and burgers has always been my dream."
Bridget Hall

71

LEMON PEPPER CHICKEN

Signature Tastes of SAN ANTONIO

If you're looking for the tastiest fried chicken in San Antonio, then Chatman's Chicken can deliver! Our southern style fried chicken will leave you begging for more; all delicious foods are seasoned with herbs and spices and cooked to perfection. Chatman's Chicken has received numerous reviews on how excellent the food tasted, and how friendly the staff treated them; we pride ourselves on delivering only the best for our customers, and hope to see you soon!

2 chicken breasts cut into bite sized pcs.
vegetable oil
1 onion sliced into thin strips
1 tin tomatoes
juice of ½ lemon

Spices:
4 arid red chillis
½ tsp. black pepper corns
½ tsp. chilli powder
½ tsp. paprika
tsp. cumin seeds
tsp. fenugreek seeds
tsp. turmeric
2 cardomoms
pinch cinnamon
4 cloves
pinch coriander power
pinch ginger powder
pinch mustard seeds

1. Fry the chicken in regards to 3-4 tablespoons of vegetable oil to colour and remove from the frying pan.

2. Add the onion until golden then add the spices. Mix the spices and blitz before adding to the pan and fry for in regards to 5 minutes, adding a little water if necessary.

3. Add the chicken and pour the lemon juice over. Stir well.

4. Chop the tomatoes and stir into the mix. Cook at medium heat for regarding 10 minutes.

5. Cook in a medium oven for 45 minutes and serve with basmati rice.

1747 S WW WHITE RD., SAN ANTONIO, TX

CHATMAN'S CHICKEN

"Eating should be done in silence, lest the windpipe open before the gullet, and life be in danger."
The Talmud

Green Chili Cheese Burger

This is a great place for a burger and a beer. The burgers taste like they cared in the kitchen. Friendly employees, excellent burgers cooked to order, and a large selection of ice cold beers. This place always has a few of the craft beers on special making it an affordable dinner.

Signature Taste of SAN ANTONIO

2 lb. Angus-quality ground beef
2 tbsp. kosher salt
1 tbsp. fresh ground black pepper
4 lb. mild green chiles, (recommended: New Mexico Hatch Chiles)
2 lb. hot green chiles, (recommended: New Mexico Hatch Chiles)
3 large white onions, peeled
6 garlic cloves, peeled
1 tbsp. fresh epazote
½ tbsp. dried Mexican oregano
½ C. grapeseed oil
1 C. water
oil, for brushing grill
4 hamburger buns
1 lb. Asadero cheese, sliced ¼-inch thick
1 lb. mozzarella cheese, sliced ¼-inch thick

1. Preheat the grill to high.
2. In a large bowl, mix the ground beef with the salt and pepper and set aside.
3. Next, brush the green chiles with oil and place them on the hottest part of the grill. Cook the chiles until they are charred on all sides about 5 minutes. Then remove them from the grill and put them in a bowl of ice water to cool. Remove the chiles from the ice water and carefully peel off the charred skin. Cut the stem off, remove the seeds and set aside. Take the onions and place them on the grill. Cook the onions until charred on all sides about 10 minutes and set aside.
4. In a blender, add half the peeled chiles and half of the charred onions. Then add in the garlic, epazote, and oregano. Blend until the ingredients come together. Add the grapeseed oil and water and continue blending until the mixture is smooth about 30 seconds. Remove mixture to a large bowl.
5. Roughly chop the remaining chiles and onions and mix them into the chile puree. Season, to taste.
6. Form the ground beef into 4 (8-ounce) patties. Brush the grill with oil and cook the patties to desired doneness, 5 minutes for medium rare, 15 minutes for well done. Put the hamburger buns on the grill until lightly toasted. Just before removing the burgers, top them with the cheese and chile mixture.
7. Remove the patties from the grill once the cheese begins to melt and place them on the hamburger buns. Garnish with your favorite toppings and enjoy!

CHESTER'S HAMBURGER CO.
1006 NE LOOP 410, SAN ANTONIO, TX

"It takes my two favorite foods -- pizza and cheeseburgers -- and blends them together."
Donald Trump

75

HUNAN BEEF OR ORANGE BEEF

China Inn is a great restaurant. The employees are very friendly and the service is great. The place seems small and nondescript but you will be pleasantly surprised. The food is fabulous, always fresh, no MSG, and very tasty. The prices are extremely reasonable especially for the lunch and dinner combos.

Signature Tastes of SAN ANTONIO

¾ lb. flank steak (sliced into thin strips)
1 egg white
1 tbsp. cornstarch
oil (for frying)
2 tbsp. soy sauce
1 tbsp. chili paste with garlic
1½ tsp. cornstarch
½ tsp. sugar
several drops sesame oil (to taste)
2 garlic cloves (minced)
4 C. broccoli florets
1 tbsp. dry sherry
⅛ tsp. salt

1. In a medium bowl combine beef, egg white and cornstarch. Mix well and set aside. In another bowl mix together soy sauce and chili paste. Mix in 1 ½ teaspoon cornstarch, sugar, sesame oil, and garlic. Set aside.

2. Heat oil in a deep fryer to 375 degrees. Deep fry strips of beef in batches for about 2-3 minutes or until golden brown. Drain on paper towels.

3. Heat a wok or skillet over medium-high heat. Add the sauce mixture to the wok and cook until it becomes thickened and bubbly. Mix in cooked beef strips and cook for 1 minute. Remove beef and sauce from the pan to a platter and set aside.

4. Wipe the fry pan clean. Heat 1 tablespoon of oil in the wok or skillet over medium high heat. Add sherry and salt. Add broccoli florets and stir fry for 1 minute. Serve broccoli with the beef mixture and white rice.

2241 NW MILITARY HWY., SAN ANTONIO, TX

CHINA INN

"They would add beef stew meat or roasted beef bones, so you'd have beef stock flavored with crab, which gave it a really good taste."
John Shields

Signature Tastes of SAN ANTONIO

In January, 1977, with the encouragement of family and friends, Chris Madrid, a University of Texas marketing major, opened Chris Madrid's Tacos and Burgers, in historic Mid-town section of San Antonio. The burgers quickly became the favorite menu item and soon the tacos were deleted from the menu and name. Today, Chris Madrid's has turned into a unique dining experience. It is a quaint, friendly restaurant offering personal attention, a quality product, and a genuine concern for customer satisfaction. Tex-Mex decor adorns the old gas station and cantina. The cantina is a full service bar featuring iced down longnecks and frozen margaritas.Chris

1 tbsp. vegetable oil
1 med. onion, chopped
1 (8 oz.) can tomato sauce
6 tbsp. bottled red taco sauce
3 C. cooked, diced chicken
1 (16 oz.) can refried beans
1 lg. clove garlic, minced
2 C. shredded sharp cheddar cheese
vegetable oil for frying
6 corn tortillas
1 recipe guacamole sauce
1 lg. tomato, peeled, seeded and diced
shredded lettuce
1 lg. onion, diced
1 C. dairy sour cream

1. Heat oven to 325 degrees. Heat 1 tablespoon oil in oven-proof skillet and saute onion until golden. Add tomato sauce and 4 tablespoons taco sauce. Simmer, uncovered, stirring often until slightly thickened, about 5 minutes. Add chicken; cover and set aside.

2. In baking dish, combine beans, garlic, remaining 2 tablespoons taco sauce and 1 cup shredded cheddar cheese; mix well. Place uncovered beans and chicken mixtures separately in oven for 30 minutes. Stir beans occasionally.

3. Heat vegetable oil, about ½-inch deep in skillet; drop in tortillas one at a time for seconds or until just softened.

4. Remove and drain; wrap in foil to keep pliable. When ready to serve, spread each tortilla with beans, guacamole, and chicken mixture in that order. Add diced tomatoes, shredded lettuce, remaining 1 cup shredded cheese, onion and sour cream as desired to each chalupa.

CHRIS MADRID'S
1900 BLANCO RD., SAN ANTONIO, TX

"In eating, a third of the stomach should be filled with food, a third with drink, and the rest left empty."
The Talmud

CHICKA-CHICKA BOOM BOOM

Signature Tastes of SAN ANTONIO

The original Chuy's restaurant started in 1982 in Austin, Texas. It all began in an old abandoned Texas barbeque joint on Barton Springs Road. There was seating about sixty, a dirty parking lot, a women's restroom the size of abroom closet & a men's room tat was, uh, outside. Founders Mike Young & John Zapp decided to turn the location into a Mexican food restaurant. They spent all of their money on getting the restaurant opened, and they only had $20.00 left to spend on decor. Fortunately, they didn't let that stop them.

10 corn tortillas
1¼ lb. cooked chicken
½ C. vegetable broth
¼ C. water salt and
pepper
¾ lb. roasted green
chilies
2 oz. tomatillos
1½ oz. cilantro
1 oz. green onion
¾ oz. serrano pepper
½ oz. lime juice
1¼ lb. American cheese

1. In a saucepan, add vegetable broth, water and spices and place over a medium to high flame. Using a food processor, puree roasted green chilies, tomatillos, cilantro, green onions, serranos and lime juice.

2. Add to saucepan, stirring in well. Bring mixture to a slow boil. Lower flame and slowly add American cheese, whipping as needed to remove clumps and make sure it doesn't stick to the bottom. When the cheese is melted and mixed, remove from heat.

3. To make enchiladas, fill a corn tortilla with 2 ounces of cooked, roasted chicken. Roll up and place in a baking pan. Top with mixed cheese, as needed. Warm in a hot oven for 4 minutes, until cheese is melted. Top with Boom-Boom Sauce.

18008 SAN PEDRO AVE., SAN ANTONIO, TX

CHUY'S

"The chief pleasure in eating does not consist in costly seasoning, or exquisite flavor, but in yourself."
Horace

Clear Springs
RESTAURANT
CATFISH SEAFOOD STEAKS
CLOSED FOR CONSTRUCTION
STARTING JANUARY 4TH
CALL FOR RE-OPENING
PARKING
HISTORICAL
MARKER

GRILLED CHICKEN SANDWICH

In the 1840's the Guadalupe and Comal River Valleys became focal points for the early German immigrant settlements. Among the earliest of the German communities was Clear Springs, named for a water source now covered by Lake Dunlap. The Land on which Clear Springs Restaurant now stands was originally surveyed by James Bowie, a hero of the Alamo, in 1825. Clear Springs Hall and Store was built in 1873 for storing cotton. At the height of cotton production it was normal to see cotton wagons backed up long distances to be weighed. It was also common for the drivers to spend their waiting time shopping and visiting at the Clear Springs Store.

1 C. mayonnaise
⅛ tsp. black pepper (ground)
⅛ tsp. garlic powder
⅛ tsp. celery salt
4 C. chicken (chopped leftover grilled)
2 celery (stalks sliced)
½ C. dried cranberries (sweetened)
⅔ C. cashews (salted)
8 slices bread (toasted)
4 tbsp. mayonnaise
4 red leaf lettuce (leaves)
1 sliced tomato (ripe)

1. Whisk together 1 cup of mayonnaise, pepper, garlic powder, and celery salt until combined. Combine the chicken, celery, cranberries, and cashews in a large bowl. Pour the mayonnaise mixture over the chicken mixture and stir until evenly combined.

2. Spread ½ tablespoon of mayonnaise on each slice of toasted bread. Divide the chicken salad between four of the slices of toast; top each with a lettuce leaf and a slice of tomato. Complete each sandwich with the remaining toast slices.

CLEAR SPRINGS RESTAURANT
1692 S TX-46, NEW BRAUNFELS, TX

"In the family sandwich, the older people and the younger ones can recognize one another as the bread. Those in the middle are, for a time, the meat."
Anna Quindlen

BRUSCHETTA

COPA WINE BAR AND TASTING ROOM
19141 STONE OAK PARKWAY, SAN ANTONIO, TX

8½ roma tomatoes
¼ C. fresh basil (stems removed)
3 garlic cloves (minced)
1 garlic clove (cut in half)
¼ red onion (chopped finely)
¼ C. olive oil
3 tbsp. balsamic vinegar
1 tsp. kosher salt
1 tsp. black pepper (freshly ground)
1 baguette (french, sliced)

1. Preheat your oven on the broiler setting.

2. Prepare a pot of salted boiling water to blanche the tomatoes. Fill a large bowl with ice water and set aside. Cut a cross shape in either end of the tomatoes and immerse them in the boiling water for about 10-15 seconds. Remove the tomatoes and place them in the ice water to stop the cooking. Then, peel the skin off the tomatoes and dice them.

3. Combine the tomatoes, basil, garlic, onion, salt, pepper and balsamic vinegar.

4. Rub the olive oil on the baguette slices with a pastry brush and place them in the oven until toasted, about 1-2 minutes.

5. Pour the rest of the olive oil into the tomatoes.

6. Remove the bread from the oven and rub them with garlic.

7. Scoop the tomatoes onto the bread and serve.

"In 'The Republic' he [Plato] states that the enjoyment of food is not a true pleasure because the purpose of eating is to relieve pain -- hunger.
Mark Kurlansky

HUMMUS SOUP

Così was founded on the idea that good food will make that journey all the more delicious. From our hand-tossed Signature Salad to our Tomato, Basil, and Mozzarella Sandwich served on delicious warm flatbread, to the comfortable, urbane and contemporary atmosphere, Così is more than a restaurant. It is a constantly surprising, always delightful experience. A place where people gather to relax, dine and share their common belief that "Life Should Be Delicious".Hummus Soup

8 C. uncooked chickpeas or 4½ C. canned and drained chickpeas 5 C. vegetable stock 3 garlic cloves, pressed 1½ tbsp. tahini (sesame paste) 4 tbsp. freshly squeezed lemon 4 tbsp. freshly grated Parmesan cheese 1 tsp. salt Italian parsley for garnish fresh thyme leaves for garnish	**1.** Soak uncooked chickpeas in pan covered with water overnight or for 12 hours. **2.** If using cooked chickpeas, drains and rinse 3-4 times. **3.** Bring vegetable stock to a boil. **4.** Add chickpeas and salt and cover. **5.** Simmer on a low heat for 2 hours or until the chickpeas are tender. **6.** If using canned chickpeas, simmer for only 10 to 15 minutes. **7.** Cool soup until it is safe to place in food processor or blender. **8.** Puree soup adding garlic, tahini and lemon juice. **9.** Pour mixture back into pot. **10.** If too thick, add additional vegetable stock or water. **11.** Add Parmesan cheese and cook for 10 minutes. **12.** Serve hot with parsley and thyme garnish.

17503 LA CANTERA PKWY., SAN ANTONIO, TX

COSI

"They have a wealth of uses, but the biggest ones are for soups, salads, sandwiches and stir-fry dishes."
Chi Lang

BEEF SOUVLAK SANDWICH

Demo's Greek Food was started in 1979 by Demosthenes Demetrius Karagas, known as Demo. Demo was only 19 years old when he started the original location on Blanco Rd. His mother Lucille Karagas was involved in the opening and the developing of the restaurant. Lucille is 1st generation of Greek descent, her mother Victoria Eugenides was known for her excellent cooking and baking in the small town of Brussa. Yia yia Eugenides receipes continue to delight our guests today. Lucille still works at the Blanco Location.

Signature Tastes of SAN ANTONIO

1 lb. round steak (sirloin tip steaks)
2 tsp. dried oregano
2 tsp. minced garlic
½ tsp. black pepper (ground)
2 tsp. oiled
¼ C. lemon juice
⅓ C. plain yogurt
½ tsp. dill (dried)
1 tsp. red wine vinegar
1 tsp. minced garlic

1. Combine spices and oil and press into meat on both sides. Cut meat into 1 inch cubes and toss with lemon juice and let stand for 5 minutes.

2. Thread on skewers. Broil or grill for about 5 minutes, turnning once. Do not overcook.

3. Combine sauce ingredients and serve with Souvlaki.

DEMO'S GREEK FOOD
2501 N SAINT MARYS ST., SAN ANTONIO, TX

"I felt like a wonderful sandwich, a slice of white bread between two slices of ham."
Dorothy Lamour

Stuffed Tomato
with Shrimp Salad

Signature Tastes of SAN ANTONIO

8 tomatoes (creole or beefsteak, cored)
salt
black pepper (freshly ground)
½ C. olive oil
2 tbsp. dijon mustard
2 tsp. honey
1½ tsp. minced garlic
1 tbsp. crab boil (liquid)
2 lemons (halved)
2 lb. shrimp (peeled and deveined)
1 sweet corn (ear, blanched and kernels removed)
½ C. diced tomatoes
½ C. vidalia onions (diced)
¼ C. black olives (pitted and halved)
1 tbsp. chervil (finely chopped fresh, leaves)
8 sprigs chervil (fresh)

1. Bring a pot of salted water to a boil.
2. Using a sharp knife, make a small X on the bottom of each whole tomato. Place the tomatoes in the boiling water and cook for 1 minute.
3. Remove and place in a bowl of ice water. Cool the tomatoes completely.
4. Remove from the water and peel the skin off each tomato.
5. Quarter each tomato ¾ of the way to the bottom. Remove the seeds.
6. Place the tomatoes in a large glass pan.
7. Season the tomatoes with salt and pepper.
8. In a small mixing bowl whisk together the oil, mustard and honey.
9. Season with salt and pepper. Pour the marinade over each tomato.
10. Cover with plastic wrap and refrigerate for at least 6 hours. Remove from the refrigerator and pour off the marinade into a medium size bowl.
11. In a saucepan, add the crab boil and lemons. Bring the mixture to a boil.

DeWese's Tip Top Cafe
2814 Fredericksburg Rd., San Antonio, TX

"Salad, freshens without enfeebling and fortifies without irritating."
Jean-Anthelme Brillat-Savarin

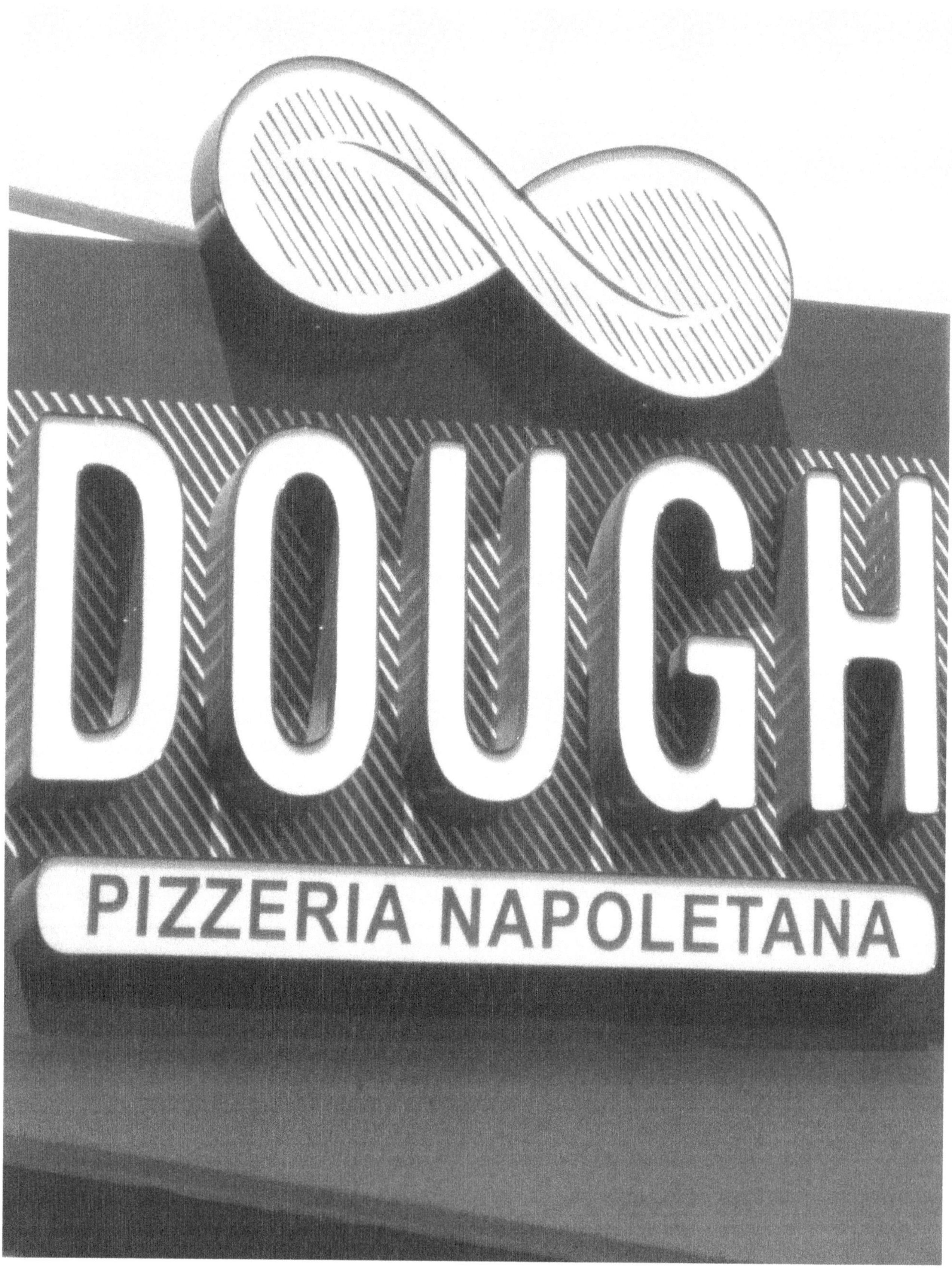
DOUGH
PIZZERIA NAPOLETANA

Baby Bibb Salad

Signature Tastes of SAN ANTONIO

Dough Pizzeria Napoletana San Antonio, Texas location is to date one of an elite 54 restaurants in the U.S. and #292 in the world to receive the prestigious certification from L'Associazione Vera Pizza Napoletana for serving authentic Pizza Napoletana. In order to be considered for certification, Doug Horn, Chef/Co-Owner of DOUGH, studied artisan pizza-making with the Director of the Verace Pizza Napoletana Americas (VPN)-Peppe Miele. Doug was taught the process of making authentic Pizza Napoletana following the strict guidelines as set forth by the Italian government.

3 large ripe Bartlett pears, divided use
⅓ C. granulated sugar
½ tsp. fresh tarragon or scant ¼ tsp. dried
1-2 tbsp. cider vinegar
1½ tbsp. lemon juice
2-3 heads Bibb lettuce, rinsed and dried
4 oz. (1 C.) crumbed gorgonzola or blue cheese

1. Peel, core, and chop one pear. Place pear, ⅓ cup water, sugar, and tarragon in a small saucepan.

2. Simmer over medium heat until pear pieces are soft, about 5 minutes depending on ripeness of pear. Do not let all the water evaporate. There should be about ⅞ cup pear and liquid. Cool.

3. Pour pear and liquid into a blender and blend until smooth. Add part of the vinegar and lemon juice to taste. Taste and adjust sugar and acid to make a sweet-tart dressing, adding a little water if needed to thin. Refrigerate until cold.

4. Core and thinly slice remaining 2 pears. For each serving arrange 3-4 lettuce leaves on a salad plate. Top with ⅓ of a sliced pear, 2-3 tablespoons Gorgonzola and drizzle with 2 tablespoons dressing. Serve immediately.

DOUGH PIZZERIA NAPOLETANA PIZZA
6989 BLANCO RD., SAN ANTONIO, TX

"Salad is never more appetizing than when served in a large wooden bowl."
Dorothy Draper

91

El Chaparral
RESTAURANT
"A TASTE LIKE NO OTHER"
HAPPY HOUR
MON FRI
3 7

CHALUPAS

Three decades and two generations of experience and passion go into every smiling face and mouth watering bite that make-up El Chaparral. Our family history is etched into everything we do. In 1972, our parents, Charlie and Mary Garcia, followed their dream to a small eatery in Helotes, Texas. We sold our home in San Antonio and moved into the modest living quarters behind the restaurant. Some of our earliest memories are playing in the kitchen with our older sister Jessica and swimming in the creek behind the restaurant.

1 lb. ground beef, crumbled
½ med. size onion, chopped
1 tbsp. chili powder
1 tsp. cumin powder
salt & pepper to taste
1 (No. 300) can pinto beans
12 frozen corn tortillas
3 tbsp. shortening
shredded lettuce
¾ lb. mild cheddar cheese, shredded
3 tomatoes, cut in small pcs.
bottled taco sauce

1. Heat lightly greased, large skillet. Add the ground beef and onion. Cook until the ground beef is browned. Drain off grease and add the chili powder, cumin, salt and pepper to the meat mixture and mix thoroughly. Blend in beans and their liquid.

2. Cover mixture and cook at simmering point for about 30 minutes.

3. Heat shortening in skillet and lightly fry tortillas on both sides. Drain on absorbent paper and stack. Keep warm in oven, moderately hot.

4. To assemble chalupas, place 2 or 3 tablespoons of the meat mixture on each tortilla. Sprinkle grated cheese over meat then arrange shredded lettuce and tomatoes on top. Serve with taco sauce in a separate bowl.

5. Yield: serves 4 allowing 3 chalupas per serving.

EL CHAPARRAL MEXICAN
15103 BANDERA RD HELOTES, TX

"If we are what we eat, with all the genetically modified and imitation foods we now eat, what the heck are we?"
Anonymous

This is your Tex-Mexican Restaurant with the standard offerings. Most of the food is pretty good and the staff are great people. That said, the food is always hot and fresh. What is very convenient is the drive-thru. Very fast, especially for large orders that we bring back to the office some mornings or lunch. Atmosphere and service is authentic Tex-Mex and the girls are always friendly. Parking is a breeze. I would say the attraction here ('cause it's always busy) is that they are reliably fast, hot and affordable. You almost always know what you're going to get, how it's going to taste and about how much its going to run you. And that's a comfortable feeling for a lot of folks.

8 poblano chiles
2 bunches green onions
(about 12), dark green
tops trimmed
2 lbs. skirt steak, cut
crosswise into 6-inch-
wide pieces
4 garlic cloves, minced
coarse kosher salt
corn or flour tortillas
2 avocados, peeled,
pitted, sliced
lime wedges

1. Prepare barbecue (high heat). Grill chiles and onions until charred all over, about 3 minutes for onions and 5 minutes for chiles. Transfer onions to plate; tent with foil. Transfer chiles to large bowl; cover with plastic and let stand 15 minutes. Peel and seed; cut into 1-inch-wide strips. Transfer to plate; tent with foil.

2. Rub steak with garlic; sprinkle with coarse salt and pepper. Grill until cooked to desired doneness, about 3 minutes per side for medium. Transfer to work surface; cool 5 minutes. Grill tortillas until warm and slightly charred, about 10 seconds per side. Cut steak crosswise into strips; transfer to plate.

3. Serve steak with tortillas, chiles, green onions, avocado slices, lime wedges, and Salsa Mexicana.

EL SABROSITO MEXICAN
9141 FM-78, CONVERSE, TX

"Before eating, always take time to thank the food."
Arapaho Proverb

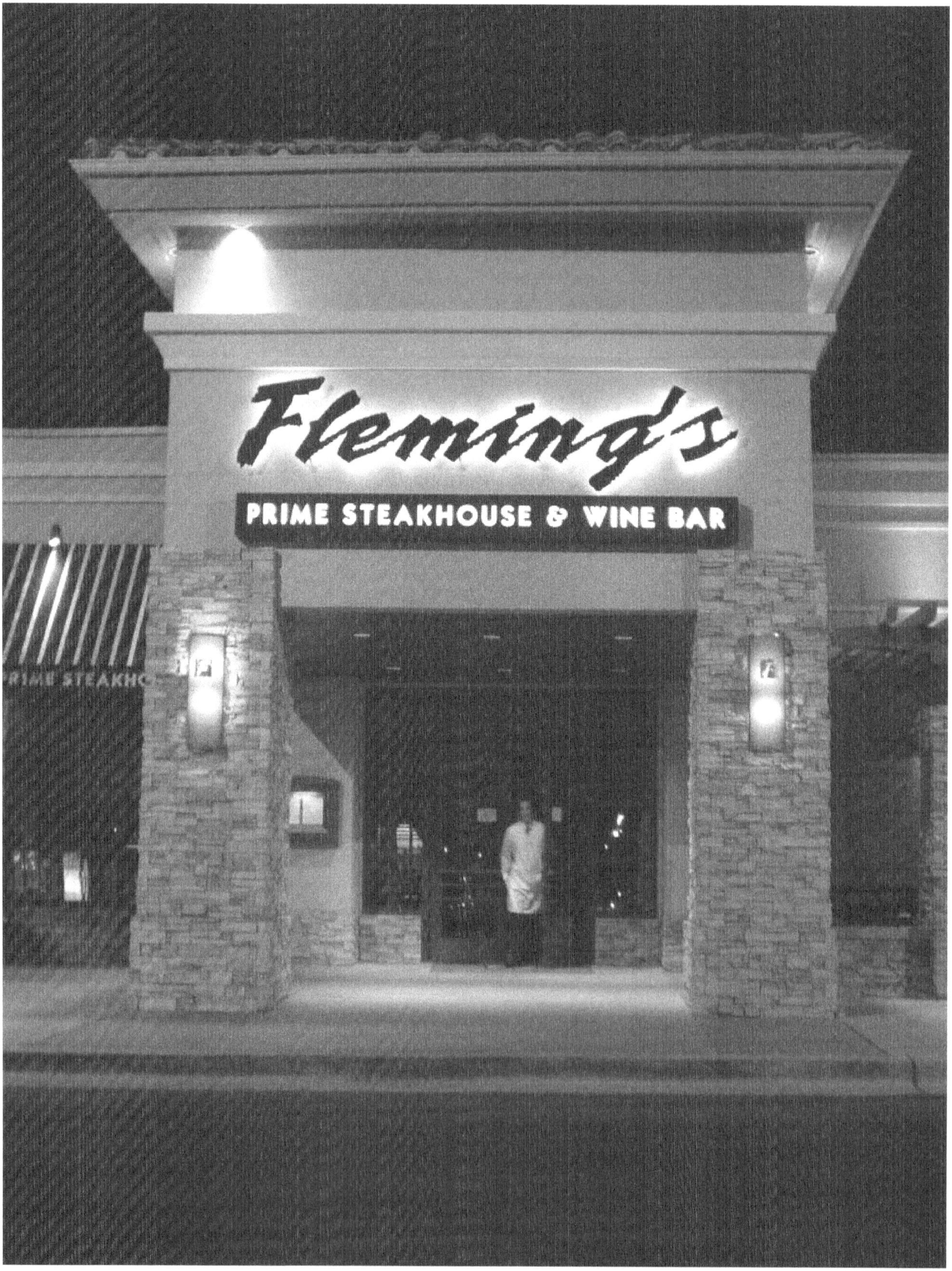
Fleming's
PRIME STEAKHOUSE & WINE BAR

THE WEDGE

As the sun fades into the West over the breathtaking beauty of the Quarry Golf Course, the night comes to life at Fleming's Prime Steakhouse & Wine Bar. Just as our city is known for its unique history and the famous Alamo, Fleming's is known for its world-class food and wine, lively and comfortable atmosphere and gracious service.

1 head iceberg lettuce
(cut into 4 wedges)
1 tbsp. dijon mustard
2 tbsp. red wine vinegar
1 clove minced garlic
¼ C. olive oil
1 tsp. sugar
2 tbsp. blue cheese
(crumbled)
kosher salt
black pepper
½ pt. grape tomatoes
2 strips cooked bacon
(crispy and crumbled)
¼ C. red onion (finely
diced)

1. Heat a grill or grill pan and place the lettuce wedges on a platter.

2. Prepare the vinaigrette by briskly whisking together the Dijon, vinegar, and garlic. Drizzle in the olive oil while whisking to create an emulsion. Add the sugar and blue cheese, and whisk gently to mix. Season with salt and pepper to taste.

3. Lightly oil the tomato slices, and season with salt and pepper. Grill until slightly charred on the outside and then transfer to the platter with the lettuce wedges.

4. Pour the vinaigrette over the lettuce and tomato and top with bacon and red onion.

"It's better that it should make you sick than that you don't eat it at all."
Catalan Proverb

FOGO
DE
CHÃO

CHURRASCARIA
BRAZILIAN STEAKHOUSE

The Gaucho Way of
Preparing Meat

SHIITAKE MUSHROOMS

The story of Fogo de Chão® began in the mountainous countryside of Rio Grande do Sul in Southern Brazil, where its founders were born. Growing up, the brothers were immersed in the centuries-old Gaucho culture, a rich blend of traditions from European immigrants and Brazilian natives. In 1979, the first Fogo de Chão opened its doors in Porto Alegre, combining the best of the centuries-old culinary tradition of churrasco with a focus on exceptional customer service.

1 lb. fresh sliced shiitake mushrooms
3 tbsp. low-sodium chicken or vegetable broth
2 cloves garlic, chopped
2 tbsp. extra virgin olive oil
salt and pepper to taste

Optional:
2 tbsp. each of fresh rosemary, oregano or feta cheese

1. Chop garlic and let sit for 5 minutes to enhance its health-promoting properties.

2. Remove stems from mushrooms and slice.

3. Heat broth in a stainless steel skillet. When broth begins to steam, add mushrooms and Healthy Sauté, covered, for 3 minutes.

4. Remove skillet cover and let mushrooms cook for 4 more minutes.

5. Toss with olive oil and season with salt and pepper and whatever optional ingredients desired. This recipe can be served as a side dish or over fish or poultry.

849 E COMMERCE ST., SAN ANTONIO, TX

FOGO DE CHÃO

"Eat not to dullness, drink not to elevation."
Benjamin Franklin

99

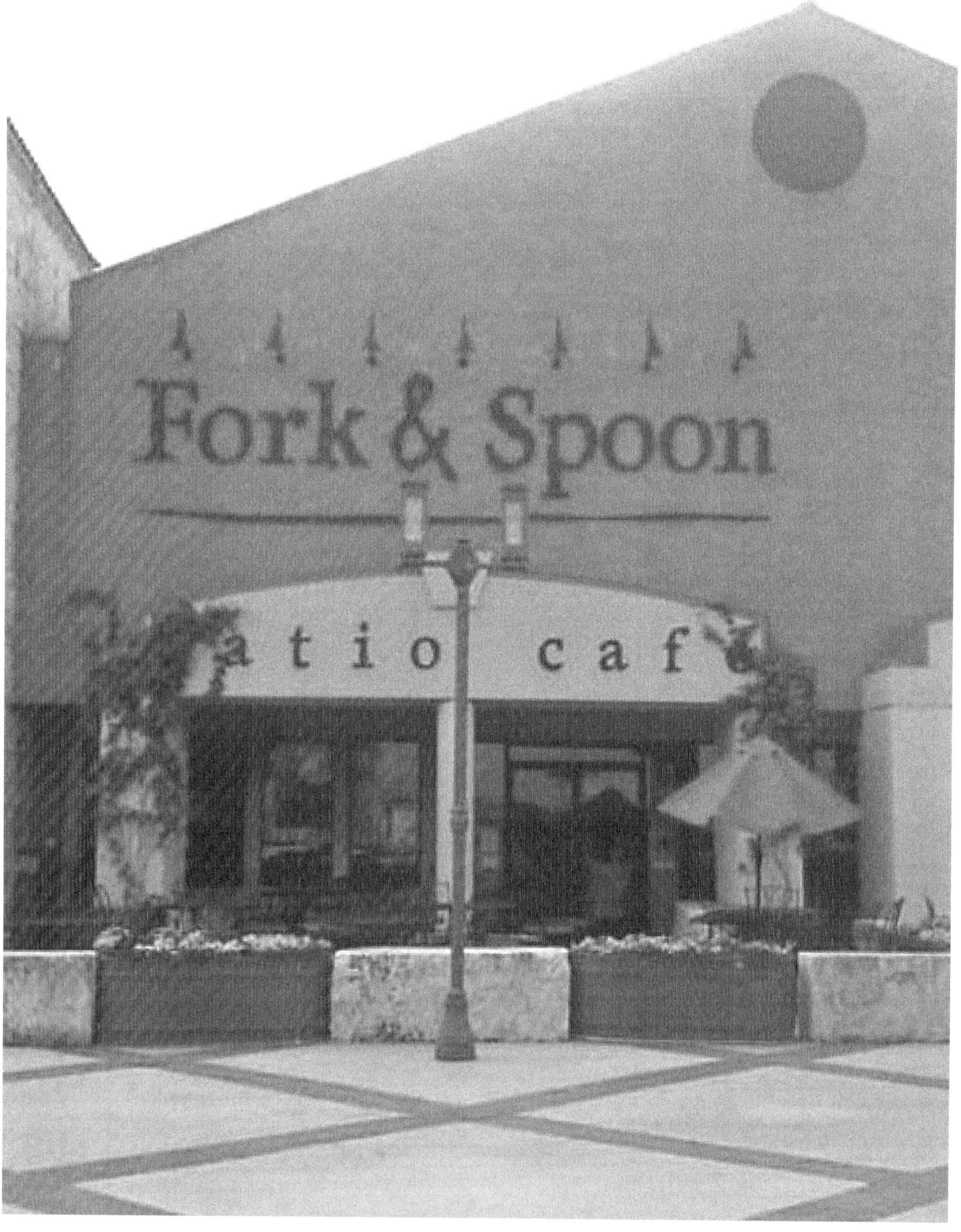
Fork & Spoon
atio caf

BELGIUM WAFFLES

Signature Tastes of SAN ANTONIO

651 NORTH BUSINESS IH35, NEW BRAUNFELS, TX

FORK AND SPOON

1 (.25 oz.) package
active dry yeast
¼ C. warm milk (110 degrees F/45 degrees C)
3 egg yolks
2 ¾ C. warm milk (110 degrees F/45 degrees C)
¾ C. butter, melted and cooled to lukewarm
½ C. white sugar
1½ tsp. salt
2 tsp. vanilla extract
4 C. all-purpose flour
3 egg whites

1. In a small bowl, dissolve yeast in ¼ cup warm milk. Let stand until creamy, about 10 minutes.

2. In a large bowl, whisk together the egg yolks, ¼ cup of the warm milk and the melted butter. Stir in the yeast mixture, sugar, salt and vanilla. Stir in the remaining 2½ cups milk alternately with the flour, ending with the flour. Beat the egg whites until they form soft peaks; fold into the batter. Cover the bowl tightly with plastic wrap. Let rise in a warm place until doubled in volume, about 1 hour.

3. Preheat the waffle iron. Brush with oil and spoon about ½ cup (or as recommended by manufacturer) onto center of iron. Close the lid and bake until it stops steaming and the waffle is golden brown. Serve immediately or keep warm in 200 degree oven.

"You know I love to talk about food I'm going to eat while I'm already eating."
Grace, on the TV show Will & Grace

Kappa Maki

Welcome to Formosa Garden, where exquisite Asian cuisine meets traditional Asian art décor to offer our diners an unforgettable experience. With daily fresh ingredients and our chefs' attention to detail, the menu is a collaboration of classic Asian flavors with a touch of exotic flare. Our mission is to create dishes that are unique, authentic and affordable; culinary creativity simply at its best.

2 sheets nori (dried seaweed)
half a cucumber, sliced horizontally

Sushi rice:
1½ tbsp. japanese rice vinegar
1 tsp. sugar
1 tbsp. salt
1 C. sushi rice

Serve with:
pickled ginger
wasabi paste
soy sauce

1. First of all, wash the rice and then make sure that for every one cup of rice, there's two cups of water. Add the water and the rice to the pot that you're cooking it in and let it cook. It usually takes around 15 minutes. Once the rice has been cooked, turn off the heat but leave it on the pot for five minutes.

2. Mix the rice vinegar, salt and sugar at the bottom of a large bowl. While the rice cools, which should take around ten minutes, prepare the filling. Remove the skin of the cucumber and cut it into long, horizontal strips. They shouldn't be too thin or too thick.

3. Spoon the rice out of the pot into the bowl and mix it with a wooden spoon.

4. Lay a sheet of nori onto a cutting board and then, wet your hands. Then, drop the rice horizontally into the middle of the sheet. Use your hands if you must, and keep a bowl of cool water ready in case your hands get too sticky. Leave one inch at the top of the sheet and at the bottom so that you can seal it properly.

5. On top of the mound of rice, add two sticks of cucumber and then roll it up. Using a sharp knife, slowly and carefully cut the roll into eight pieces. If the knife becomes difficult or sticky, then pour a little of the rice vinegar onto the knife.

Formosa Garden
1011 NE Loop 410, San Antonio, TX

Signature Taste of San Antonio

"Cooking is like love, it should be entered into with abandon or not at all"
Harriet van Horne

CAESAR SALAD

At Four Kings, the sandwiches start with house-baked bread and just get better from there. This small place is tucked away in an inconspicuous strip shopping center not far from Joint Base San Antonio-Randolph, and it takes a little effort to spot it from Pat Booker Road, but it's worth it. Not only does this place bake its own bread, it makes nearly all the items from scratch, including roasting its own meats for salads and sandwiches. About the only thing the cooks don't bake themselves is ham, as if it matters.

½ C. high quality extra virgin olive oil
4 cloves fresh garlic, peeled, smashed, then minced
1 baguette, preferably a day old, sliced thin
¼ C. freshly juiced lemon juice (plus more to taste)
4 oz. Parmesan cheese, grated
1 tsp. anchovy paste, or 1-2 anchovies, smashed and minced
2 eggs
freshly ground black pepper (¼ tsp. or to taste)
½ tsp. salt
4-6 small heads of romaine lettuce, rinsed, patted dry, wilted outer leaves discarded

1. In a very large bowl, whisk together the olive oil and garlic. Let sit for half an hour.

2. While the oil is sitting, make the croutons. Spread the baguette slices out over a baking sheet (may need to do in batches), lined with parchment paper or Silpat. Brush or spray with olive oil (or melted butter, or if you want garlicky croutons, dip pastry brush in the garlic infused oil you have sitting in step 1). Broil for a couple of minutes until the tops are lightly browned. (Note: do not walk away, these can easily go from browned to burnt.) Remove and let cool.

3. Add anchovies and eggs to the oil garlic mixture. Whisk until creamy. Add salt and pepper and ¼ cup of lemon juice. Whisk in half of the Parmesan cheese. Taste, add more lemon juice to taste. The lemon should give an edge to the dressing, but not overwhelm it.

4. Using your hands, tear off chunks of lettuce from the heads of lettuce (do not use a knife to cut). Add to the oil mixture and toss until coated. Add the rest of the Parmesan cheese, toss.

5. Coarsely chop the toasted bread and add (with the crumbs from the chopping) to the salad. Toss. Serve immediately.

6. Serves 4-6 for a main course or up to 8-12 for a side salad.

2047 UNIVERSAL CITY BLVD., UNIVERSAL CITY, TX

FOUR KINGS

"To remember a successful salad is generally to remember a successful dinner; at all events, the perfect dinner necessarily includes the perfect salad."
George Ellwanger

Spanako Pizza

At the foothills of the fabled Texas Hill Country, Leon Springs is a proverbial Wide Spot in the Road. However, its reputation for knowing how to have a good time has earned the tiny community a big dot on the map. Visit Leon Springs and find Rudy's, Home of the World's Worst Barbecue and Somatic Therapies Massage Center. As a recent addition to the Leon Springs landscape, Fralo's Art of Pizza is earning a spot in the hearts of locals with casual dining among lazy moss-draped oaks and picnic tables, a scene often rounded out with a live musician at least four nights a week year 'round.

1 tbsp. extra-virgin olive oil
1 tbsp. unsalted butter
2 garlic cloves, chopped
1 red onion, thinly sliced
1 pizza dough, refrigerated or from your favorite pizzeria
2 10 oz. boxes frozen chopped spinach, defrosted
1 sack (10 oz.) shredded mozzarella cheese
1 tsp. dried oregano
¼ lb. feta crumbles
1 tbsp. grill seasoning
2 plum tomatoes, diced
salt and fleshly ground black pepper

Topping:
2 roasted red peppers, drained
¼ C. fresh flat-leaf parsley
¼ C. pitted kalamata olives
1 C. coarsely chopped arugula
hot pepper rings (optional)

1. Preheat the oven to 425 degrees F. In a large nonstick skillet preheated over medium heat add 1 tablespoon of the EVOO and the butter. When the butte melts, add the garlic and all of the onions and cook for 5 minutes.

2. Transfer the garlic and onions to a bowl to cool. Form the dough into a 12-inch pizza. Place on a pizza pan or a large cookie sheet. Place the topping ingredients in a small food processor, season with salt and pepper, and process until a thick paste forms. Spread the topping over the dough in a thin layer.

3. Dot the pizza with the 2 boxes of defrosted and wrung spinach and sautéed garlic and onions. Top with the mozzarella cheese and the feta crumbles. Sprinkle the oregano over the cheese.

4. Bake the pizza until golden and bubbly all over, about 17 minutes. Scatter the arugula, diced tomatoes and, if using, the hot peppers over the pizza, cut into wedges, and serve.

FRALO'S ART OF PIZZA
23651 W I-10, SAN ANTONIO, TX

"Better cut the pizza in four pieces because I'm not hungry enough to eat six."
Yogi Berra

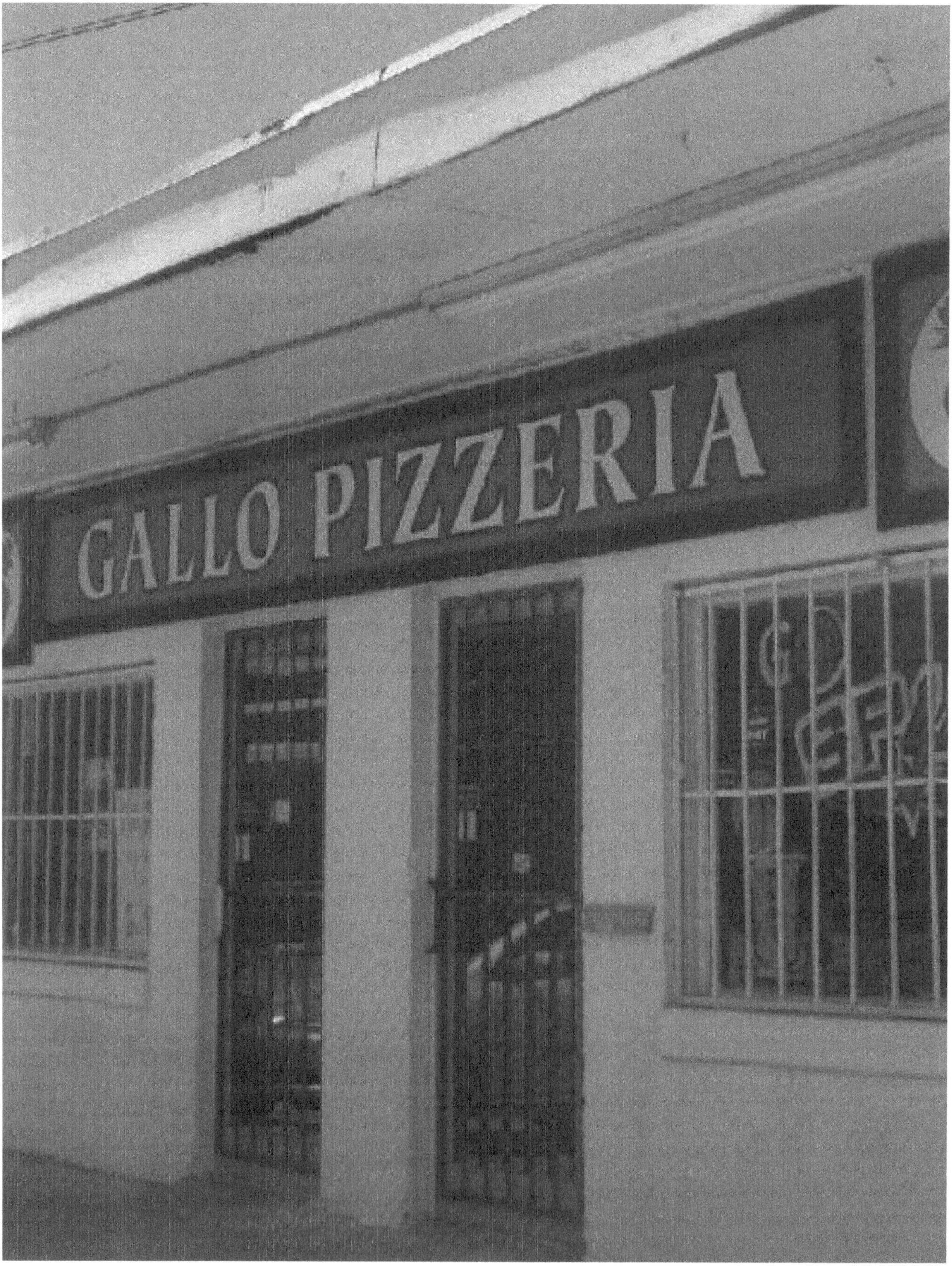
GALLO PIZZERIA

SALSA MEXICANA

Signature Tastes of SAN ANTONIO

Our goal here at Gallo Pizzeria is to serve the highest quality food with the freshest, finest ingredients at the most affordable price. Our fresh vegetables, authentic calzones, and unique specialty pizzas will make your mouth water. In fact, our special Diablo pizza will likely make your eyes water, as well! We believe freshness, quality, and affordability are key to your enjoyable dining experience.

2 ea. large ripe tomatoes, finely chopped
6 ea. serranochiles, finely minced and seeded
½ white onion, finely minced, or more to taste
½ small bunch cilantro, finely chopped
pinch of salt

1. Mix all ingredients thoroughly. For a smoother texture (that I prefer) use your standup or hand blender. Let sit for 12 hours or more before serving. Use within three days or so.

2. I don't like the texture of chile seeds but I leave in part/most of the veins (pith) for good heat. Don't worry, the acid in the tomatoes will temper the heat some.

3. I prefer a higher percentage of onion to tomato than seems common in local restaurants.

4. A 16 oz can of diced or whole tomatoes, drained and chopped, can be substituted for fresh (reluctantly). Fresh is the key concept here. Never use tomato sauce, stewed tomatoes or anything cooked. Lately I'm suspicious of tomato puree as well. Never use pickled chiles in this recipe.

5. Garlic and lime juice are seen in some recipes including one from Rick Bayless. I don't think they are necessary.

164 CASTROVILLE ROAD, SAN ANTONIO, TX

GALLO PIZZERIA

"I don't like recipes that are complicated. It's better to make a few things well and enjoy the process and the people around you."
Pascale Beale

107

POLLO FUNDIDO

This restaurant, family owned and operated, puts out some of the best, authentic Mexican food in San Antonio. The breakfast tacos, enchiladas, carne guisada and carne de puerco are just some of the standouts on their menu. Known for their Mexican food, they also have a variety of local favorites including the Garcia Burger, chicken-fried steak and the brisket plate. I've been eating brisket my whole life and Garcia's gets it right. Their brisket has a real smoky flavor and a juicy tenderness that sets theirs apart. And the service will make you feel like a welcomed guest in someone's kitchen.

Signature Tastes of SAN ANTONIO

GARCIA'S MEXICAN FOOD TO GO

842 FREDERICKSBURG RD., SAN ANTONIO, TX

Filling:
1 medium red onion
1 red pepper
1 green pepper
2 lb. boneless chicken breasts
¼ tsp. ground cumin
¼ tsp. chili seasoning mix
garlic, salt, pepper hot sauce (to taste)
12 small flour tortillas
2 C. vegetable oil

Sauce:
0.5 (8 oz.) package cream cheese
½ C. sour cream
1 jalapeno
¼ C. half-and-half
1 tsp. chopped garlic
1 C. grated monterey jack and cheddar cheese blend

1. Dice your peppers, onion, and the chicken. Add seasonings. Cook in a saucepan until vegetables are soft and the chicken is fully cooked. Remove from heat.

2. If you have a deep fryer start to heat it up.

3. If you don't, use a big pot and heat the 2 cups of vegetable oil. You will be deep frying! (Tip:Flour tortillas are easier to work with when they are warm)

4. Fill the tortillas with the chicken mixture and roll. (Tip: You might want to use tooth picks to keep the tortillas closed in the deep fryer).

5. Place the filled tortilla in the deep fryer until crispy and brown. When done place on a paper towel to soak some of the grease. Put the finished tortillas in a baking dish large enough to fit all 12; set aside.

6. Preheat oven to 325°F.

"Eating is really one of your indoor sports. You play three times a day, and it's well worth while to make the game as pleasant as possible."
Dorothy Draper

Genghis Grill-The Mongolian Stir Fry is a build your own bowl, fast casual, asian stir-fry concept. The atmosphere is colorful, lively, and a lot of fun! It's actually not a cuisine, but an INTERACTIVE style of exhibition cooking modeled after a centuries-old legend. According to this legend, 12th century Mongol warriors, led by the mighty warrior, GENGHIS KHAN heated their shields over open fires to grill food in the fields of battle!

Signature Tastes of SAN ANTONIO

2½ tbsp. peeled fresh ginger (grated)
2 tbsp. low sodium soy sauce
¼ tsp. crushed red pepper
8 oz. flank steak (thinly sliced and cut into 1½ in. lengths)
2 garlic cloves (minced)
cooking spray
7 C. bok choy (thinly sliced bok choy about 1 lb.)
1 C. shiitake mushrooms (thinly sliced, 2 oz.)
1 C. carrot (slices)
½ C. green onions (thinly sliced)
2 C. hot water
2 tbsp. hoisin sauce
28 oz. less sodium beef broth
4 oz. buckwheat noodles (uncooked soba)
1 tbsp. rice vinegar
1½ tsp. dark sesame oil (divided)

1. Combine the first 5 ingredients in a large zip-top plastic bag, and seal. Marinate in refrigerator 2½ hours, turning bag occasionally.

2. Heat a small Dutch oven over high heat. Coat pan with cooking spray. Add beef mixture to pan; stir-fry 1 minute or until browned. Remove beef mixture from pan; set aside.

3. Add bok choy, mushrooms, carrot, and green onions to pan; stir-fry 2 minutes or until bok choy begins to wilt. Add water, hoisin, and broth; bring to a boil. Stir in noodles. Reduce heat; simmer 5 minutes or until noodles are done. Stir in beef mixture and vinegar. Ladle 1½ cups soup into each of 6 bowls; drizzle each serving with ¼ teaspoon sesame oil.

1903 N LOOP 1604 E SUITE 1106, SAN ANTONIO, TX

GENGHIS GRILL

"Nothing would be more tiresome than eating and drinking if God had not made them a pleasure as well as a necessity."
Voltaire

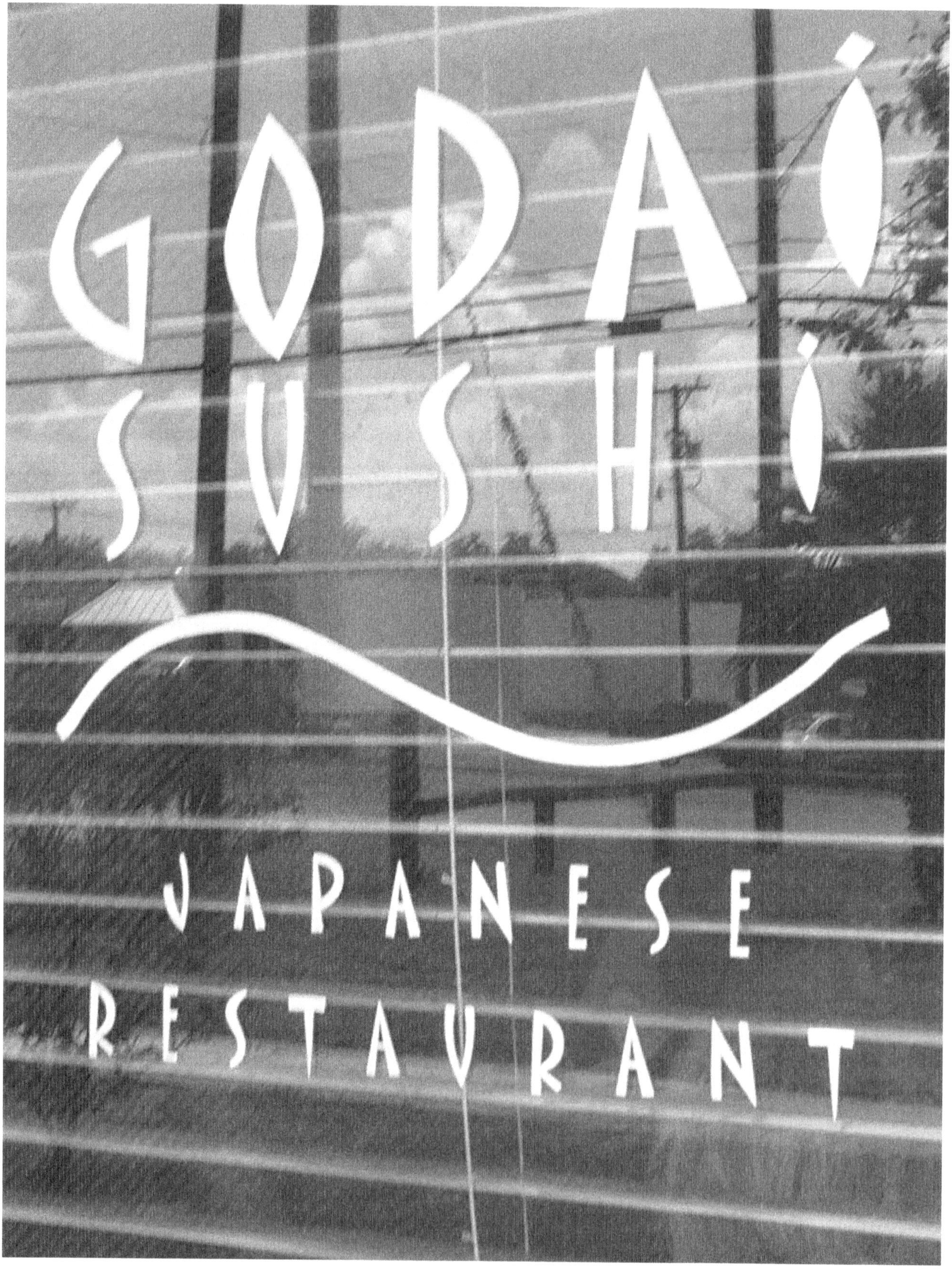
GODAI
SUSHI
JAPANESE
RESTAURANT

YAKIMESHI

Godai Sushi Bar & Japanese Restaurant is a unique restaurant located in San Antonio, Texas that serves authentic Japanese cuisine. Chef/Owner Goro will ensure you that you will enjoy a hearty meal that will delight your tastebuds and satisfy the largest of appetites. Combined with the delicious dishes, wonderful aromas, and outstanding service – you will be able to enjoy a dining experience that is beyond compare!

2 balls of rice (½ lb)
¼ medium onion (chopped)
⅛ C. green onion (chopped)
0.2 lb. ham (minced)
2 eggs (beaten)

Spices:
1 tsp. chicken soup powder
2 tsp. sake
2 tsp. soy sauce
½ tsp. salt (for mixing with egg and rice)
dash of salt and pepper

1. Mix eggs with steamed rice and add salt.

2. Heat oil in frying pan then grill onions, ham, and green onions for two minutes over high heat.

3. Add rice, and cook for 3 minutes over medium heat and add sake and chicken soup for 2 minutes.

4. Sprinkle salt and pepper, add soy sauce, and cook for 1 minute on low.

Signature Tastes of SAN ANTONIO

GODAI SUSHI BAR AND RESTAURANT

11203 WEST AVE., SAN ANTONIO, TX

"Cooking is like love. It should be entered into with abandon or not at all."
Harriet Van Horne

TARO ROOT CAKE

Signature Tastes of SAN ANTONIO

In 1972, Connie Andrews dreamed of owning her own small Chinese restaurant. It didn't matter that she was not Asian, had no cooking experience and had never cooked on a Chinese stove before. Her dreams became a reality on September 7, 1972, when her first Golden Wok restaurant opened in San Antonio. After struggling on a shoestring budget for the first two years, Connie's long days and determination paid off as the restaurant began to gain popularity. Kenneth Lau joined Golden Wok in 1974 and became a partner in 1976. The second Golden Wok location opened later that same year on Fredricksburg Road.

¼ C. scallops (chinese dried, gown yu chee about 1 oz.)
8 mushrooms (chinese dried)
¼ C. dried shrimp (chinese, 1 oz)
6 oz. bacon (chinese, store bought or homemade)
1 root (taro, 2¼ lb.)
1½ tsp. salt
2 C. rice flour
vegetable oil
oyster-flavored sauce

1. In a small bowl, soak the scallops in ⅓ cup cold water for about 2 hours, or until softened. Drain, reserving the soaking liquid. Remove and discard the small hard knob from the side of the scallops. Finely shred the scallops.
2. Meanwhile, in a medium bowl, soak the mushrooms in ½ cup cold water 30 minutes, or until softened. Drain and squeeze dry, reserving the soaking liquid. Cut off and discard stems and mince the caps. In a small bowl, soak the dried shrimp in ⅓ cup cold water for 30 minutes, or until softened. Drain, reserving soaking liquid. Finely chop shrimp and set aside.
3. Cut the bacon into 3 equal pieces and place in a 9-inch shallow heatproof dish. Bring water to a boil over high heat in a covered steamer large enough to fit the dish without touching the sides of the steamer. Carefully place the dish in the steamer, cover, reduce heat to medium, and steam 15 to 20 minutes, or just until bacon is softened and there are juices in the dish. Check the water level from time to time and replenish, if necessary, with boiling water. Carefully remove the dish from the steamer and set aside to cool.
4. Meanwhile, wearing rubber gloves, peel taro root and cut into ½-inch cubes to make about 7 cups. In a 4-quart saucepan, combine the taro root, 1 teaspoon salt, and about 1½ quarts cold water, and bring to a boil over high heat. Reduce heat to low, cover, and simmer 15 to 20 minutes, or until taro has turned a pale lavender color and is just tender when pierced with a knife.
5. Remove the bacon from its dish and reserve the juices in the dish. Cut off and discard the rind and thick layer of fat underneath. Cut the remaining meat into paper-thin slices and then finely chop. In a 14-inch flat-bottomed wok or skillet, stir-fry the chopped bacon over medium heat for 2 to 3 minutes, or until meat releases fat and just begins to brown. Add the minced mushrooms and shrimp, and stir-fry 2 to 3 minutes. Stir in pan juices from the bacon and remove from heat.
6. Drain the taro in a colander, reserving the cooking liquid. Return the taro to the saucepan, add the bacon and mushroom mixture, and stir to combine. In a large bowl, combine the rice flour and the reserved mushroom, scallop, and shrimp soaking liquids, stirring until smooth. Stir in 1 cup of the reserved hot taro broth. Pour this batter over the taro mixture in the saucepan. Add the remaining ½ teaspoon salt and stir until combined. Consistency will resemble that of thick rice pudding. Pour the mixture into a heatproof 8-inch round, 3- to 4-inch-deep, straight-sided bowl, such as a soufflé dish.
7. Bring water to a boil over high heat in a covered steamer large enough to fit the dish without touching the sides of the steamer. Carefully place the dish into the steamer, cover, reduce heat to medium-low, and steam 1 hour, or just until cake is set and is firm to the touch. Check the water level and replenish, if necessary, with boiling water. Carefully remove the bowl from the steamer and cool on a rack about 1 hour. Cover and refrigerate at least 3 to 4 hours.
8. Run a knife along the edge of the cake to loosen sides. Place a cake rack over the bowl and invert to unmold. Flip the cake right-side up onto a cutting board. Wrap the cake in plastic wrap and refrigerate until ready to use.
9. When ready to eat, cut the cake into quarters. Cut each quarter crosswise, not into wedges, but into two 2-inch-wide strips. Cut each strip crosswise into scant ½-inch-thick slices. This is the typical way of slicing a cake Chinese style.
10. Heat a 14-inch flat-bottomed wok or skillet, over medium heat until hot but not smoking. Add just enough vegetable oil to barely coat the wok. Add the taro cake slices in batches and cook for 2 to 3 minutes per side, until golden brown. Serve immediately with oyster sauce.

8822 WURZBACH RD SAN ANTONIO, TX

GOLDEN WORK

"Love is like a good cake; you never know when it's coming, but you'd better eat it when it does!"
JoyBell C.

BARBEQUE CHICKEN

Signature Tastes of SAN ANTONIO

GONZALES FOOD MARKET BBQ & SAUSAGE

2530 W.W. WHITE ROAD SAN ANTONIO, TX

Richard Lopez is the third-generation proprietor of the Gonzales Food Market in Gonzales, Texas, a storefront barbecue restaurant located on the town's historic Texas Heroes Square. Richard grew up in Gonzales, working in the market alongside numerous cousins and extended family members. When his father decided to retire, Richard, who spent twenty years working for the corporate grocery chain Albertson's, was eager to continue a family tradition. In spite of the long hours, Richard wouldn't have it any other way.

4 lb. of your favorite chicken parts (legs, thighs, wings, breasts), skin-on
salt
vegetable oil
1 C. barbecue sauce, store-bought or homemade

1. Coat the chicken pieces with vegetable oil and sprinkle salt over them on all sides. Prepare your grill for high, direct heat. If you are using charcoal or wood, make sure there is a cool side to the grill where there are fewer coals.

2. Lay the chicken pieces skin side down on the hottest side of the grill in order to sear the skin side well. Grill for 5-10 minutes, depending on how hot the grill is (you do not want the chicken to burn). Once you have a good sear on one side, move the chicken pieces to the cooler side of the grill, or, if you are using a gas grill, lower the heat to medium low. Cover the grill and cook undisturbed for 20-30 minutes.

3. Turn the chicken pieces over and baste them with with your favorite barbecue sauce. Cover the grill again and allow to cook for another 30 minutes. Repeat, turning the chicken pieces over, basting them with sauce, covering, and cooking for another 30 minutes.

4. By now the chicken should be cooked through. You can check with a meat thermometer inserted into the thickest part of the chicken piece. Look for 165°F for breasts and 170°F for thighs. Or insert the tip of a knife into the middle of the thickest piece, the juices should run clear. If the chicken isn't done, turn the pieces over and continue to cook at a low temperature. If you want can finish with a sear on the hot side of the grill. To do this, put the pieces, skin side down, on the hot side of the grill. Allow them to sear and blacken slightly for a minute or two.

5. Paint with more barbecue sauce and serve. Yield: Serves 4-6.

"Food is our common ground, a universal experience."
James Beard

117

FRIED CATFISH

Good Time Charlie's started serving San Antonio in 1979 from a simple menu of burgers and chili. While Charlie's still serves the best burger in town, the menu has grown to include something for all taste buds -- from the chicken fried steak with homemade cream gravy to a wide selection of nothing-but-fresh veggies. Charlie's has always been open 7 days from 11AM to Midnight and has built a reputation for serving up great food whenever you're ready. Conveniently located in the heart of the San Antonio Cultural District, Charlie's is a favorite for anyone looking for a homecooked meal and a cold, refreshing beverage in a friendly, down-home atmosphere.

vegetable oil, olive oil, or butter (your choice)
4 medium freshwater catfish fillets
1 C. cold milk
1 C. yellow cornmeal
2 to 3 tsp. salt
1 tsp. freshly-ground black pepper
1 tsp. red (cayenne) pepper
lemon wedges

1. Rinse the fillets under cold water and dry thoroughly with paper towels. In a pie place, lay fillets and pour milk over the top. In another pie plate, combine cornmeal, salt, pepper, and cayenne pepper.

2. Remove the fillets one at a time from the milk and roll in the cornmeal mixture to coat evenly; place on a large platter to dry leaving space between them. Let dry at least 5 minutes.

3. Heat the oil or butter in a large skillet (I like to use my cast-iron frying pan). Add the coated catfish filets and cook for 5 to 7 minutes on each side, sprinkling additional salt on the catfish after each turn. Cook until golden brown and fish flakes easily with a fork. Drain on paper towels. After draining, place the fillets on another platter covered with paper towels; place in preheated oven to keep warm while frying the remaining fillets. The fillets will remain hot and crisp for as long as 35 minutes. Serve with lemon wedges.

"Never eat anything that you can't lift."
Miss Piggy

Bi Bim Bob

We are a fine dining establishment specializing in traditional Japanese delicacy and contemporary fusion food technique. We are serving variety of Japanese savory dishes and famous Asian fare by our artisans utmost endeavors.

bean sprouts
1-1.5 lb. ground beef
9-10 oz. bag fresh spinach
2 zucchinis, cut into thin strips, 2 inches long
mushrooms, sliced thinly
2 carrot, cut into thing strips, 1-2 inches long
eggs, sunny side up or over easy
rice
gochujang (Korean hot pepper paste)
sesame oil

1. First get your rice going. Proper bibimbap would use Korean style sticky rice and making process (mainly soaking the rice before cooking it–here's a good page explaining how they do it, but it is missing the step that you drain the soaking water before adding fresh to cook.) but jasmine rice works with this, albeit not as well. Julienne the zucchini, sprinkle with salt and set aside. Next get the well-rinsed sprouts into boiling salted water. After 20 minutes, drain the sprouts, mix in a little minced garlic, sesame oil and a pinch of salt. Reserve.

2. While the sprouts are boiling. Heat a pan and when it's hot, put in 2 tablespoons of water and the spinach. Cover/stir until the spinach is completely wilted (about 1 minute). Remove and squeeze out extra water. Add 1 teaspoon of soy sauce, a little minced garlic and sesame oil. Reserve.

3. Wipe out that same pan, and back on the heat, add a little oil and sauté the zucchini you cut and salted earlier. When it's done, reserve. Do the same thing with the mushrooms and the carrots. Reserve both. Get the pan hot and add the ground beef, 2-3 cloves of the minced garlic, 1 tablespoon of soy sauce, ½ table spoon of sugar, black pepper and ½-1 teaspoon sesame oil. Cook and reserve. Get the eggs frying while assembling the bowls.

4. Assembly. Put a portion of steaming hot rice in a big bowl. Arrange about 3-4 oz of beef and a portion of each of the vegetables around the center of the bowl. Place the freshly fried egg in the center and serve.

5. To eat, you would drizzle more sesame oil, add a tablespoon of gochujang (Korean hot pepper paste, see pic below. It's not really a very hot paste!) and mix the whole thing together. Eat.

Goro's Sushi
2619 Mossrock, San Antonio, TX

"The perfect date for me would be staying at home, making a big picnic in bed, eating Wotsits and cookies while watching cable TV."
Kim Kardashian

Strawberry Banana Smoothie

Green is more than just our name. It also stands for the way we do business. What we have done: installed an energy efficient thermal roof barrier to reduce energy consumption, reused an existing circa 1896 structure to help revitalize an area of downtown. green has also reused the majority of its restaurant equipment from refrigerators to booths/tables. green has a recycling dumpster for cardboard, a large bike rack, fair trade organic coffee, free range eggs, uses biodegradable packaging when possible, and will eventually install a cistern to capture rainwater for landscape maintenance. We have free wifi and plenty of places to plug in your power cord.

**10 strawberries, hulled, washed
2 ripe bananas, peeled, coarsely chopped
1½ C. of soy milk
¼ C. low-fat natural yogurt
1 tbsp. honey
½ tsp. of vanilla extract
6 ice cubes**

1. Place all ingredients into a blender and blend on high for about 40 seconds or until smooth and frothy.

2. Taste the smoothie and add more honey if necessary. Blend for another 10 seconds.

3. Pour into glasses and serve immediately.

Green Vegetarian Cuisine
1017 N Flores St., San Antonio, TX

"Cookery is become an art, a noble science; cooks are gentlemen."
Robert Burton

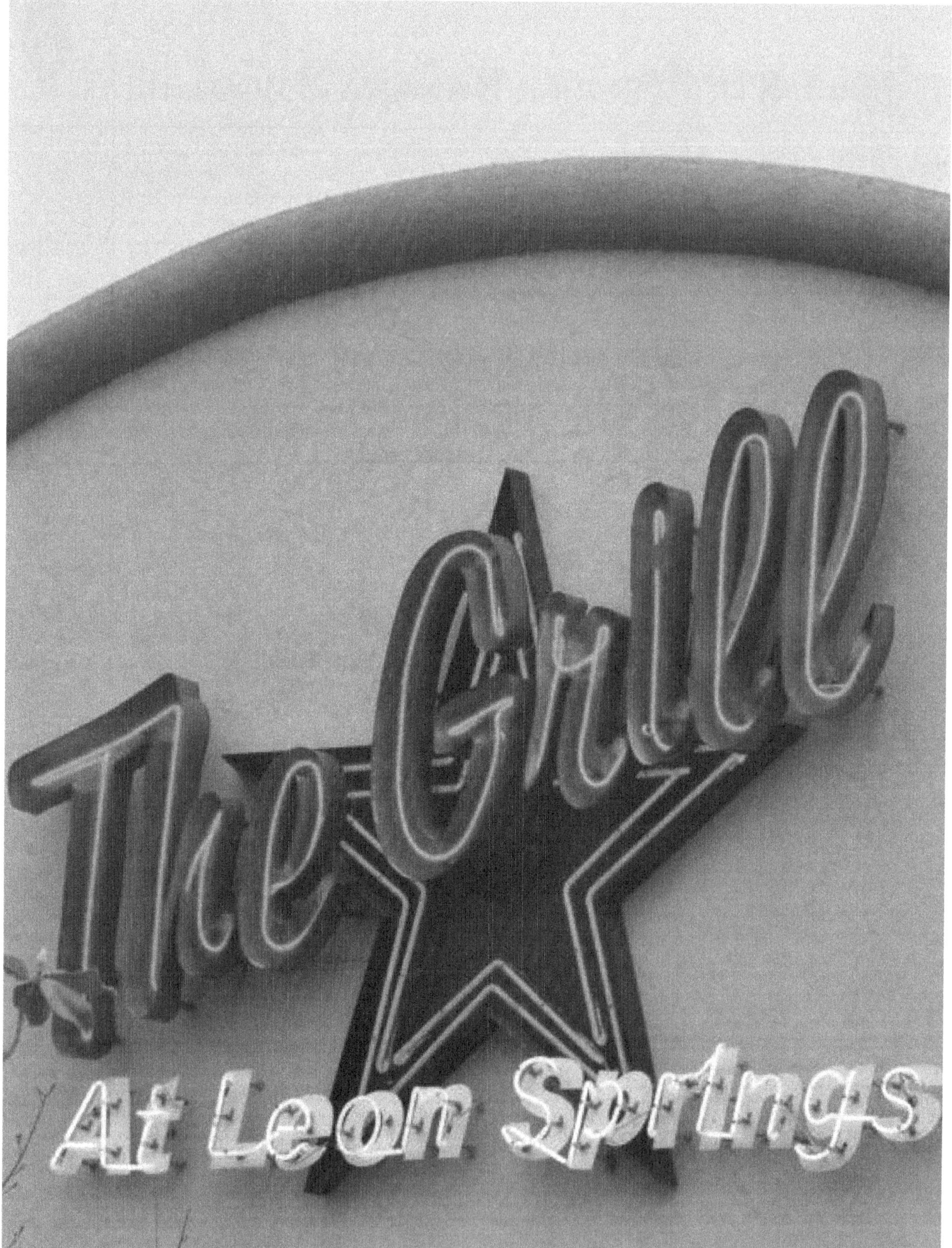
The Grill
At Leon Springs

SMOKED SALMON MOUSSE

Welcome to the Grill at Leon Springs. Step inside our big wooden doors to a bright, lively and vibrant atmosphere filled with friendly people, expertly crafted cocktails, top-notch plates, a deep wine list, and music, music, music. Fall in love with the Hill Country Terrace and become part of the energy that is The Grill!

12 oz. smoked salmon (brown part next to the skin) *½ c. melted butter* *8 oz. sour cream* *8 oz. cream cheese* *1 lemon juice* *pepper (fresh cracked, lots)* *dill (chopped)* *red onion (chopped)* *egg (chopped)* *capers* *cracker (serve with)*	**1.** Put in ingredients into food processor, blend until smooth. **2.** Pour into mold lined in plastic wrap. **3.** Chill several hours before serving. **4.** Unmold onto a pretty plate. **5.** Serve with condiments.

GRILL AT LEON SPRINGS
24116 W INTERSTATE 10, SAN ANTONIO, TX

"Eat (water)cress and gain wit."
Greek proverb

CARAMEL APPLE CHEESECAKE

Over seventy-five years ago all pizzerias cooked with coal because it gave the pizza a unique, smoky flavor and a crisp crust that is just not possible from gas, convection or wood ovens. Baking in a coal fired brick oven gives Grimaldi's pizza a flavorful and authentic taste. Grimaldi's fresh ingredients, handmade mozzarella, "secret recipe" sauce and hand tossed dough have made Grimaldi's the most award-winning pizzeria in the United States.

Crust:
1 C. graham cracker crumbs (about 8 cookie sheets)
1 tbsp. egg white
1 tbsp. water
cooking spray

Cheesecake:
1¾ C. sugar
½ C. light sour cream
3 tbsp. all-purpose flour
½ tsp. ground cinnamon
1½ tsp. vanilla extract
¼ tsp. ground nutmeg
2 (8-oz.) blocks ⅓-less-fat cream cheese, softened
1 (8-oz.) block fat-free cream cheese, softened
4 large eggs

Topping:
⅓ C. sugar
3 tbsp. water
½ tsp. fresh lemon juice
1 tbsp. butter
2 tbsp. half-and-half
1¾ C. thinly sliced peeled Granny Smith apple (about 8 oz.)
dash of nutmeg

1. Preheat oven to 400°.
2. To prepare crust, combine the first 3 ingredients in a bowl; toss with a fork until moist. Press mixture lightly into bottom of a 9-inch springform pan coated with cooking spray. Bake at 400° for 6 minutes. Remove from oven; cool on a wire rack. Wrap outside of pan with a double layer of foil. Reduce oven temperature to 325°.
3. To prepare cheesecake, place 1¾ cups sugar and next 7 ingredients (through fat-free cream cheese) in food processor; process until smooth. Add eggs, 1 at a time; process until blended. Pour cheese mixture into prepared pan. Place springform pan in a large roasting pan; add hot water to larger pan to a depth of 1 inch.
4. Bake at 325° for 1 hour or until cheesecake center barely moves when pan is touched. Remove from oven; let stand in water bath 10 minutes. Run a knife around outside edge of cheesecake. Remove pan from water bath; cool on a wire rack to room temperature. Cover and chill at least 8 hours.
5. To prepare topping, combine ⅓ cup sugar, 3 tablespoons water, and lemon juice in a small, heavy saucepan; cook over medium-high heat until sugar dissolves, stirring frequently. Cook 4 minutes or until golden (do not stir). Remove from heat. Add butter to pan; gently stir until butter melts. Stir in half-and-half. Cool slightly.
6. Heat a large nonstick skillet over medium-high heat. Coat pan with cooking spray. Add apple to pan; sauté 5 minutes or until lightly browned. Stir in sugar mixture and nutmeg. Serve topping with cheesecake.

GRIMALDI'S PIZZERIA, SAN ANTONIO, TX
15900 LA CANTERA PARKWAY, SAN ANTONIO, TX

"The discovery of a new dish does more for human happiness than the discovery of a new star."
Anthelme Brillat-Savarin

HOMEMADE SPICY QUESO

Located in the historic district of Gruene just beneath the famous Gruene water tower, we opened in 1977, serving steaks and hamburgers from a tiny kitchen in the corner of the building. Our menu still features thick steaks and large hamburgers, but the restaurant also serves up popular South Texas fare like chicken fried steak, fried catfish, grilled chicken, enormous sandwiches, fresh fish and special dishes like tomatillo chicken and bronzed catfish. Fudge pie, the enormous strawberry shortcake and our signature Jack Daniel's Pecan Pie are famous desserts. A full bar with a good wine list and fresh squeezed lime margaritas are also big hits.

1 small onion, diced
1 tbsp. oil
1 garlic clove, minced
1 (16-oz.) package pepper Jack pasteurized prepared cheese product, cubed
1 (10-oz.) can diced tomatoes and green chiles
2 tbsp. chopped fresh cilantro
tortilla chips

1. Cook onion in hot oil in a large nonstick skillet over medium-high heat 8 minutes or until tender. Add garlic, and cook 1 minute. Remove from heat.

2. Combine cheese, tomatoes, and onion mixture in a large microwave-safe glass bowl. Microwave at high 5 minutes, stirring every 2½ minutes. Stir in cilantro. Serve with tortilla chips.

"Hope is a good breakfast, but it is a bad supper."
Francis Bacon

CHICKEN PICATTA

Signature Tastes of SAN ANTONIO

⅓ C. all-purpose flour
¼ tsp. fresh ground black pepper
¼ tsp. paprika
1 lb. skinless, boneless chicken breast halves, pounded thin and cut into 2-inch pcs.
2 tbsp. olive oil
1 clove garlic, minced
¼ C. butter, divided
1 C. dry white wine
⅓ C. chicken broth
¼ C. fresh lemon juice
2 tbsp. capers
2 tbsp. chopped fresh parsley
1 (8 oz.) package angel hair pasta, cooked and drained

1. Whisk together flour, black pepper, and paprika in a shallow dish. Dredge the chicken pieces in the flour mixture, coating evenly; set aside. Heat olive oil in a large skillet over medium-high heat; stir and cook the garlic until light brown, about 1 minute. Remove the garlic from the skillet and set aside.
2. Place 2 tablespoons of butter into the skillet with the olive oil. Cook the chicken pieces in the oil and butter over medium-high heat until brown, about 5 minutes per side. Remove the chicken from the pan and set aside.
3. Pour the wine into the hot skillet and bring to a boil over high heat, scraping the browned pieces from the bottom and sides of the pan. Boil the wine until it is reduced by half, about 5 minutes. Whisk in the chicken broth, reserved garlic, lemon juice and capers. Cook for 5 minutes over medium-high heat. Stir in the remaining 2 tablespoons butter and parsley. Return the chicken pieces to the skillet and continue cooking over medium heat until the sauce thickens, about 15 minutes.
4. Meanwhile, fill a large pot with lightly salted water and bring to a rolling boil over high heat. Once the water is boiling, stir in the angel hair pasta, and return to a boil. Cook the pasta uncovered, stirring occasionally, until the pasta has cooked through, but is still firm to the bite, 4 to 5 minutes. Drain well.
5. Remove the chicken pieces to a serving dish and drizzle with a few tablespoons of the sauce and capers. Place the cooked angel hair pasta into the skillet with the remaining piccata sauce and toss to coat.

GRUENE DOOR RESTAURANT
2360 GRUENE LAKE DRIVE, NEW BRAUNFELS, TX

"If you think about a Thanksgiving dinner, it's really like making a large chicken."
Ina Garten

FRIED CATFISH FILLET

The relaxed setting of New Braunfels, Texas, the historic town of Gruene, and the fun of the Guadalupe River just seemed to be the perfect place for the newest member of the Clear Springs Restaurant Family, The Gruene River Grill. Even though we don't offer the award winning fried catfish and hand breaded onion rings that Clear Springs is famous for, we do keep the tradition going by offering a selection of mouthwatering dishes that are soon to be favorites.

For the Fish:
2 lb. catfish fillets, cut into 2" pcs.
1 bottle dark beer, 12 oz. bottle
peanut oil for deep frying
1½ C. cornmeal
1 C. flour
2 tbsp. Cajun Spice (recipe follows)-may add more if you like things really spicy

For The Cajun Spice Mixture:
2 tbsp. brown sugar
1 tbsp. chili powder
1 tsp. garlic powder
1 tsp. onion powder
1 tsp. seasoned salt
½ tsp. paprika
½ tsp. cayenne pepper
½ tsp. kosher salt
½ tsp. black pepper

1. Soak the catfish in beer for 30-60 minutes before cooking, but it's not necessary.
2. When you are ready, preheat oil in deep fryer or skillet.
3. In a large plastic bag, combine cornmeal, flour and Cajun spice, mixing well. Add fish nuggets and toss until fish is well coated.
4. When oil has reached the proper temperature (375 F), add 10-12 pieces of fish at a time. Cook for 3-4 minutes until they are a deep golden brown. Remove the fried fish from the oil using a slotted spoon and set on a paper towel lined plate. Repeat with the remaining fish. Serves 4-6. Enjoy!

Cajun Spice:
1. Combine brown sugar, chili powder, garlic powder, onion powder, seasoned salt, paprika, cayenne pepper, salt and pepper. Mix well. Store extra in airtight container until ready to use.

GRUENE RIVER GRILL
1259 GRUENE RD, NEW BRAUNFELS, TX

"Do not dismiss the dish saying that it is just, simply food. The blessed thing is an entire civilization in itself."
Abdulhak Sinasi

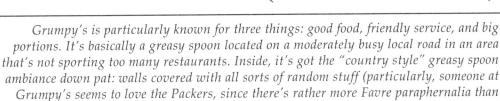

PICADILLO (SEASONED BEEF)

SIGNATURE TASTES of SAN ANTONIO

Grumpy's is particularly known for three things: good food, friendly service, and big portions. It's basically a greasy spoon located on a moderately busy local road in an area that's not sporting too many restaurants. Inside, it's got the "country style" greasy spoon ambiance down pat: walls covered with all sorts of random stuff (particularly, someone at Grumpy's seems to love the Packers, since there's rather more Favre paraphernalia than I'd expect for Texas), and a whole lot of little tables.

1 lb. ground beef
½ an onion, sliced
4-5 cloves of garlic, peeled and chopped
2 jalapenos seeded and diced
4 medium tomatoes, seeded and diced
8 green olives, pitted and sliced into quarters
2 tbsp. of the olive liquid
¼ C. raisins (softened by soaking in warm water for 20 minutes)
1 poblano chile or green bell pepper, seeded and chopped
1 tsp. cumin
¼ tsp. ground cloves
1 small cone of piloncillo or 1 tsp. brown sugar mixed with 1 tsp. molasses.
2 potatoes peeled and cubed (optional, see below)
¼ C. oil (optional for potatoes)

1. Cook the ground beef, jalapenos and onions over medium heat until the beef is about ½ cooked and only some pink remains.

2. Add the garlic and cook for mixture for 2 more minutes. Add the remaining ingredients and cook over low heat until the beef is well browned and crumbly and the tomatoes and onions are softened and begin to combine with the other ingredients.

Optional:
1. Cook the potatoes in the oil over medium heat in a large pan. When the potatoes have softened and are browned, fold into the beef mixture.

GRUMPY'S MEXICAN CAFE
18817 FM-2252, SAN ANTONIO, TX

"The primary requisite for writing well about food is a good appetite."
A.J. Liebling

TACOS DE ALAMBRE

Signature Tastes of SAN ANTONIO

8 slices bacon
1 tbsp. olive oil
1 onion, diced
1 tbsp. minced garlic
4 jalapeno peppers, seeded and chopped
1½ lb. ground beef
½ tsp. salt
¼ tsp. ground black pepper
1 tbsp. olive oil
32 corn tortillas
4 roma (plum) tomatoes, diced
1 (8 oz.) package shredded Monterey Jack cheese

1. Place the bacon in a large, deep skillet, and cook over medium-high heat, turning occasionally, until evenly browned, about 10 minutes. Drain the bacon slices on a paper towel-lined plate, reserving grease in the skillet. Crumble the bacon strips once cool.

2. Meanwhile, heat 1 tablespoon of olive oil in a large skillet over medium heat. Stir in the onion, garlic, and jalapeno peppers; cook and stir until the onion has softened and turned translucent, about 5 minutes. Increase the heat to medium-high, and stir in the ground beef; season with salt and pepper. Cook and stir until the ground beef is crumbly and no longer pink, 10 to 12 minutes. Drain off any excess liquid.

3. the beef mixture into the skillet of bacon grease. Crumble the bacon into the beef, and stir until thoroughly combined. Keep warm over low heat.

4. Heat 1 tablespoon of olive oil in a clean skillet over medium-high heat until hot. Place a tortilla into the pan, and place a generous spoonful of the meat filling onto the lower half of the tortilla.

5. Cook until bubbles begin to form in the tortilla, then fold over the meat. Continue cooking until the taco is crisp and lightly browned on each side, 1 to 2 minutes total. Repeat with the remaining tortillas and meat mixture. Top the tacos with diced tomatoes and shredded Monterey Jack cheese to serve.

1001 NW LOOP 410, SAN ANTONIO, TX

GUAJILLO'S

"A daydream is a meal at which images are eaten. Some of us are gourmets, some gourmands, and a good many take their images precooked out of a can and swallow them down whole, absent-mindedly and with little relish."
W. H. Auden

The Guenther House

· RESTAURANT ·
· RIVER MILL STORE ·
· MUSEUM ·

205 East Guenther Street

Restaurant Hours Mon - Sun 7am - 3pm
Museum and Store Hours Mon - Sat 8am - 4pm
Sun 8am - 3pm

ORIGINAL GUENTHER HOUSE
CHEWY BROWNIE

In 1848, a twenty-three-year-old apprentice millwright boarded Europe bound for America. His name was Carl Hilmar Guenther. Hilmar traveled through the Midwest before embarking down the Mississippi River to Louisiana and, ultimately, Texas. During this time, he was involved in a variety of work experiences including lumbering, farming and flour milling. In America, Guenther had found that "You seize the opportunity that presents itself." Three years after his arrival, with the financial help from his parents, he did just that, building a flour mill seventy-five miles northwest of San Antonio on the Live Oak Creek in Fredericksburg, Texas.

Brownie:
¾ C. butter
1¾ C. sugar
¾ C. cocoa
½ tsp. vanilla
3 eggs
1¾ C. Pioneer® Original Biscuit & Baking Mix

Brownie:
1. Preheat oven to 350°F. Oil a 9x13-inch pan.
2. Cream butter, sugar, cocoa and vanilla until well blended.
3. Add eggs, mixing thoroughly. Stir in Biscuit & Baking Mix, adding gradually and mixing until batter is smooth.
4. Pour into prepared pan.
5. Bake 22 to 25 minutes. Remove from oven. Cool in pan on a wire rack.

Chocolate Topping:
¼ C. butter, melted
5 tbsp. evaporated milk
3 tbsp. cocoa
1½ C. powdered sugar, sifted
¼ tsp. vanilla

Chocolate Topping:
1. Mix butter, milk and cocoa in a medium saucepan; heat until boiling, stirring constantly.
2. Remove from heat and stir in powered sugar, blending well. Stir in vanilla. (If topping thickens too much, microwave for 15-20 seconds.)

Creme de Menthe Topping:
3 oz cream cheese, softened
1 tbsp. butter, softened
2 tbsp. green Creme de Menthe
1½ C. powdered sugar, sifted
¼ tsp. vanilla
green food coloring

Creme de Menthe Topping:
1. Beath cream cheese, butter and Creme de Methe until creamy.
2. Stir in powdered sugar, blending well. Stir in vanilla and food coloring.
3. Frost brownies by drizzling a row of Chocolate Topping along the 9-inch width of the pan; beside the row of Chocolate Topping drizzle a row of Creme de Menthe Topping. Repeat, alternating toppings, until brownie is covered. Score through the toppings lengthwise (criss-wise to rows of toppings) in even parallel lines about 1-inch apart, using a light touch with a toothpick, alternating lines going right to left then left to right, to give an alternate swirl effect. Let toppings set before cutting.

205 E GUENTHER ST., SAN ANTONIO, TX

GUENTHER HOUSE

"Eat as much as you'd like. My philosophy has always been that all women desire to be as fat as myself but just have a great fear of doing so. Because they think they won't get any men, but you will. You'll get more men, and better men."
Roseanne Barr

CALZONES

Signature Taste of SAN ANTONIO

I started Guillermo's in 1995 after graduating from college. My name is William Garza but most people refer to me as Billy or Guillermo. At age 12 I began working at Luca Pizza in Windsor Park Mall. I graduated from Central Catholic High School and received my degree from the University of Texas at San Antonio. I am in the restaurant business because I enjoy serving people. We strive hard everyday to find better ways to serve you. Guillermo's consist of Tony (who has been with Guillermo's for 14 years), a staff of 21, family, friends, and customers that make all of Guillermo's come together. We look forward to serving and having you enjoy your experience with us.

GUILLERMO'S
618 McCullough Avenue San Antonio, TX

batch of calzone dough
cornmeal for sprinkling
1 C. ricotta cheese
1 egg, beaten
¼ C. grated Parmesan cheese
1 C. cubed mozzarella cheese
1½ tbsp. minced Italian parsley
⅛ tsp. salt
20 to 28 slices pepperoni

1. Heat the oven to 425°.
2. Mix all filling ingredients except pepperoni in a medium bowl.
3. When the dough is ready, punch it down and form into 4 equal balls. On a lightly floured surface, roll or pat each ball into a 6- to 6 ½-inch-diameter circle.
4. Place one fourth of the filling (about ½ cup) on half of each dough circle, keeping a 1-inch border free. Place 5 to 7 slices of pepperoni in each calzone.
5. Dampen the dough edges with water. Fold the dough semicircle over the filling and seal the edges by pinching them together. Place the completed calzones on an ungreased baking sheet sprinkled with cornmeal.
6. Bake for 12 to 15 minutes, until golden.
7. If you don't plan on eating the calzones right away, let the calzones cool and store them individually in small resealable plastic bags. Package the smaller bags in a large resealable freezer bag.
8. Label and tape your bag of calzones to the container of Simple Sauce already in the freezer.

To serve:
1. Thaw the sauce and calzones. Heat the sauce for about 10 minutes in a pan until bubbly. Meanwhile, heat the calzones in a 400° oven for 15 to 18 minutes. When they're heated through, place the calzones on individual plates and ladle Simple Sauce over each.

"A gourmet who thinks of calories is like a tart who looks at her watch."
James A. Beard

FUDGE PECAN BROWNIES

Signature Tastes of SAN ANTONIO

½ C. (1 stick) unsalted butter, plus more for pan
1 C. all-purpose flour, (spooned and leveled)
¼ tsp. baking powder
⅛ tsp. salt
2 oz. unsweetened chocolate, coarsely chopped
1 oz. semisweet chocolate, coarsely chopped
1 C. packed dark-brown sugar
¼ C. granulated sugar
2 large eggs
1 tsp. pure vanilla extract
1 C. pecans, coarsely chopped

1. Preheat oven to 350 degrees. Butter an 8-inch-square baking pan. Line bottom with parchment paper, leaving an overhang on two sides. Butter paper; set pan aside. In a medium bowl, whisk together flour, baking powder, and salt; set aside.

2. Place butter and chocolates in a large heatproof bowl set over (not in) a saucepan of simmering water. Heat until smooth, 2 to 3 minutes, stirring occasionally. Remove from heat, and stir in sugars, eggs, vanilla, flour mixture, and half of pecans. Transfer batter to prepared pan; smooth top. Sprinkle with remaining pecans.

3. Bake until a toothpick inserted in center comes out clean, 30 to 35 minutes. Set pan on a wire rack; let cool completely. Using paper overhang, lift brownie onto a cutting board; cut into 16 squares.

HEARTHSTONE BAKERY CAFE
8096 AGORA PKWY., SELMA, TX

"I just figured if I was going to make the world a better place, I'd do it with cookies."
Ana Pascal

139

After years in the local restaurant business and undertaking the renovation of several historic homes in New Braunfels, we decided to combine our eclectic blend of our experiences and try constructing and operating a restaurant of our own. Aside from wanting to establish creative and comfortable space, we wanted to draw from the diverse cultural and culinary influences of the Texas Hill Country for a fresh, new dining experience.

1 lb. uncooked large shrimp, peeled and deveined
1 tsp. salt
1 (15 - 16 oz.) can tomato sauce
1 C. chopped tomato (1 medium)
¼ C. chopped white onion
1 jalapeño, seeded and finely chopped
¼ C. chopped cilantro
¼ C. fresh lime juice
1 tsp. hot pepper sauce
2 avocados, seeded and peeled
lime wedges, for garnish
cilantro, for garnish
tortilla chips

1. Bring 3 quarts water to a boil in 4 quart saucepan. Add 1 teaspoon salt. Cook shrimp in boiling water until they form into the shape of the letter "C". Do not overcook. Remove from heat; drain and cool, then cut shrimp in half.

2. Combine tomato sauce, tomato, onion, jalapeño, cilantro, lime juice and hot pepper sauce in a large glass bowl. Add cooled shrimp and refrigerate at least one hour.

3. Chop avocados coarsely; stir into shrimp mixture and serve.

HUISACHE GRILL & WINE BAR
303 W SAN ANTONIO ST., NEW BRAUNFELS, TX

"Food is our common ground, a universal experience."
James A. Beard

Pan Seared Halibut

Il Sogno, a five-star Italian Osteria, features Italian fare found in the trattorias and osterias of Rome and Florence. Renowned chef Andrew Weissman opened the restaurant in the historic Pearl Brewery in 2009. The menu features a range of Italian classics from espresso drinks, yogurt with muesli, and coddled eggs for breakfast to pizzas, salads and entrees such as pan-seared halibut and house-made ravioli for lunch or dinner.

1 egg
1 C. all-purpose flour
2 tbsp. dried herbes de Provence
1 tsp. seafood seasoning (such as Old Bay)
1 tsp. salt
ground black pepper
1 lb. skinless, boneless halibut fillets
2 tbsp. olive oil

1. Whisk egg in a small bowl.

2. Combine flour, herbes de Provence, seafood seasoning, salt, and black pepper in a separate small bowl.

3. Cut halibut into 4 equal pieces.

4. Heat olive oil in a large frying pan over medium-low heat.

5. Dip each piece of halibut in whisked egg.

6. Dredge all sides of each piece in flour mixture to evenly coat; tap off excess flour.

7. Place coated pieces immediately in the hot olive oil.

8. Cook the halibut until lightly browned, about 5 minutes; turn and cook until fish is opaque and flakes easily with a fork, another 2 minutes.

200 East Grayson No. 100, San Antonio, TX

Il Sogno Osteria

"The food in Yugoslavia is fine if you like pork tartare."
Ed Begley, Jr.

CHICKEN TERIYAKI

OINONIO

Signature Tastes of SAN ANTONIO

Chef Young opened Il Song Garden Korean BBQ and Sushi in 2006 with much fanfare. Since opening, the accolades have continued to pour in. Her delicate approach to Korean cuisine has garnered numerous San Antonio Express News Critic's and Reacher's Choice awards as well as a yearly selection as the Best Korean BBQ from the San Antonio Current.

4 skinless, boneless chicken breast halves
1 C. teriyaki sauce
¼ C. lemon juice
2 tsp. minced fresh garlic
2 tsp. sesame oil

1. Place chicken, teriyaki sauce, lemon juice, garlic, and sesame oil in a large resealable plastic bag. Seal bag, and shake to coat. Place in refrigerator for 24 hours, turning every so often.

2. Preheat grill for high heat.

3. Lightly oil the grill grate. Remove chicken from bag, discarding any remaining marinade. Grill for 6 to 8 minutes each side, or until juices run clear when chicken is pierced with a fork.

6905 BLANCO RD., SAN ANTONIO, TX

IL SONG GARDEN

"If you are killing a chicken and cooking a chicken, it has to taste like chicken. Veal has to taste like veal. You have to be able to identify what you're eating. One of my worst experiences is when I can't tell what I'm eating. It is a waste."
Joel Robuchon

Chicken Tikka Masala

Signature Tastes of SAN ANTONIO

Marinade ingredients:
2 tbsp. cummin seeds
2 tbsp. coriander seeds
2 tbsp. paprika
1 tsp. mango powder (optional)
1 tsp. chilli powder (optional or to taste)
pinch of red food colouring
juice of a lime (or lemon, but lime is better)
about 10 oz. good thick yogurt
salt to taste

Other Ingredients:
about 1.5 lb. chicken, diced
3-6 cloves garlic, chopped (to taste - I like loads!)
1 large onion, very finely chopped
chicken stock or water
oil or ghee for frying

1. Grind the spices and mix with marinade ingredients. Immerse chicken in marinade and leave in the fridge for 24 hours Heat Oil in a frying pan (skillet!) or wok until very hot Stir fry chicken vigorously for about 5 mins (you may need to do it in 2 batches, depending on the size of your pan).

2. Remove chicken and keep warm.

3. Fry onion and garlic until just browning and return chicken with any remaining marinade, plus stock, plus more spices if you think the sauce needs it; an extra teaspoon of cummin and coriander may lift it a little.

4. Simmer until chicken is cooked and Sauce is nice and thick. Serves 4 with rice.

1031 Patricia Dr., San Antonio, TX

India Oven

"Your words are my food, your breath my wine. You are everything to me."
Sarah Bernhardt

147

AGED PRIME RIB

J. Alexander's is a contemporary American restaurant, known for its wood-fired cuisine. Our core philosophy is to provide you with the highest possible quality dining experience. The menu features a wide selection of American classics including prime rib of beef, steaks, fresh seafood, sandwiches and entrée salads. The menu in each restaurant includes a varied and rotating selection of features like Seafood Czarina, Tuscan Steak, Grilled Fish with Mango Papaya Salsa and Chicken Milanese. The restaurant has a full-service bar that includes an outstanding selection of wines both by the glass and bottle.

1 7 bone prime rib, dry aged **1 C. kosher salt** **¼ C. cracked black pepper** **2 tbsp. olive oil** **2 tbsp. chopped fresh thyme**	**1.** Let rib come to room temperature. Rub with olive oil and spread with kosher salt, black pepper and thyme. **2.** Preheat oven to 500 degrees, place rib in oven and turn down temperature to 275 degrees and cook for 2 hours or until internal temperature 105 degrees. **3.** Let rest for 20 minutes.

Signature Tastes of SAN ANTONIO

J. ALEXANDER'S

255 E BASSE RD., SAN ANTONIO, TX

"Let us eat and drink; for tomorrow we shall die."
Bible - Isaiah 22:13

GYRO SANDWICH

Signature Tastes of SAN ANTONIO

Jerusalem Grill brings culture and excitement to your taste buds! Here you'll enjoy the freshest, most flavorful entrees with true Middle Eastern spices all fitting in a low fat low calorie diet without sacrificing authentic Middle Eastern taste. We offer a pleasant Family atmosphere, great tasting food with fresh and quality ingredients, a full Middle Eastern-Lebanese menu, as well as Halal Meat.

Marinade:
⅓ C. lemon juice
¼ C. olive oil
¾ tsp. oregano, dry
2 cloves garlic, minced
½ tsp. kosher salt
¼ tsp. black pepper

Finished Gyros:
1 lb. boneless, skinless chicken breasts
½ red onion, diced
2 plum tomatoes
2 oz. feta cheese, crumbled
8 tbsp. Tzatziki sauce
4 whole wheat pita bread

1. Cut your chicken breasts across the grain into strips.
2. Mix together lemon juice, olive oil, oregano, garlic, salt, and pepper in a resealable bag, and then shake vigorously to combine.
3. Add your chicken breast strips to the plastic bag and seal it up, removing as much air as possible. Massage the chicken through the bag to ensure that the marinade is evenly dispersed and that there is as much coverage with the chicken as possible.
4. Stash your marinating meat mixture in the refrigerator for one hour so the flavors can combine and get to know themselves and the chicken.
5. Remove the chicken from the refrigerator and discard the leftover marinade.
6. Cook the chicken in a nonstick skillet at medium-high heat, in this case my beloved electric frying pan, until the chicken is done and the juices run clear. This usually takes me about five to seven minutes and I flip the chicken a few times during the process.
7. Note: At this point, your kitchen will start smelling so good that everyone comes running. Keep them out of your hair and out of the chicken by setting them to pulling out their favorite gyro toppings.
8. Now it's time to assemble the final gyro sandwiches, and there are two different ways that you can do it. Traditionally, you would leave the pita bread whole and wrap it around the meat and toppings, but for variety's sake, I chose to cut the bread in half and fill them like little pockets.

3259 Wurzbach Rd., San Antonio, TX

JERUSALEM GRILL

"You don't need a pack of wild horses to learn how to make a sandwich."
Phil McGraw

Tzatziki

Over the years, the new customers as well as regular customers have commented on how the food and service are of the highest quality and has the most extensive Green menu in town. Authentic food, such as Pastitsio and Mousaka, making your taste buds feel like they've traveled straight to Greece. Come in for the food and fun without traveling overseas!

Signature Tastes of SAN ANTONIO

3 tbsp. olive oil
1 tbsp. vinegar
2 cloves garlic, minced
finely
½ tsp. salt
¼ tsp. white pepper
1 C. greek yogurt,
strained
1 C. sour cream
2 cucumbers, peeled,
seeded and diced
1 tsp. chopped fresh dill

1. Combine olive oil, vinegar, garlic, salt, and pepper in a bowl. Mix until well combined.

2. Using a whisk, blend the yogurt with the sour cream.

3. Add the olive oil mixture to the yogurt mixture and mix well.

4. Finally, add the cucumber and chopped fresh dill.

5. Chill for at least two hours before serving.

16602 SAN PEDRO AVE., SAN ANTONIO, TX

John the Greek

"They shall hunger no more, neither thirst any more;
Neither shall the sun light on them, nor any heat."
Bible Revelation 7:16

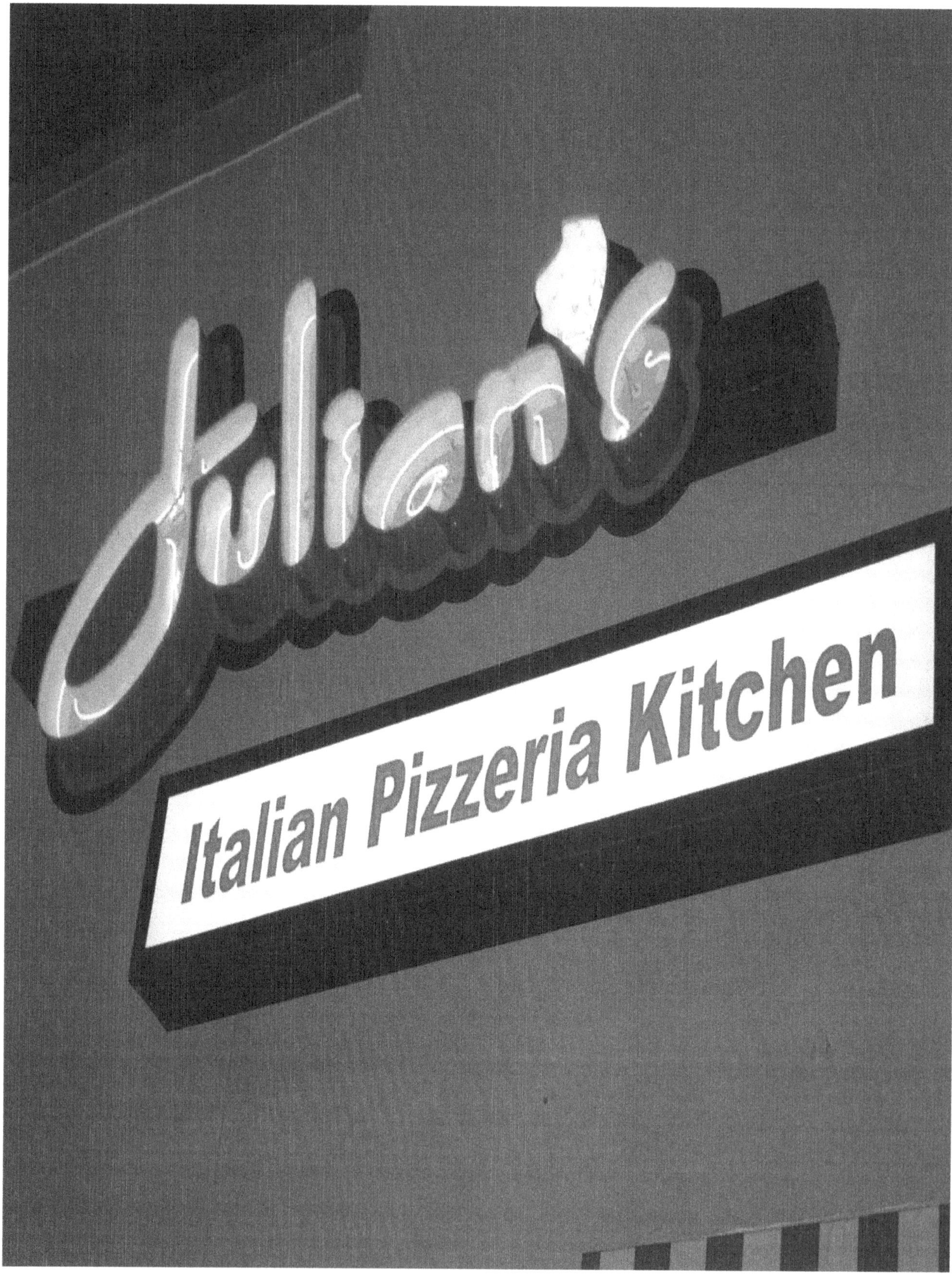
Julian's
Italian Pizzeria Kitchen

Signature Tastes of SAN ANTONIO

Julian's Italian Pizzeria & Kitchen is a unique concept that allows customers the opportunity to dine in a relaxed family atmosphere while enjoying a quality product for reasonable prices. Our mission at Julian's has always been to provide delicious food, using the highest quality ingredients, while providing outstanding customer service. Pizza is what Julian's is known for, but other house specialties include Calzones, Stromboli, Subs, Homemade Lasagna, Eggplant Parmigiana, Chicken Parmigiana, a variety of Fresh Salads, and several authentic Pasta Dishes. Our pizza crust is made thin and crispy, topped with homemade pizza sauce, whole milk mozzarella cheese, and the freshest toppings. A favorite of our lunch crowd is our generous pizza by the slice!

extra-virgin olive oil
2 large eggplant, 2 lb.
salt and pepper
2 C. basic tomato sauce, recipe follows
1 bunch fresh basil leaves, chiffonade
1 lb. fresh mozzarella, sliced ⅛-inch thick
½ C. freshly grated Parmigiano-Reggiano
¼ C. fresh bread crumbs, lightly toasted under broiler

Basic Tomato Sauce:
¼ C. extra-virgin olive oil
1 Spanish onion, ¼-in. dice
4 garlic cloves, peeled and thinly sliced
3 tbsp. chopped fresh thyme leaves, or 1 tbsp. dried
½ medium carrot, finely grated
2 (28-oz.) cans peeled whole tomatoes, crushed by hand and juices reserved
salt

1. Preheat the oven to 450 degrees F.
2. Using some extra-virgin olive oil, oil a baking sheet.
3. Slice each eggplant into 6 pieces about 1 to 1 ½ inches thick. Lightly season each disk with salt and pepper and place on the oiled sheet. Bake the eggplant at 450 degrees F until the slices begin turning deep brown on top, about 12-15 minutes. Remove the eggplants from the oven. Remove the slices from the baking sheet and place them on a plate to cool.
4. Lower oven temperature to 350 degrees F. In an 8 by 12-inch brownie pan, place the 4 largest eggplant slice evenly spaced apart. Over each slice, spread ¼ cup of tomato sauce and sprinkle with a teaspoon of basil. Place one slice of mozzarella over each and sprinkle with 1 teaspoon grated Parmigiano. Place the smaller slices of eggplant over each of the disks and repeat with tomato sauce, basil, and the 2 cheeses. Repeat the layering again until all the ingredients are used.
5. Sprinkle the toasted bread crumbs over the top of the eggplant dish, and bake uncovered until the cheese is melts and the tops turn light brown, about 20 minutes. Serve immediately.

Tomato Sauce:
1. In a 3-quart saucepan, heat the olive oil over medium heat. Add the onion and garlic and cook until soft and light golden brown, about 8 to 10 minutes. Add the thyme and carrot and cook 5 minutes more, until the carrot is quite soft. Add the tomatoes and juice and bring to a boil, stirring often.
2. Lower the heat and simmer for 30 minutes until as thick as hot cereal. Season with salt and serve. This sauce holds 1 week in the refrigerator or up to 6 months in the freezer.

JULIAN'S ITALIAN PIZZERIA
13444 WEST AVE., SAN ANTONIO, TX

"One can say everything best over a meal."
George Eliot

Avocado Egg Rolls

Kona Grill offers diners freshly prepared food, personalized service, and a warm contemporary ambiance that creates an exceptional, yet affordable dining experience. The diverse menu includes a wide variety of mainstream American dishes, as well as a variety of entrees and appetizers with an international influence. Specialties include Baked Sea Bass in a miso-sake marinade, Filets, Almond Crusted Pork Tenderloin, and Kona Grill's signature dish - Macadamia Nut Chicken. Kona Grill also features an award-winning sushi menu containing all of the traditional favorites plus several unique dishes created by talented sushi chefs.

Kona Grill
15900 La Cantera Pkwy., San Antonio, TX

Egg Rolls:
1 large avocado, peeled, pitted, & diced
2 tbsp. sun-dried tomatoes, chopped
1 tbsp. finely chopped red onions
½ tsp. fresh cilantro, chopped
1 dash salt
4 egg roll wraps (can also use won ton wraps)
1 egg, beaten
Oil for deep-frying

Dipping Sauce:
¼ C. olive oil
4 tsp. white vinegar
1 tsp. balsamic vinegar
½ tsp. tamarind pulp
½ C. honey (I use slightly less)
1 pinch turmeric
½ C. chopped cashews
⅔ C. fresh cilantro
2 garlic cloves
2 green onions
1 tbsp. sugar
1 tsp. freshly ground black pepper
1 tsp. ground cumin

Egg Rolls:
1. Stir together avocado, tomatoes, onion, cilantro, and salt. Distribute filling evenly on the center of each egg roll wrapper.
2. Fold one corner up, ¼ of the way over the filling. Brush the remaining corners and edges with beaten egg, roll up the left and right side, then fold top corner over all and press to seal.
3. Repeat with the remaining wrappers. Deep-fry the egg rolls in 375 degree oil for 3-4 minutes, or until browned.
4. Drain on paper towels. Slice egg rolls diagonally in half and serve with the prepared dipping sauce.

Dipping Sauce:
1. Combine vinegars, honey, tamarind in a microwave safe bowl. Stir until tamarind is dissolved completely.
2. Microwave for 1 minute. Using a blender, Puree tamarind mixture, cashews, cilantro, garlic, onions, sugar, pepper, and cumin.
3. Pour mixture into a bowl and stir in oil. Cover and refrigerate until ready to use.

"Egg whites are good for a lot of things – lemon meringue pie, angel food cake, and clogging up radiators."
MacGyver

CHALUPAS

Signature Tastes of SAN ANTONIO

A few specialties you will find on the menu include puffy tacos, enchiladas, and of course fajitas, pollo con queso, and much more. Being famous for their puffy tacos, the golden, crisp hand pressed shells will be stuffed and overflowing with your choice of toppings: lettuce, tomato, cheese, onion, and jalapeño. Fillings include beef, chicken, guacamole, tofu, or bean. Served up with the classic rice (made with natural, whole grain brown rice) and beans, you are sure to leave this restaurant with a full stomach and a big smile.

corn tortillas, white, yellow, or red
hot oil for frying (350°)
16 oz. can Rosarita refried beans
¼ C. pace picante sauce
1 tbsp. Gebhardt chili powder
1 tbsp. fiesta fajita seasoning
1 tbsp. ground cumin
1 tbsp. bacon grease
1 tbsp. salt
1 tbsp. fresh ground pepper
½ C. water
4 oz. grated cheese (Cheddar, Monterey jack, or mixed)
iceberg lettuce, sliced thin
ripe tomatoes, chopped ½"

1. The first step is to 'doctor' up the refried beans.
2. Into a small saucepan, heat the bacon grease. When hot, add the canned beans, water, salt, pepper, chili powder, cumin, fajita seasoning and picante sauce.
3. Stir well and reduce the heat to medium low and 'simmer' for 20 to 30 minutes while
4. preparing all the other items. Stir several times to avoid burning.
5. Fry the corn tortillas, one at a time, in hot oil (350°). Put the tortilla into the oil, let fry for about 20 seconds, then turn over with tongs. Let fry for about 2 minutes, then turn over again.
6. The white or yellow corn tortilla should turn a 'golden' brown, but not a dark brown. The red tortilla's will turn a darker shade of red and all will quite 'bubbling' when they are completely fried throughout.
7. Remove when done and place on a paper towel to absorb the excess oil.
8. Allow 1 chalupa per person if serving as an appetizer, two if for the entree.
9. Grate the cheese using a 'fine' grater or processor blade. Place in a plastic bag or cover and refrigerate until ready to assemble the chalupas.
10. Core, wash, and dry the iceberg lettuce. You will cut the lettuce into fine 'strips' (⅛" or less). Take a large 'chunk' and hold in one hand while carefully slicing off thin strips.
11. Refrigerate until ready to assemble.
12. Core the tomato, then cut into quarters. Slice each quarter down the center, then cut across both these pieces so that you have ½" or smaller pieces. Refrigerate until ready to use.
13. Remove the beans from the heat and pour into a glass bowl. This will help them thicken before using on the chalupas. They should be fairly thick, but not 'runny'.
14. Turn on the broiler and preheat oven while preparing the shells. With a rubber spatula or large spoon, spread a thin layer of beans (¼" or less) on each shell.
15. Spread a thin layer of cheese on top of the beans. Place on a cookie sheet and place under the broiler until the cheese is hot and 'bubbly'.
16. Remove and place a small handful of the shredded lettuce on top of the cheese. Next, sprinkle some chopped tomatoes on top of the lettuce. It should resemble a 'mound'.
17. Last, sprinkle some of the remaining grated cheese and top with paprika.
18. Serve immediately with picante sauce and ranch dressing.

LA FIESTA PATIO CAFE
1421 PAT BOOKER RD., SAN ANTONIO, TX

"Kill no more pigeons than you can eat."
Benjamin Franklin

157

Pastel de Tres Leches

Signature Tastes of SAN ANTONIO

La Fonda's long and colorful history began on Main Avenue in 1930 when resourceful sisters Virginia Berry and Nannie Randall opened a Mexican food-to-go shop. These two ladies supplied take-home Tex-Mex favorites to the neighborhood. In spite of the Great Depression, their little business prospered and an opportunity presented itself to purchase the house across the street at 2415 North Main Avenue. Converting this home to a full-service restaurant seemed a risk worth taking, and in 1932, La Fonda on Main formally opened.

Cake:
1½ C. flour
1 tsp. baking powder
½ C., or 8 tbsp. unsalted butter, room temperature
¾ C. sugar
5 eggs, room temperature
½ tsp. vanilla
1 C. whole milk
1 C. sweetened, condensed milk
⅔ C. evaporated milk

Whipped Cream Frosting:
1½ C. whipping cream
½ C. sugar
1 tsp. vanilla

1. Preheat oven to 350°F and grease and flour an 8x11-inch baking pan.
2. Sift the flour and baking powder into a large mixing bowl. Cream the butter and sugar together in a mixer on medium speed until light and fluffy.
3. Reduce mixer speed to medium-low and add the eggs one at a time, allowing each one to get incorporated before adding the next. Finally add the vanilla and continue beating until foamy.
4. Remove the bowl from mixer and fold in the sifted flour until it is well incorporated.
5. Pour the batter into the prepared pan and bake 30 minutes, or until done. Remove from oven and set aside to cool.
6. Pierce cake all over with a fork, toothpick or skewer. Mix the whole, sweetened, condensed, and evaporated milk together and pour the mixture over the whole cake.
7. Refrigerate cake for anywhere from 2 to 8 hours, or until liquid is completely absorbed and cake is well chilled.
8. Beat the cream, sugar and vanilla together until the cream holds soft peaks. Frost the cake with the whipped cream and serve.

LA FONDA ON MAIN
2415 N MAIN AVE., SAN ANTONIO, TX

"Great eaters and great sleepers are incapable of anything else that is great."
Henry IV of France

POULET PICATTA

Signature Tastes of SAN ANTONIO

La Frite is San Antonio's premier and only Belgian Bistro. La Frite Belgian Bistro offers crowd pleasing, masterfully prepared, traditional Belgian/French fare, in a warm, welcoming and friendly atmosphere. Zagat rates this bistro with the "best mussels since Brussels". French inspired daily specials are offered in addition to the traditional Belgian treats. La Frite is where the locals come to enjoy a tasty meal in a casual European atmosphere. The outside tables are ideal for people watching.

**3 large lemons, divided
4 small chicken breasts boneless and Skinless (1 lbs / 450 g)
¼ C. of sauce Miracle Whip Calorie-Wise
22 crackers Ritz, finely crushed (1 C.)
2 tbsp. olive oil
2 tsp. chopped fresh parsley
½ C. chicken broth with 25% less sodium
1 tbsp butter**

1. Cut half of a lemon into 4 thin slices. Squeeze the juice of lemons; reserve. Coat chicken with sauce Miracle Whip, then crackers crumbs.

2. Heat oil in a large frying pan to fire mi-vif. Add chicken and cook for 5 minutes. Return the chicken and cook for 5 minutes at medium heat or until it is golden and well-done (170 ° F). Put the chicken in a dish. The sprinkle with parsley and cover to retain heat.

3. Carefully wipe the crumbs in the pan.

4. Develop reserved lemon juice and broth in the pan. Cook everything to fire mi-vif for 6 to 8 minutes or until the liquid has reduced slightly, stirring from time to time. Add butter and lemon slices.

5. Cook it stirring over low heat for 3 to 4 minutes or until the butter is melted and the lemons are hot. Serve the sauce over the chicken.

LA FRITE BELGIAN BISTRO
728 S ALAMO ST., SAN ANTONIO, TX

"Money brings you food, but not appetite; medicine, but not health; acquaintances, but not friends."
Henrik Ibsen

Ceviche Veracruzano

A place that was created to celebrate the rich and delicious street foods from interior Mexico. From tacos al pastor in Mexico City, tlayudas in Oaxaca, to cocteles de mariscos from Veracruz, Mexico's street foods are as unique and colorful as its traditions, culture and people. Come enjoy the food and drinks and you'll soon realize... no hace falta morir para llegar a la Gloria.

¾ lb. very fresh white fleshed ocean fish, such as cod
½ C. fresh lime juice
1 ½ tbsp. (about 2) minced Serrano peppers
½ C. chopped tomato
½ C. small diced avocado
1 tbsp. minced onion
2 tbsp. chopped fresh cilantro
1 tbsp. olive oil
½ tsp. salt
8 corn tortillas, cut into thick strips and fried until crisp
lime wedges

1. Cut the fish into ½-inch dice.

2. Place in a glass dish with the lime juice.

3. Cover and refrigerate for 6 hours, stirring occasionally.

4. Drain the fish and add the peppers, tomato, avocado, onion, cilantro, olive oil, and salt.

5. Fold gently to mix. Serve with some fried tortilla strips, thick cut, garnish with lime wedges.

100 E. Grayson, San Antonio, TX

La Gloria

"When the stomach is full, it is easy to talk of fasting."
Saint Jerome

163

ENCHILADAS VERDES

La Hacienda is the second restaurant brought to you by the Barrios family! We opened in February of 2004, and quickly became as popular as the original Los Barrios Restaurant on Blanco Road. La Hacienda offers a spacious indoor dining room, a beautiful patio covered by majestic oak trees, two children's play areas, and the best Mexican food San Antonio has to offer! We can accommodate any size group, from a table for 1 to a party for 200! Join us at La Hacienda de Los Barrios in North Central San Antonio, where families come together under our roof!

Green Tomatillo Sauce:
1 lb. tomatillo
2 garlic cloves
1 tbsp. vegetable oil
½ onion, finely chopped
salt and pepper to taste

Enchiladas:
vegetable oil for frying
12 corn tortillas, home-made or store-bought
2 C. shredded cooked chicken or shredded queso Chihuahua or Monterey Jack cheese
¾ C. sour cream
chopped cilantro

1. To make the sauce, soak the tomatillos in a bowl of cold water to loosen the husks. Drain, and peel off the husks.

2. Place the tomatillos and garlic in a sauce pan with water to cover the tomatillos halfway and bring to a boil. Boil until the tomatillos are soft, about 10 minutes. Drain. Transfer the tomatillos and garlic to a blender and blend to a puree.

3. Heat the 2 tablespoons oil in a medium saucepan over medium heat. Add the pureed tomatillos and onion, and season with salt and pepper. Bring to a simmer, and simmer for about 5 minutes.

4. Meanwhile, pour ½ inch of vegetable oil into a large skillet and heat over medium-high heat until hot. One at a time, dip tortillas into the hot oil to soften them, just a few seconds. Transfer to paper towels to drain.

5. Fill the center of the tortillas with chicken or cheese and fold over the sides. Place seam side down on individual plates and top with warm sauce. Garnish with sour cream and enjoy.

LA HACIENDA DE LOS BARRIOS
18747 REDLAND RD., SAN ANTONIO, TX

"A smiling face is half the meal."
Latvian Proverb

GARDEN BEAN BURGER

Signature Tastes of SAN ANTONIO

A hop, skip, and stagger from the Blue Star Art Gallery is La Tuna Grill. Located just across the railroad tracks, this tin-clad eatery dishes up amazing food at great prices. Load up the arteries with the "Loaded Fries," topped with bacon, sour cream, and cheddar - these spuds are worth it! The "La Tuna Trio" is another fave. Three mini burgers grilled to your preference, these would make Wimmpy whimper. And the freshly made bread pudding is supurb. Whether you want to hang out on the patioand people watch, or eat inside - it's all good. TIP: Don't make your first visit to La Tuna on the First Friday of each month - too loco!!!

½ C. quinoa
1 small onion, finely chopped (1 C.)
6 oil-packed sun-dried tomatoes, drained and finely chopped (¼ C.)
1½ C. cooked black beans, or 1 15-oz. can black beans, rinsed and drained, divided
2 cloves garlic, minced (2 tsp.)
2 tsp. dried steak seasoning
8 whole-grain hamburger buns

1. Stir together quinoa and 1½ cups water in small saucepan, and season with salt, if desired. Bring to a boil. Cover, reduce heat to medium-low, and simmer 20 minutes, or until all liquid is absorbed. (You should have 1½ cups cooked quinoa.)

2. Meanwhile, place onion and sun-dried tomatoes in medium nonstick skillet, and cook over medium heat. (The oil left on the tomatoes should be enough to sauté the onion.) Cook 3 to 4 minutes, or until onion has softened. Stir in ¾ cup black beans, garlic, steak seasoning, and 1½ cups water. Simmer 9 to 11 minutes, or until most of liquid has evaporated.

3. Transfer bean-onion mixture to food processor, add ¾ cup cooked quinoa, and process until smooth. Transfer to bowl, and stir in remaining ¾ cup quinoa and remaining ¾ cup black beans. Season with salt and pepper, if desired, and cool.

4. Preheat oven to 350°F, and generously coat baking sheet with cooking spray. Shape bean mixture into 8 patties (½ cup each), and place on prepared baking sheet. Bake 20 minutes, or until patties are crisp on top. Flip patties with spatula, and bake 10 minutes more, or until both sides are crisp and brown. Serve on buns.

LA TUNA GRILL
100 PROBANDT, SAN ANTONIO, TX

"We take the hamburger business more seriously than anyone else."
Ray Kroc

CASHEW CHICKEN

Signature Tastes of SAN ANTONIO

Right in the medical center, this family owned restaurant definitely isn't bad. You won't get 4 star service, or a fancy atmosphere, but the food is great and the people are just very genuine. The food tastes just and good or even better with a much smaller check at the end of the night, they also deliver for a few extra bucks within a certain distance. Well worth giving it a try- you will be hooked- much better in so many ways than another Chinese restaurant nearby!

4 skinless, boneless, chicken breasts (about 1½ to 1¾ lb. total), cut into 1-inch cubes
peanut oil (about ¾ C., can substitute other vegetable oil)
chili powder (abt. 3 tbsp.)
tamari (about ½ C.)
(if you don't have access to tamari you can substitute soy sauce, use wheat-free tamari or soy sauce if you need to cook gluten-free)
honey (about ½ C.)
2 C. raw cashews
salt
3 C. roughly chopped onions (about 2 medium large onions)
3 C. roughly chopped mushrooms

Optional:
1-2 tsp. minced fresh ginger
¼ C. chopped green onion greens

1. Marinate the chicken. Place the cubed chicken in a medium bowl. Add the oil. Add the tamari until the marinade turns dark brown (about 2 Tbsp per breast). Sprinkle the chili powder over the chicken pieces while stirring, so that each piece of chicken gets well coated with the chili powder and marinade. Stir in the honey, about 2 tablespoons for each breast. Add chopped ginger if using. Marinate for ½ hour to several hours, the longer the better.
2. Place cashews in a saucepan, cover with water, add a teaspoon of salt. Bring the water to a boil and simmer until the cashews are soft, a couple of minutes (the water will get foamy). Remove from the heat, strain and set aside.
3. Heat a large skillet on medium high heat. Working in batches if needed so you don't crowd the pan, use tongs to remove the chicken pieces from the marinade and place them in the pan, reserving the extra marinade. Sauté the chicken pieces until just cooked through, remove from the pan and set aside. Place any extra marinade back in the pan and simmer for several minutes (to kill any bacteria). Pour off all but 1 Tbsp of the marinade into a separate bowl and reserve.
4. In the same pan, sauté the onions on medium high to high heat for several minutes. Add mushrooms and continue to sauté until onions are translucent and mushrooms are cooked, several minutes more. Add some reserved marinade to the pan if necessary.
5. Combine chicken, mushrooms, onions, with the cashews. Stir in onion greens (if using) right before serving. Serve over rice.

LEE'S GARDEN CHINESE
7271 WURZBACH RD., SAN ANTONIO, TX

"At a dinner party on should eat wisely but not too well.
And talk well but not too wisely."
W. Somerset Maugham

169

Goat Cheese with Garlic, Chile Morita & Piloncillo Sauce

Serious Food prepared right here in the building. Established in 1985 when Dwight Hobart heard Lydia Mendoza cry out "¡Que bueno!" after tasting Drew Allen's cooking in 1982. There's more to it, but I wouldn't want to bore you with the details. Join us for Breakfast, Brunch, Lunch and Dinner. Reservations for groups, catering, and private dining welcome. It's never too late to enter a convent.

Signature Tastes of SAN ANTONIO

For Cheese Spread:
6 oz. soft mild goat cheese, at room temperature
12 oz. cream cheese, at room temperature
1 small garlic clove, minced and mashed to a paste with ¼ tsp. salt
1 tsp. chile morita paste or minced canned chiles chipoltes in adobo sauce

For Sauce:
1 tbsp. chile morita paste or minced canned chiles chipoltes in adobo sauce
8 oz. piloncillo (Mexican unrefined sugar)
1 C. heavy cream

Accompaniment:
grilled bread, corn chips or crackers

Make Cheese Spread:
1. In a bowl with an electric mixer beat together cheeses, garlic paste, and chile morita paste or minced chipolte chiles. Transfer mixture to a small serving bowl and chill, covered, at least 4 hours or overnight.

Make Sauce:
1. In a small saucepan combine chile morita paste or minced chiles chipoltes, piloncillo, and cream and cook over low heat, stirring occasionally and breaking up sugar, until piloncillo is melted and sauce is smooth, about 20 minutes. Transfer sauce to a small serving bowl and chill, covered, for at least 4 hours or up to overnight.

2. Spread cheese on grilled bread, corn chips or crackers and lightly drizzle with sauce.

IIII S Alamo St., San Antonio, TX

LIBERTY BAR

"Kissing don't last: cookery do!"
George Meredith

CAESAR SALAD

Liberty Bistro serves Contemporary American Cuisine. Ours is a seasonally changing menu focusing on wild seafood, local meats and produce from small farms. Everything is made in-house including all of our bread, pastas, and desserts. We emphasize quality over quantity.

Parmesan Crisps:
¾ C. (3-oz.) grated parmesan

Dressing:
½ C. extra-virgin olive oil
4 anchovy fillets, rinsed and patted dry, optional
2 tbsp. freshly squeezed lemon juice
2 cloves garlic
3 dashes hot sauce (recommended: Tabasco)
1 tsp. dijon mustard
¾ tsp. salt
½ tsp. Worcestershire sauce
freshly ground black pepper

Salad:
2 hearts romaine lettuce, chopped
3 hard-boiled eggs, peeled and quartered
1 C. cherry tomatoes, halved

Parmesan Crisps:
1. Heat a nonstick skillet over medium-high heat and sprinkle the cheese, by the tablespoon, into the skillet. Cook until lacy and slightly set; about 1 minute. Flip and cook until crisp, about 2 minutes more. Transfer to a wire rack to cool.

Dressing:
1. Combine the olive oil, anchovies, lemon juice, garlic, hot sauce, mustard, salt, Worcestershire sauce, and pepper, to taste, in blender or food processor. Blend until smooth.

Salad:
1. Put the lettuce, eggs, and tomatoes into a large serving bowl and crumble in the Parmesan crisps. Pour enough dressing on the salad to coat well, toss, and serve.

Signature Tastes of SAN ANTONIO

200 N. SEGUIN AVE., NEW BRAUNFELS, TX

LIBERTY BISTRO

"We may live without friends; we may live without books, but civilized men cannot live without cooks."
Owen Meredith

173

FRENCH TOAST

Little Gretel, a 20 minute drive from San Antonio, is located on River Road across from a park bordering the Guadalupe River – alive with ducks and geese. Their small patio garden has 12 tables surrounded by potted, climbing roses. Fran and I took a break during our day of shopping the "Texas Hill Country" and had an incredible lunch at the very charming Little Gretel. Their menu has been featuring German and Czech cuisine since 1983.

4½ C. all-purpose flour, divided
¼ C. sugar
1 tsp. salt
1 tsp. grated lemon rind
1 (¼ oz.) package active dry yeast
1 C. butter
½ C. water
6 large eggs
3 tbsp. butter, softened
⅔ C. firmly packed brown sugar
2 tbsp. milk
¼ tsp. vanilla extract
2 egg yolks, lightly beaten
2 C. finely chopped pecans melted butter powdered sugar

1. Combine 1¾ cups flour, ¼ cup sugar, and next 3 ingredients in a large mixing bowl; stir well. combine 1 cup butter and water in a saucepan; heat until butter melts, stirring occasionally. Cool to 120F to 130°F.
2. Gradually add liquid mixture to flour mixture, beating well at low speed with an electric mixer. Beat an additional 2 minutes at medium speed. Add 6 eggs; beat well. Gradually stir in remaining flour. cover and let rise in a warm place (85F), free of drafts, 1 hour or until doubled in bulk. Cover and chill at least 8 hours.
3. Combine 3 tablespoons butter and next 4 ingredients in a medium bowl; stir well. Stir in pecans, and set aside.
4. Punch dough down; turn out onto a lightly floured surface, and knead 4 to 5 times. Divide dough in half. Work with 1 portion of dough at a time, refrigerating other portion. Roll dough into a 14 x 9 inch rectangle; brush with melted butter.
5. Spread half of pecan mixture over dough to within ½ inch of edge. Roll up 1 side of dough, starting at short side and ending at middle of dough. Roll up remaining side of dough until rolls meet in the middle.
6. Place dough in a well greased 9 x 5 inch loafpan, rolled side up. Gently brush loaf with melted butter. repeat process with remaining portion of dough and pecan mixture. Cover and let rise in a warm place, free of drafts 45 minutes or until doubled.
7. Bake at 350F for 20 minutes; cover with aluminum foil and bake 15 more minutes or until golden. Remove from pans immediately, cool on a wire rack. Sprinkle with powdered sugar.

LITTLE GRETEL
518 RIVER ROAD, BOERNE, TX

"One must eat to live, not live to eat."
Moliere

PEACH–PECAN UPSIDE-DOWN CAKE

Signature Tastes of SAN ANTONIO

Los Barrios opened in 1979 in a small boat garage in downtown San Antonio. Success quickly followed, and six months later, we moved into an old Dairy Queen just north of downtown. From these humble beginnings, matriarch Viola Barrios built a thriving Mexican restaurant that has been locally and nationally recognized. Los Barrios Restaurant's secret to success is our casero-style cooking. All of our recipes are prepared in the traditional Mexican home-cooking style that has been used for generations of families in Mexico. This is the cooking style that Viola Barrios knew, and this is the cooking style that our customers love!

Cake:
2 C. Bisquik mix
2 eggs
1 C. sugar
1 C. milk
¾ C. vegetable oil
2 tsp. vanilla extract

Topping:
¼ lb. (1 stick) butter, melted
1 C. packed brown sugar
one 15¼-oz. can sliced peaches, drained
about ½ C. pecan halves

1. Preheat the over to 375°F.

2. To make the cake batter, combine all the ingredients in a large bowl, whisking together until blended. Set aside.

3. To make the topping, pour the melted butter into a Bundt pan. Sprinkle the brown sugar evenly over the butter. Arrange the peaches on top. Place a pecan halfway between each peach slice.

4. Carefully pour the batter over the peaches. Bake for 40 minutes, or until a toothpick inserted in the center of the cake comes out clean. Transfer the pan to a wire rack to cool for 10 minutes, then invert.

5. Serve the cake warm, with ice cream, if desired.

LOS BARRIOS MEXICAN
4223 BLANCO RD., SAN ANTONIO, TX

"It's difficult to believe that people are still starving in this country because food isn't available."
Ronald Reagan

175

FRIED GREEN TOMATO AND SHRIMP REMOULADE SLIDERS

Chef John Besh welcomes you to Lüke San Antonio, on the city's famed River Walk. This is Besh's first restaurant outside of his home state of Louisiana, and it features a menu of authentic Old World cuisine, combining classic German and French cooking techniques with a New Orleans touch. Lüke is conveniently situated in San Antonio's popular downtown district.

1 large egg
1 C. buttermilk
1 C. yellow cornmeal
½ tsp. salt, or to taste
¼ tsp. freshly ground pepper, or to taste
8 (½-in.-thick) slices all-green tomatoes (about 2 medium tomatoes)
6 tbsp. vegetable oil
24 medium shrimp (about ½ lb.) peeled, cooked, and chilled
1 C. Remoulade sauce, chilled

Garnish:
mixed greens

1. Whisk together egg and buttermilk in a medium bowl. Combine cornmeal, salt, and pepper in a shallow dish. Dip tomato slices in egg mixture, then coat with seasoned cornmeal.

2. Heat oil in a large sauté pan over medium heat. Place tomato slices in pan in a single layer, and cook until golden brown on bottom, about 3 minutes. Flip and brown other side, about 3 minutes more. Interior should be cooked through but not mushy.

3. Place 2 tomato slices on each of 4 serving plates and top each slice with 3 shrimp. Spoon 1½ tablespoons. Remoulade sauce over each slice, and garnish, if desired. Serve immediately.

125 E. HOUSTON ST., SAN ANTONIO, TX

LÜKE

"Nothing stimulates the practiced cook's imagination like an egg."
Irma Rombauer

M.K. Davis
Restaurant & Bar

SERVING SAN ANTONIO SINCE 1956

T-BONE STEAK

Signature Tastes of SAN ANTONIO

The nachos were excellent just as good as some Mexican Food restaurant. They were the old fashion way & not just things put on top of them. The meat & beans were season well & layer high. The chicken fried steak & HB steaks were excellent & lot of it. It's a great value for your money & the beers are huge & very cold. The service is good & staff is very friendly & helpful. All the food had a great taste & large quantity.

4 - 24 oz. T - bone steaks cut 1 ½ inches thick
1 small onion
4 cloves of garlic
1 C. worchestire sauce
1 stick of butter
salt and pepper to taste
1 tbsp. vinegar
louisiana hot sauce to taste

1. Start the Grill...must be cooked on an outdoor grill. I use charcoal and mesquite. I cook my steaks on pretty high heat - you be the judge.
2. In a small sauce pan add your butter, onions and garlic - saute til they are translucent.
3. Add the vinegar, worchestire and Louisiana hot sauce - bring to a simmer.
4. Folks, this only takes 7 minutes PER SIDE to cook. This will get you a medium to medium-rare steak that don't need no steak sauce !!!! :)
5. Brush your steaks down with the sauce mixture.
6. Place steaks on the grill , directly over the heat.
7. Brush liberally and very often with the rest of the sauce mixture while your steak is cooking.
8. After 7 minutes turn your steak over only once and do the same on the other side.
9. This will get you a medium rare to medium steak that will melt in your mouth !
10. Serve with a big baked potato and a fresh garden salad.

1302 N FLORES ST., SAN ANTONIO, TX

M.K. DAVIS

"When men reach their sixties and retire they go to pieces. Women just go right on cooking."
Gail Sheehy

179

CHEESE LASAGNA

1 (16 oz.) package lasagna noodles
4 C. ricotta cheese
¼ C. grated Parmesan cheese
4 eggs
salt and pepper to taste
1 tsp. olive oil
3 cloves garlic, minced
1 (32 oz.) jar spaghetti sauce
1 tsp. Italian seasoning
2 C. shredded mozzarella cheese

1. Preheat oven to 350 degrees F (175 degrees C). Bring a large pot of lightly salted water to a boil. Add pasta and cook for 8 to 10 minutes or until al dente; drain and lay lasagna flat on foil to cool.

2. In a medium bowl, combine ricotta, Parmesan, eggs, salt and pepper; mix well.

3. In a medium saucepan, heat oil over medium heat and sauté garlic for 2 minutes; stir in spaghetti sauce and Italian seasoning. Heat sauce until warmed through, stirring occasionally, 2 to 5 minutes.

4. Spread ½ cup of sauce in the bottom of a 9x13 baking dish. Cover with a layer of noodles. Spread half the ricotta mixture over noodles; top with another noodle layer. Pour 1½ cups of sauce over noodles, and spread the remaining ricotta over the sauce. Top with remaining noodles and sauce and sprinkle mozzarella over all. Cover with greased foil.

5. Bake 45 minutes, or until cheese is bubbly and top is golden.

Signature Tastes of SAN ANTONIO

MAAR'S PIZZA & MORE
14218 NACOGDOCHES RD., SAN ANTONIO, TX

"Chameleons feed on light and air.
Poets' food is love and fame."
Percy Bysshe Shelley

TEA SMOKED
CHICKEN BREAST SALAD

Gina purchased the restaurant from Rene Guerrero in July 2009. She began with Madhatters many years ago as a "cook," then became "kitchen manager" before working up to "front of house" manager. She is joined by her husband Joey, daughters Melissa and Olympia, her son Joseph, and newest addition, granddaughter Emeri.

Signature Tastes of SAN ANTONIO

3 boneless, skinless free-range chicken breasts
100 g loose leaf tea
100 g soft brown sugar
200 g dried butter beans, soaked overnight
200 g dried yellow split peas, soaked overnight
200 g dried green lentils, soaked overnight
1 medium onion, peeled and chopped
1 lemon, quartered
2-3 bay leaves
1 tbsp. finely chopped fresh thyme leaves, plus 3-4 sprigs
1 bag mixed watercress, spinach and rocket salad
5 tbsp. rapeseed oil
1 tbsp. red wine vinegar
small bunch of fresh mint, leaves chopped
1 tbsp. finely chopped fresh marjoram leaves
1 tbsp. wholegrain mustard
100 g walnuts, roughly chopped
salt and freshly ground black pepper
edible flowers, to garnish (optional)

1. Double line a wok with aluminium foil. Add the tea and sugar and toss lightly. Place a metal grill over the wok and a tight fitting lid over that. Place over a medium heat. Do not leave unattended. Use in a well ventilated area.

2. Put the chicken on a board and bash with a rolling pin until around 1cm thick. Smoke on the grill over the wok. Depending on the size of the wok and the thickness of the chicken, this can take up to an hour to cook thoroughly. Keep checking and remove as soon as the chicken is cooked all the way through but still moist.

3. Rinse the soaked pulses in cold water and put in a saucepan with the onion, lemon, bay leaves and 2-3 sprigs of thyme. Bring to the boil and cook for about 45 minutes or until tender but not mushy.

4. While the pulses are cooking, make a dressing by whisking the rapeseed oil, red wine vinegar, chopped mint, chopped thyme and marjoram leaves and mustard. Season with salt and pepper.

5. Drain the pulses and return to the pan. Stir in the dressing and allow to absorb the flavours while cooling. Toss the salad through the pulses and spoon into four shallow bowls. Shred the chicken and add to the salad. Sprinkle with walnuts and garnish with edible flowers if liked.

320 BEAUREGARD ST., SAN ANTONIO, TX

MADHATTERS

"Serenely full, the epicure would say, fate cannot harm me; I have dined today."
Sydney Smith

DENVER FRITTATA

What started with a wild idea back in 1998 has turned into San Antonio's favorite spot for breakfast. In early 2000 we started looking for a small spot to open a "little place" where we could focus on (with all respect to Frank Sinatra) doing it our way. We found a great little spot that had everything we needed and off to the races we went. On September 19, 2000 The Magnolia Pancake Haus opened it's doors for business. A menu that reflected our numerous years in the business built around a recipe for "The World's Best" buttermilk pancakes and items as unique as you might find anywhere you travel became the new standard for breakfast in San Antonio.

8 eggs
¼ C. half and half
1 tbsp. butter
1 C. cheddar cheese, shredded
1 small green pepper, diced
1 small onion, diced
½ C. ham, diced
salt and pepper to taste

1. Preheat oven to broil. Spray 10 inch non-stick skillet with cooking spray (If pan is not oven proof, cover handle with foil)

2. Over medium heat, melt butter and add peppers and onions. Saute until tender crisp. Add ham to heat through.

3. In mixing bowl, whisk eggs, half and half, ½ cup cheese, salt and pepper. Lower heat to low.

4. Pour egg mixture into skillet over veggies and ham. Place lid on pan. Cook for 6-8 minutes.

5. Remove cover and sprinkle remaining cheese over top. Place under broil until cheese melts.

6. Remove from oven. Slide frittata onto serving plate and cut into wedges.

MAGNOLIA PANCAKE HAUS
606 EMBASSY OAK, SUITE 100, SAN ANTONIO, TX

"When we lose, I eat. When we win, I eat. I also eat when we're rained out."
Tommy Lasorda

185

FUJI APPLE SALAD

Signature Tastes of SAN ANTONIO

In 1915, William G. McAdoo, then the Secretary of the Treasury, was commissioned to build the city of New Braunfels its first federally built United States Post Office. Once completed, the Post Office quickly became a first-class facility for locals to send and receive mail, conduct financial business in the Treasury Department, and as many have told it, "to catch up on the news and gossip around town".

2 C. apple cider 1 star anise 1 cinnamon stick 1 large slice of ginger ¼ C. rice wine vinegar ½ C. canola oil 3 fuji apples 1 tbsp. chopped chives, save a little for garnish salt and black pepper to taste	**1.** In a non-reactive pan over low heat reduce apple cider with star anise, cinnamon and ginger by 75 per cent. Strain out solids and pour liquid into a blender. Add vinegar and while blender is running, drizzle in oil. **2.** Season with salt and pepper. Peel and julienne the apples and immediately toss with the emulsion. Check for seasoning. Add the chives.

McAdoo's Seafood Company

196 N. Castell, New Braunfels, TX

"Salad is not a meal. It is a style."
Frances Ann Lebowitz

Barbacoa Mexicana

In 1941, Pete and Cruz Cortez opened a little three-table café for early-rising farmers and workers at San Antonio's Mercado. Sixty years later Mi Tierra Café is a world-famous landmark – the place hometown regulars and hungry tourists go for authentic Mexican food and a warm Texas welcome. Pete's and Cruz's children and grandchildren continue the family tradition of good food and big-heart hospitality at Mi Tierra, which now seats over 500 and is still located in Market Square, El Mercado.

Barbacoa:
⅓ C. apple cider vinegar
3 tbsp. lime juice
3-4 chipotle peppers – canned
4 cloves garlic
4 tsp. cumin
2 tsp. oregano – dried Mexican variety is best
1½ tsp. ground black pepper
1½ tsp. salt
½ tsp. ground clove
2 tbsp. vegetable oil
4-5 lb. beef roast (chuck roast is fine)
¾ C. chicken broth
3 bay leaves

Pico de Gallo:
4 tomatoes – diced
½ C. red onion – diced
¼ C. cilantro – diced
2 tbsp. jalapenos – diced
2 tbsp. lime juice – or just squeeze some lime over until it's flavored right.
¼ tsp. salt

Pinto Beans:
3 cans (15 oz each) pinto beans – canned are fine or make some fresh.
3 tbsp. bacon fat – cook up about 4 pcs. of bacon and you should have enough.
½ tsp. oregano – dried Mexican variety is best.

Rice – Cilantro Lime Flavored:
3 C. water
2 C. uncooked white rice
3 tbsp. butter
1½ tsp. salt
⅓ C. cilantro – chipped
2 tbsp. lime juice

Burrito:
8 Flour Tortillas – 12"
shredded Monterey Jack cheese
guacamole – if desired
sour cream – if desired

1. Combine the lime juice, vinegar, chipotle peppers, garlic, cumin, oregano, black pepper, salt and clove in a blender (you can also use a food processor) and blend at the highest speed until it's smooth and creamy.

2. Cut the roast up into several smaller pieces and remove any excess fat. In a large dutch oven, heat approximately 2 tbsp of oil and cook each side of the pieces of meat until lightly browned.

3. Pour the adobo sauce sauce over the meat and ad in the chicken broth and bay leaves. Cover and let simmer for about 4 hours, turning every 30 to 40 minutes. Uncover and cook an additional 1 to 2 hours until the meat is easily pulled apart.

4. While the baracoa is cooking, prepare the pico de gallo by combining all of the listed ingredients in a large bowl.

5. Let this chill in the refrigerator until everything is ready to serve. In a medium pan heat the bacon fat over a medium to medium low heat and add in the pinto beans and oregano.

6. Simmer for 45 minutes stirring periodically. Cover and lit sit until you're ready to assemble the burritos. In another large sauce pan prepare the rice. Combine the water, rice, salt and butter.

7. Bring the water and rice to a boil and then cover. Reduce the heat to low and simmer for 20 minutes. Remove the cover and stir in the lime juice and cilantro. Cover and let sit until you're ready to make your burritos.

8. To make your burrito, start with a warmed flour tortilla. This is best done on a dry skillet or in a ziplock bag in the microwave. It shouldn't take more than a minute, but keep an eye it so you don't overheat them.

9. Place a good pile of the barbacoa in the middle of the burrito. Next put a few spoons of the rice, beans and then the pico de gallo. If you'd like cheese, guacamole and/or sour cream, place that on top.

10. Fold in both sides of the tortilla and then roll up as tight as possible from bottom to top, keeping the sides closed in as you go. There's a bit of an art to it, so you may have to practice some. If you mess up, start over. Or enjoy it in bowl.

MI TIERRA CAFE & BAKERY
218 PRODUCE ROW, SAN ANTONIO, TX

Signature Tastes of SAN ANTONIO

"Worthless people live only to eat and drink; people of worth eat and drink only to live."
Socrates quotes

Mina & Dimi's Greek House, we have carefully selected some of our favorite dishes, as well as others from popular Greek tavern seaside resorts. From the garlicky taste of Tzatzsiki to the cinnamon spice of Baklava, we provide the wonderful atmosphere of Greece. Clearly dining at Mina & Dimi's Greek House is a thing for all senses: Taste, smell, sight, touch, and certainly sound. We don't expect everybody to be our customer, but we expect them to at least have the chance.

*half red onion, chopped
1 English cucumber or
2 field cucumbers
2 tomatoes, chopped
1 sweet pepper, chopped
½ C. (125 mL.)
kalamata olives
¼ C. (60 mL.) extra-
virgin olive oil
2 tbsp. (30 mL.) lemon
juice
2 tbsp. (30 mL.) red
wine vinegar
1½ tsp. (7 mL.) dried
Greek oregano
¼ tsp. (1 mL.) salt
pinch pepper
5 oz. (150 g.) cubed feta
cheese*

1. Soak onion in cold water for 20 minutes; drain and transfer to large bowl. Cut cucumber lengthwise into quarters (seed field cucumbers, if using) and chop; transfer to bowl along with tomatoes, pepper and olives.

2. Toss with olive oil, lemon juice, vinegar, oregano, salt and pepper; mix well. Transfer to serving bowl; top with cheese.

MINA & DIMI'S GREEK HOUSE

7159 W US-90, SAN ANTONIO, TX

"Vegetables are interesting but lack a sense of purpose when unaccompanied by a good cut of meat."
Fran Lebowitz

MOROCCAN BITES
TAGINE
MOROCCAN CUISINE

Hallal   TAGINE   حلال

OPEN

5
7
1
4

MOROCCAN CHICKEN BITES

Moroccan Bites Tagine is an exotic oasis offering highest standards of food and service in a luxurious environment. By having you, we extend of casual comfort. It is our hope to take you back in time and place into our world, where cuisine and hospitality are cherished matters of health, happiness and cultural heritage.

1 tsp. cinnamon
1 tsp. cumin
½ tsp. turmeric
¼ C. extra virgin olive oil
¼ C. cilantro
2 tsp. honey
4 cloves garlic, chopped
6 whole chicken breast halves without skin, boneless, cut into 32 pcs.
32 dried apricot halves, cut in half

1. Combine all ingredients except chicken and apricots in a blender until smooth, adding a little water if needed. Toss chicken with marinade and let stand overnight in the refrigerator.

2. Bake chicken bites until cooked through, about 15-20 minutes.

3. Serve with an apricot on a toothpick. If desired, make a second batch of the cilantro vinaigrette for drizzling or dipping.

MOROCCAN BITES
5714 EVERS RD., SAN ANTONIO, TX

"I love lean meats like chicken, turkey. I'm obsessed with sushi and fish in general. I eat a lot of veggies and hummus."
Shawn Johnson

GULF COAST SHRIMP

Signature Tastes of SAN ANTONIO

First opened in 2009, Mr. Tim's Country Kitchen has turned into a staple of fine Comfort Food dining in the Southtown San Antonio area for the last three years. Owned and operated by Tim Smith, Mr. Tim's Country Kitchen prides itself on providing the freshest, tastiest food with friendly efficient service. Raised in Alice Texas, Tim first started in the food preparation business when he was only 15 years old and started his first restaurant at the ripe young age of 18 after professionally migrating to Houston.

1 tbsp. clarified butter
1½ tbsp. minced garlic
1 lb. large shrimp shelled
2 tbsp. lemon juice
1½ tbsp. Worcestershire sauce
¼ C. beer
3 tbsp. cold butter cut into pieces
.
Seasoning Mixture:
1 tsp. ground cayenne pepper
2 tsp. ground black pepper
1 tsp. salt
1 tsp. dried leaf thyme, crumbled
1 tsp. rosemary, crumbled
¼ tsp. basil
¼ tsp. sweet paprika

1. Combine seasoning ingredients. Using a heavy skillet, heat butter until hot and foamy. Sauté garlic for 20 seconds; stir in shrimp, lemon juice, Worcestershire sauce, and 2 tablespoons of seasoning mix.

2. Mix together well; sauté for about a minute. Add beer; simmer until shrimp are cooked, about a minute or 2 longer; remove from heat. Add cold butter; stir until butter is melted.

3. Place mixture into a large bowl and serve with bread.

MR. TIM'S COUNTRY KITCHEN

620 S PRESA ST., SAN ANTONIO, TX

"Food is your body's fuel. Without fuel, your body wants to shut down."
Ken Hill

Signature Tastes of SAN ANTONIO

Welcome friends and newcomers. We're excited you're visiting us. Guests come to Myron's for more than a great steak, they come for a truly memorable experience. So don't be surprised when we call you by name, or remember your drink order. Just settle in, relax, and enjoy your evening. We're proud to serve only the best USDA Prime beef - and we're just as proud of how we serve it. Myron's - the prime steakhouse of USDA Prime steakhouses.

2 tbsp. Old Bay seasoning
1 lemon, halved
1 tsp. granulated garlic
1 clove garlic, finely minced
½ tsp. chili powder
1 tsp. salt
24 extra large tail-on raw shrimp (more if you are using smaller shrimp)

For the Cocktail Sauce:
½ C. Heinz chili sauce
1 C. ketchup
1 tbsp. horseradish
1 dash Worcestershire sauce
juice of ½ lemon
½ tsp. Tabasco
½ clove garlic, finely minced
1 tbsp. cilantro, chopped

1. To prepare the cocktail sauce, mix all the cocktail sauce ingredients together in a medium bowl and refrigerate until ready to serve.

2. Have a large bowl of ice water ready and set near the sink. To a 8-quart pot of water, add the Old Bay, lemon, granulated garlic, garlic, chili powder, and salt. Bring to a boil. Add the shrimp to the pot and when the water returns to a boil, the shrimp should be done! The shrimp should be bright pink.

3. Immediately drain and place the shrimp into the ice bath to cool for 2 minutes. Peel the shrimp (leaving the tail-on.) Drain and serve with the cocktail sauce.

MYRON'S PRIME STEAKHOUSE
136 N CASTELL AVE., NEW BRAUNFELS, TX

"I love food and feel that it is something that should be enjoyed. I eat whatever I want. I just don't overeat."
Tyra Banks

TOMATILLO CHICKEN

Signature Tastes of SAN ANTONIO

**4 boneless skinless chicken breast halves
garlic powder
salt and pepper
¼ tsp. cumin seed
½ medium onion, halved and sliced
1 (1 pt.) jar tomatillo salsa (mild or hot)
4 slices monterey jack pepper cheese
¼ C. loosely packed chopped cilantro
4 tbsp. sour cream
8 flour tortillas**

1. Line baking tray with aluminum foil. Place chicken breasts on foil. Sprinkle with garlic powder, salt, and pepper to taste. Sprinkle with cumin seed. Place ¼ of onion slices on each chicken breast half.

2. Cover all with tomatillo salsa. Place another sheet of aluminum foil on top of chicken breasts and fold all four sides until sealed very tight. Bake foil packet on tray in 375 oven for 30 minutes. Remove from oven and carefully remove top foil sheet.

3. Place a slice of pepper jack cheese on each chicken breast half. Sprinkle all with chopped cilantro. Return to the oven uncovered. Remove from the oven when cheese has melted.

4. Meanwhile heat tortillas. Serve one chicken breast per person.

5. Place a tbsp of sour cream on top of each chicken breast half. Serve with hot tortillas and refried or borracho beans.

NICHA'S COMIDA MEXICANA
3119 ROOSEVELT AVE., SAN ANTONIO, TX

"I love food and I love everything involved with food. I love the fun of it. I love restaurants. I love cooking, although I don't cook very much. I love kitchens."
Alma Guillermoprieto

CINNAMON ROLLS

Signature Tastes of SAN ANTONIO

The Olmos Perk Coffee Bar ('OP') opened its doors in September 2006. OP was the brain-child of two accounting executives who had over 40 years of combined experience working in the fast-food industry. Mike Mendez is one of the owners who decided after 30 years he no longer wanted to be a 'bean counter'. Instead, he was thinking of beans of another sort - coffee beans. Mike developed a business plan to open a coffee shop and spent over a year searching for the perfect location. Once that location was found in Olmos Park, Mike worked with a contractor and an architect to turn a former nail salon into a space suitable for an upscale coffee shop. Mike devotes 100% of his time to managing the coffee shop, while the other owner continues to work as an accounting executive and acts as a silent partner for OP.

Rolls:
2½ C. all purpose flour, plus extra for the counter
2 tbsp. white granulated sugar
1¼ tsp. baking powder
½ tsp. baking soda
½ tsp. salt
1¼ C. buttermilk
6 tbsp. unsalted butter, melted

Cinnamon Filling:
¾ C. packed dark brown sugar
¼ C. white granulated sugar
3 tsp. cinnamon
⅛ tsp. salt
1 tbsp. unsalted butter, melted

Cream Cheese Frosting:
8 oz. cream cheese
½ C. butter
1 tsp. vanilla
3 C. confectioner's sugar
1 tbsp. milk

1. To make frosting, mix all ingredients until smooth
2. Preheat the oven to 425 degrees F. Generously coat a 9 inch round cake pan and a wire cooling rack with vegetable oil spray.
3. Make the filling: combine together the brown sugar, ¼ cup granulated white sugar, cinnamon, salt, and the 1 Tablespoon melted butter until the mixture resembles wet sand.
4. Make the dough: In a large bowl, whisk together the flour; 2 Tablespoons white granulated sugar, baking powder, baking soda, and salt.
5. In a separate bowl, whisk the buttermilk and 2 Tablespoons of the melted butter together.
6. Stir the buttermilk mixture into the flour mixture with a wooden spoon until absorbed, about 30 seconds. The dough will look shaggy.
7. Turn the dough out onto a generously floured counter and knead until smooth, about 1 minute.
8. Press the dough out into a 9 by 12 inch rectangle using your hands.
9. Brush the dough with 2 Tablespoons melted butter. Sprinkle the dough evenly with the filling, leaving a ½-inch border. Press the filling firmly into the dough.
10. Loosen the dough from the counter using a bench scraper or a metal spatula.
11. Starting at a long side, roll the dough, pressing lightly, to form a tight log.
12. Pinch the seam to seal. Slice the dough into 8 even pieces.
13. Place the slices in the greased pan.
14. Brush with the remaining 2 Tablespoons melted butter. Bake until the edges are golden brown, 20-25 minutes.
15. Use a knife to loosen the buns from the pan. Flip the buns out onto the prepared wire rack, then turn buns upright and let cool for 10 minutes before frosting with cream cheese icing. Prepare the icing while rolls are cooling.

5223 N McCullough Ave., San Antonio, TX

OLMOS PERK COFFEE

"Man seeks to change the foods available in nature to suit his tastes, thereby putting an end to the very essence of life contained in them."
Sai Baba

Moo Shu Pork

Our family opened the doors to our first Chinese restaurant in 1989. Our mission back then, and still is today, is to offer our diners generous portions of freshly made dishes at reasonable prices. We pride ourselves in offering guests fast efficient service with a personal touch. Our goal is to keep our customers happy while satisfying their appetites for flavorful Chinese food.

10 dried wood ear mushrooms
2 (4-oz.) boneless pork loin chops, trimmed
1½ tsp. cornstarch
3 tbsp. soy sauce
2 tbsp. peanut or vegetable oil, divided
2 large eggs, lightly beaten
1 C. shredded napa cabbage
1 (8-oz.) can bamboo shoots, drained and chopped
½ C. sliced fresh mushrooms
2 green onions, cut into 1-inch pcs.
9 moo shu pancakes
¼ C. hoisin sauce

1. Soak wood ear mushrooms in hot water to cover 15 minutes or until soft; drain and slice. Set aside.

2. Freeze pork chops 30 minutes or until firm. Remove from freezer, and cut into 1/8-inch-thick strips. Toss with cornstarch and soy sauce; set aside.

3. Heat 1 tablespoon oil in a large skillet or wok at medium-high heat 2 minutes. Add eggs; stir-fry 1 minute or until done. Remove eggs from wok.

4. Add remaining 1 tablespoon oil to skillet, and heat over medium-high heat 2 minutes. Add pork, and stir-fry 3 to 4 minutes or until done. Add wood ear mushrooms, cabbage, bamboo shoots, and fresh mushrooms. Stir-fry 2 to 3 minutes.

5. Add eggs and green onions, and stir-fry 30 seconds. Spoon evenly down center of each pancake; roll up. Serve with hoisin sauce. 1 cup sliced fresh mushrooms may be substituted for wood ear mushrooms; omit soaking.

OOLONG CHINESE BISTRO
12411 BANDERA RD., HELOTES, TX

"My philosophy from day one is that I can sleep better at night if I can improve an individual's knowledge about food and wine, and do it on a daily basis."
Emeril Lagasse

GRINGO CHICKEN TACOS SALAD

Signature Tastes of SAN ANTONIO

We start with the classics, but we elevate them. We make all of our food fresh from our own recipes, and use only the best ingredients. Like hand-pressed patties and buns toasted with butter for our burgers. Our own sauce and fresh basil on our pizzas. A special-recipe marinade for our chicken tacos. As for our ice cream, pralines, and chocolate chip cookies — we make them all in house.

crispy white corn chips:
Generous handful
(crumbled optional)
hearty portion of or-
ganic spring lettuce mix
scoop of chopped red
tomatoes
scoop of chopped white
onions
3 oz. shredded blended
cheese
1 or 2 shredded chicken
breasts (slow roasted
with various herbs and
spices)
3 oz. mild taco sauce
3 oz. chipotle white
sauce

1. Place chips on plates.

2. Spread lettuce evenly over chips.

3. Place tomatoes and onions in separate corners.

4. Place cheese in center. Place hot chicken over cheese.

5. Top with taco sauce and chipotle white sauce.

6. Preferably scramble all together and enjoy.

ORDERUP: EAT IN, TAKE OUT

999 E BASSE RD., SAN ANTONIO, TX

"Sharing food with another human being is an intimate act that should not be indulged in lightly."
M. F. K. Fisher

VEGETABLE TEMPURA

Signature Tastes of SAN ANTONIO

350 g. kumara (orange sweet potato), peeled, thinly sliced
1 large carrot, peeled, thinly sliced diagonally
450 g. pumpkin, peeled, seeds removed, thinly sliced
125 g. green beans, trimmed
1 large green capsicum, seeds removed, cut into 2cm-wide strips
125 g. button mushrooms
½ C. rice flour
½ C. plain flour
½ tsp. baking powder
1 egg
300 ml. bottle soda water, chilled
vegetable oil, for deep-frying
soy sauce, to serve

1. Refrigerate vegetables until cold.

2. Place flours and baking powder into a large bowl. Add egg and soda water. Stir until just combined (don't over-mix, mixture doesn't have to be smooth).

3. Pour oil into a large saucepan or wok until it is one-third full. Heat over medium-high heat until a small piece of bread sizzles when dropped into oil.

4. Dip vegetables, 1 piece at a time, into tempura batter, allowing excess to drain. Gently lower into hot oil. Cook, 3 to 4 at a time, for 2 to 3 minutes, or until batter is crisp and light golden. Drain on paper towels. Repeat until all vegetables are cooked. Serve immediately with soy sauce.

OSAKA STEAK & SUSHI
11851 BANDERA RD., SAN ANTONIO, TX

"The disparity between a restaurant's price and food quality rises in direct proportion to the size of the pepper mill."
Bryan Miller

BEEF WITH BROCCOLI

As Director of Beverage for P.F. Chang's China Bistro, Mary Melton brings more than 25 years of industry experience to her role. She is responsible for the overall strategy of the beverage program across 190 restaurants and manages the creation of beverage menus, the wine program, drink innovation and development, wine education and bartender training. Prior to joining P.F. Chang's in 2005, Mary worked with the Henry Wine Group as a fine wine specialist and gained experience in wine sales with the Regal Wine Company. Mary's first venture into the industry included restaurant and nightclub management in San Diego.

⅓ C. green onion (chopped)
1 tbsp. splenda artificial sweetener
1 tbsp. brown sugar
3 tbsp. low sodium soy sauce
2 tbsp. rice wine vinegar
1 tsp. sesame oil
1 tsp. minced garlic
¼ tsp. ground ginger (1 tsp. minced fresh)
1 lb. flank steak
1 tbsp. olive oil
2 C. broccoli
2 C. chow mein noodles (cooked chow mein noodles not fried)

1. Combine first 8 ingredients.

2. Heat a wok or large frying pan to medium high.

3. Cut flank steak into thin strips.

4. Put flank steak into green onion marinade.

5. Blanche broccoli florets by putting in a bowl with a little bit of water and microwaving on high for 3 minutes.

6. Add olive oil to pan.

7. Stir fry beef mixture with broccoli for about five minutes or until beef is desired doneness.

8. Spoon over cooked chow mein noodles.

Signature Taste of SAN ANTONIO

"There is no sincerer love than the love of food."
George Bernard Shaw

SHRIMP PAESANO WITH LEMON BUTTER GARLIC

Signature Tastes of SAN ANTONIO

When you visit or entertain on the River, you want to be at Paesanos RiverWalk. You and your guest will enjoy the comfortable and contemporary enclave at the bend in the River Walk. Paesanos Riverwalk Ristorante breaks the boundaries of traditional Italian cuisine to explore modern Mediterranean specialties. Enjoy the legendary Shrimp Paesano, it's almost as famous as the Alamo. Our prime Riverside location puts you and your guests at the center of the action, with indoor or al fresco private dining spaces- relaxed yet refined settings. We're sure you will agree that Paesanos Riverwalk is one of the best riverwalk restaurants in San Antonio.

1 lb. shrimp raw, deveined and shelled
1 pint light cream 10% or half and half
2 tbsp. olive oil or butter
2 c. flour, all-purpose
1 large egg yolk
1 stick butter
1 clove garlic minced
¼ C. parsley leaves fresh, chopped
1 chives fresh
¼ C. lemon juice

1. Preheat oven to 400.

2. Reserved some cream for the sauce. Soak shrimp in the remaining cream for at least 30 minutes in the refrigerator.

3. Drain and roll shrimp in flour then sauté in oil over medium heat for 5 minutes. Do not turn shrimp!

4. Remove and place shrimp in baking dish with the sautéed side down in preheated oven. Turn oven to broil and broil for 5 minutes.

For sauce:
1. Mix egg yolk and lemon juice in half the butter and stir over low heat until melted, take off heat.

2. Add garlic and rest of butter and stir briskly until butter melts and sauce thickens. (Add small amount of ½ and ½ to thicken). Add chives and parsley.

3. Serve the sauce with the crispy shrimp.

PAESANOS RIVERWALK
111 W CROCKETT ST., SAN ANTONIO, TX

"What I've enjoyed most, though, is meeting people who have a real interest in food and sharing ideas with them. Good food is a global thing and I find that there is always something new and amazing to learn - I love it!"
Jamie Oliver

ENCHILADAS DE MOLE

Signature Tastes of SAN ANTONIO

The core reason for the success of Paloma Blanca Mexican Cuisine isn't our cuisine or atmosphere – it's our family of good people. Many of us have been with the company since its inception, and yes, many of us are actually related to one another! Each of us takes pride in providing each guest with an exceptional experience by endeavoring to live up to the sign you'll find in the back of the house: Paloma Blanca practices the Golden Rule. We will always work to treat our guests as we would want to be treated. We're working to better our community. Since our opening in 1997, Paloma Blanca Mexican Cuisine has prioritized assisting various area charitable organizations.

Enchilada:
8-10 corn tortillas, small size
1½ C. shredded chicken (can substitute shredded beef or pork if desired)
¼ C. sour cream
¼ C. green onions, sliced
2 C. grated white cheese, halved in 2 equal parts (queso fresco or chihuahua)
kosher salt and fresh ground black pepper, to taste

Mole Sauce:
2 slices thick-cut bacon
1 large onion, chopped
2 ribs celery, chopped
1 medium carrot, chopped
4 dried guajillo peppers, seeds & stems removed
4 cloves garlic
¼ C. warm water
1 – 14 oz. can stew Mexican tomatoes
2 C. chicken broth
¼ C. premium dark chocolate, chopped fine
kosher salt and fresh ground black pepper
cilantro and diced white onions, for garnish

Mole Sauce:
1. Preheat a saucepan over medium high heat and cook bacon until fully cooked and crispy. Remove bacon from pan and save for another purpose. Add onion, carrot and celery and sauté until soft and translucent, about 6-8 minutes.
2. Meanwhile, puree chilies, garlic and water in a food processor. Strain the puree through a fine mesh strainer, reserving juices. Add tomatoes, broth and strained chili puree to vegetable mixture in the saucepan and cook on high heat for 20-30 minutes.
3. Let the sauce reduce and thicken, then strain the sauce again, pressing on solids.
4. Stir in the dark chocolate to the sauce until melted. Add salt and pepper to taste; keep warm.

For Enchiladas:
1. Mix chicken, sour cream, green onions and half of the cheese in a bowl. Add salt and pepper to taste.
2. Lay out the tortillas on a baking sheet and fill each one with chicken mixture down the middle. Roll the tortillas tightly and lay in a ceramic or clay baking dish that has a thin layer of mole sauce already spread on the bottom (to prevent sticking and burning).
3. Cover with remaining sauce and top with remaining cheese. Bake at 325 for 30 minutes, or until golden brown and bubbling. Let stand a few minutes before serving.
4. Serve with chopped cilantro and green onions for garnish and extra sour cream, if desired.

PALOMA BLANCA MEXICAN CUISINE
5800 BROADWAY ST., SAN ANTONIO, TX

"When I eat with my friends, it is a moment of real pleasure, when I really enjoy my life."
Monica Bellucci

TORTILLA SOUP

Check out this Mexican Restaurant in the Texas Hill Country, located ten minutes from Boerne and downtown San Antonio. Papa Nacho's Cantina has everything you need to enjoy a great meal! From tasty appetizers, nachos, soups, Mexican Dinners and Chef's Specials, it's no wonder Papa Nacho's Cantina is a favorite for locals and travelers alike. You won't want to miss the Cheese Chile Relleno, a Poblano pepper filled with Monterey Jack and Panela Cheese, dipped in egg butter and topped with Tampiquena sauce.

1 tbsp. vegetable oil, plus more for frying
2 large onions, chopped
8 cloves garlic, minced
1 tbsp. plus 1½ tsp. coarse kosher salt
1 tsp. ground cumin
½ tsp. red chile flakes
12 C. reduced-sodium chicken broth
1 can (28 oz.) diced tomatoes
juice of 2 limes
1 pckg (8 oz.) small corn tortillas, cut into ¼-in.-thick strips
2 lb. boneless, skinless chicken breast, cut into ¼-in.-thick strips
1 C. chopped fresh cilantro
sliced avocado, sour cream, grated Monterey jack cheese, additional chopped cilantro, and/or sliced green onions for topping

1. Heat 1 tbsp. vegetable oil in a large pot (at least 5 qts.) over medium heat. Add onions and cook until translucent, 5 to 7 minutes. Stir in two-thirds of the garlic, 1 tbsp. salt, cumin, and chile flakes and cook 2 minutes.

2. Add broth, tomatoes, and half the lime juice and increase heat to a gentle simmer; cook 20 minutes.

3. Meanwhile, pour about 1 in. of vegetable oil into a small frying pan set over medium-high heat. When oil is hot but not smoking, add one-third of the tortilla strips and cook until golden brown and crisp, about 2 minutes. With a slotted spoon, transfer strips to a paper towel-lined baking pan. Repeat with remaining tortilla strips in two batches. Sprinkle with 1 tsp. salt. Set aside.

4. Purée soup in batches in a blender. Return soup to pot and resume simmering. In a small bowl, toss chicken with remaining lime juice, garlic, and ½ tsp. salt. Marinate at room temperature for 10 minutes, then add to soup and simmer 5 minutes, until chicken is just cooked through. Stir in cilantro. Serve hot with tortilla strips and your choice of toppings.

Signature Tastes of SAN ANTONIO

PAPA NACHOS CANTINA
24145 INTERSTATE 10, SAN ANTONIO, TX

"I no longer prepare food or drink with more than one ingredient."
Cyra McFadden

CHICKEN FRIED BREAST

Papouli's Greek Grill was borne of a long legacy of restaurateurs in San Antonio, Texas. Papouli Tom Anthony arrived in the United States in 1911, and like most Greek-born immigrants of his time, opened a restaurant. His "Manhattan Café.rose rapidly to legendary status, built upon the tradition of offering excellent food, hospitality, and atmosphere. And it is these same values that carried the Manhattan Café through three generations of San Antonians that Papouli.s Greek Grill was conceived and built. The name, "Papouli's" was chosen not only out of respect and honor for the man who inspired this third generation of Anthony family restaurateurs, but more so for the values in which Papouli Tom, as well as his son Dan, believed and instilled in generations to come.

Signature Tastes of SAN ANTONIO

Falafel:
1 (15 oz.) can garbanzo beans, drained
½ yellow onion, diced and lightly sautéed
5 garlic cloves, minced and lightly sautéed
½ bunch cilantro
¼ bunch flat leaf parsley
¼ C. plus 2 tbsp. all purpose flour
1 tsp. baking powder
1 tbsp. ground cumin
2 tsp. ground coriander
1½ tsp. salt
¾ tsp. black pepper

Tzatziki:
2 tbsp. extra virgin olive oil
1½ tbsp. apple cider vinegar
½ tsp. ground cumin
1 garlic clove, minced
1¼ C. Greek yogurt
½ hothouse cucumber, grated
½ lemon, juiced
salt and pepper to taste

2 whole pitas, cut in half
4 romaine leaves, thinly sliced
2 roma tomatoes, seeded and diced
vegetable oil for frying

1. Fill a heavy bottom skillet with ½ inch oil and preheat to 350°F.
2. Place garbanzo beans, onion, garlic, cilantro, and parsley in a food processor and process until finely ground.
3. Scoop mixture into a mixing bowl and add remaining falafel ingredients and stir together until fully combined. Cover with plastic wrap and place in refrigerator for about 2 hours.

Fortzatziki:
1. Place oil, vinegar, cumin, and garlic in a small mixing bowl and whisk together. Add yogurt and cucumber to the mixture, season with salt and pepper and continue to whisk together. Set aside.
2. Form 2 tablespoon sized patties with the falafel mixture and fry for 3 to 4 minutes. Flip each patty and fry for an additional 2 minutes. Drain on paper towels and season with salt and pepper.
3. To assemble: Smear the insides of each pita with a small amount of tzatziki and fill with 3 falafels, a small amount of lettuce and a sprinkle of diced tomatoes. Top with more tzatziki and serve.

PAPOULI'S GREEK GRILL

11224 HUEBNER RD STE 201, SAN ANTONIO, TX

"We don't get fat because we overeat; we overeat because we're getting fat."
Gary Taubes

STUFFED POBLANO PEPPER

Signature Tastes of SAN ANTONIO

This is a family owned authentic San Antonio type Mexican restaurant. The food is consistently fantastic and the regular menu is supplemented with daily specials that range from hamburgers to chili cheese enchiladas. Have been eating there for years and have never been disappointed. A local favorite and is always busy but well worth any wait.

4 poblano peppers
1 C. uncooked brown rice (or 4 C. of any cooked grain)
1½ C. salsa
1 15 oz. can of black beans
1½ C. frozen or canned corn kernels
3 green onions (optional)
1 tsp. cumin
1 tsp. chili powder
cayenne to taste
salt and freshly ground pepper
shredded cheese (we used a Mexican blend)
chopped cilantro for serving (optional)

1. Combine 1 cup uncooked rice with 2 cups water. Bring to a boil, then simmer according to package instructions. (Or, prepare the rice or grain ahead of time.)
2. While the rice cooks, prepare the peppers: slice them in half and remove the seeds and ribs. Make sure to wear gloves! I learned this the hard way (don't ask).
3. Place the peppers in a baking dish skin side up. Broil about 7 minutes, then flip the peppers and broil 7 minutes more.
4. Chop the 3 green onions (if using), and drain and rinse the black beans.
5. In a large microwave safe bowl, combine: beans, onions, 1 ½ cups salsa, 1 ½ cups corn, a bit of the shredded cheese, 1 teaspoon cumin, 1 teaspoon chili powder, a couple dashes of cayenne (if you like it spicy!). Season with salt and pepper to taste. When the rice is finished, combine with the filling.
Note: Remember that quantities and ingredients are all to taste, so feel free to adjust as needed!
6. Heat the filling a few minutes in the microwave (or on the stove) until warm, depending on the heat of the rice.
7. Place the pepper halves skin side down in a baking dish, and spoon the filing into each half. Top with shredded cheese and broil until the cheese is melted, for about 1 ½ to 2 minutes.
8. If desired, garnish with chopped cilantro and serve with sour cream.

PAPPA GALLO'S MEXICAN RESTAURANT
29782 US HWY., 281 N STE 2, BULVERDE, TX

"It's important to begin a search on a full stomach."
Henry Bromel

TABBOULEH SALAD

In 2008 two families came together with the dream of providing a culinary experience fit for a Pasha. Comparable to knighthood, the term Pasha was bestowed upon those who earned prestigious recognition. Throughout history the Eastern Mediterranean has been famous for producing world renowned chefs and gastronomical delights. In honor of this great heritage, Pasha Mediterranean Grill strives to bring you a unique and healthy alternative that does not disappoint.

¼ C. olive oil
¼ C. fresh lemon juice
3 large garlic cloves, minced
1 C. bulgur (cracked wheat)
1 C. boiling water
1 C. chopped seeded plum tomatoes
½ C. chopped fresh Italian parsley
2 large green onions, chopped
2 tbsp. chopped fresh mint

1. Whisk oil, lemon juice, and garlic in small bowl to blend; set aside. Place bulgur in large bowl. Mix in 1 cup boiling water. Let stand until bulgur is tender and water is absorbed, about 15 minutes.

2. Mix in tomatoes, parsley, green onions, and mint. Add oil mixture; toss to blend. Season with salt and pepper. Let stand at least 30 minutes to blend flavors. (Can be made 1 day ahead. Cover; chill.)

PASHA MEDITERRANEAN GRILL
9339 WURZBACH RD., SAN ANTONIO, TX

"Nothing will benefit human health and increase the chances for survival of life on Earth as much as the evolution to a vegetarian diet."
Albert Einstein

Coconut Pancakes

Patty Lou's has an excellent lunch and breakfast menu that is delicious and cheap! You won't spend more than 10 dollars total. The waitstaff is very friendly and personable, and it's never busy so the food comes out fast. They have many different specialty pancakes and they are really good.

1 C. whole wheat pastry flour
1 tbsp. sugar
2 tsp. baking powder
¼ tsp. salt
2 tbsp. unsweetened coconut flakes
1 C. fresh coconut water from a mature coconut, or 1 C. light coconut milk, which is available, canned, in the Asian section of grocery or health food stores
1½ tbsp. melted coconut oil or vegetable oil
1 egg

1. Mix the dry ingredients in one bowl.

2. Whisk together the liquid ingredients (coconut milk, oil and egg) in another bowl.

3. Combine until just mixed.

4. Make the coconut pancakes as you would any other pancake. Enjoy!

PATTY LOU'S RED BARON PUB
914 BURR RD., SAN ANTONIO, TX

"Food is our common ground, a universal experience."
James Beard

N O W   H I R I N G
www.pericosgrill.com
or CALL 210.691.3636

PERiCOS
MEXICAN CUISINE

PASTEL DE TRES LECHES

Put a little salsa in your life! Pericos relaxed atmosphere and delicious Mexican Cuisine can be the right spice after a long day. With over 50 delicious Mexican dishes we have something for everyone in the family. So come on over to Pericos - Because life Tastes Better with Salsa.

1½ C. flour
1 tsp. baking powder
½ C. or 8 tbsp. unsalted butter, room temperature
¾ C. Sugar
5 eggs, room temperature
½ tsp. vanilla
1 C. whole milk
1 C. sweetened, condensed milk
⅔ C. evaporated milk

Whipped Cream Frosting:
1½ C. whipping cream
½ C. sugar
1 tsp. vanilla

1. Preheat oven to 350°F and grease and flour an 8x11-inch baking pan.

2. Sift the flour and baking powder into a large mixing bowl. Cream the butter and sugar together in a mixer on medium speed until light and fluffy.

3. Reduce mixer speed to medium-low and add the eggs one at a time, allowing each one to get incorporated before adding the next. Finally add the vanilla and continue beating until foamy.

4. Remove the bowl from mixer and fold in the sifted flour until it is well incorporated.

5. Pour the batter into the prepared pan and bake 30 minutes, or until done. Remove from oven and set aside to cool.

6. Pierce cake all over with a fork, toothpick or skewer. Mix the whole, sweetened, condensed, and evaporated milk together and pour the mixture over the whole cake.

7. Refrigerate cake for anywhere from 2 to 8 hours, or until liquid is completely absorbed and cake is well chilled.

8. Beat the cream, sugar and vanilla together until the cream holds soft peaks. Frost the cake with the whipped cream and serve.

Signature Tastes of SAN ANTONIO

PERICOS MEXICAN CUISINE
11075 IH-10 W, SAN ANTONIO, TX

"Water is the most neglected nutrient in your diet but one of the most vital."
Kelly Barton

CRAB RANGOON

PHO 4 STARS VIETNAMESE NOODLE HOUSE
21038 US HWY 281 N, SAN ANTONIO, TX

The Service has all the elements of a 5 star restaurant. You are greeted when you arrive, seated quickly and never forgotten. The Food is consistent and excellent! All types of dishes, soup, rolls, rice and noodle plates have had excellent food ever time. If you have never eaten Pho they are understanding and help you make decisions that will meet your taste. If you are thinking of trying Vietnamese food this would be the place to try. Atmosphere is casual, smiles are abundant and you leave wanting to return.

Filling:
8 oz. cream cheese
8 oz. fresh crab meat or canned crab meat, drained and flaked
½ tsp. Lea & Perrins Worcestershire sauce
½ tsp. light soy sauce
⅛ - ¼ tsp. freshly ground white pepper, to taste
1 - 1½ green onions, finely sliced
1 large clove garlic, finely minced
1 tsp. red onion, chopped
1 pkg wonton wrappers
1 small bowl filled with water for wetting wontons
oil for deep-frying

1. Combine the crab and the cream cheese. Mix in the remaining filling ingredients one at a time.
2. On a flat surface, lay out a wonton wrapper in front of you so that it forms a diamond shape. Wet the edges of the wonton.
3. Add a heaping teaspoon of filling to the middle, and spread it out toward the left and right points of the diamond so that it forms a log or rectangular shape (otherwise the wrapper may break in the middle during deep-frying).
4. Fold over the edges of the wrapper so that it forms a triangle shape. Seal the edges, adding more water if needed.
5. Cover the completed Crab Rangoon with a damp towel to prevent them from drying out while preparing the rest.
6. Heat wok and add oil for deep-frying. When oil is ready (the temperature should be between 360 - 375 degrees), carefully slide in the Crab Rangoon, taking care not to overcrowd the wok. Deep-fry until they are golden brown, about 3 minutes, turning once. Remove with a slotted spoon and drain on paper towels. Cool and serve.

To Make Ahead: The filling can be prepared up to a day ahead of time and stored in a sealed container in the refrigerator, or the wontons can be filled and refrigerated up to one day ahead of time before cooking. The wontons can also be prepared up to the deep-frying stage and frozen for up to 3 months. Cook the frozen wonton according to the instructions above, adding a few minutes to the cooking time.

"New Orleans food is as delicious as the less criminal forms of sin."
Mark Twain

Pho Bo Vien

We would like to thank you for coming to Pho Ha Long Vietnamese Restaurant and appreciate your continued support. We hope you will find the warmth and tradition of this authentic Vietnamese kitchen your pleasure stop for lunch and dinner. We proudly use only the freshest ingredients and we continuously strive to improve the quality of both our food and service. We welcome your feedback/comments of our restaurant on how we can provide only the best for you, your family, and friend.

Signature Tastes of SAN ANTONIO

1 lb. chuck steak
½ tsp. pepper
1 tsp. salt
1 tbsp. cornstarch
1 tbsp. oil
1 tsp. baking powder
⅓ C. chopped green onion
½ C. fresh cilantro stem sesame oil ¼ C. hoisin sauce
¼ C. black bean sauce
1 tbsp. lemongrass, minced
¼ C. hot chili sauce (Sriracha)

1. Slice meat thinly; mix with pepper, salt, cornstarch, oil, and baking powder.
2. Let meat stand for 1 hour, then place meat in a plastic ziplock bag and set in freezer for 45 minutes, turning each 10 minutes to keep from freezing.
3. Remove from freezer and mince very fine in small quantities, or grind in a mortar.
4. Boil 2 cups of water in a saucepan, then reduce to a simmer.
5. Mix 1 cup of cold water with 1 teaspoon salt; oil your hands, and place about a tablespoonful of meat in your palm and squeeze tightly.
6. Dip soup spoon into salty water, then use to lower meatball into boiling water; remove meatballs when they turn white or rise to the surface.
7. Repeat method until all meatballs are finished.
8. After all the meatballs are done, add 1 quart of water and 1 teaspoon of salt to the water and bring to a boil.
9. Skim off the foam.
10. Reduce the heat to low, add the beef balls to the stock and simmer for 3-5 minutes.
11. To serve, put 5-6 beef balls and some soup in a bowl and sprinkle with some green onions, chopped cilantro, and 1-2 drops of sesame oil.
12. Make 3 bowls of dipping sauces for the meatballs: 1 with hoisin sauce, 1 with black bean sauce, and 1 with Sriracha chile sauce and lemongrass stirred together.
13. Sip the soup and dip the meatballs into the bowls of dipping sauces.

6424 NW Loop 410, San Antonio, TX

Pho Ha Long

"Food is the most primitive form of comfort."
Sheila Graham

PHO SURE

VIETNAMESE RESTAURANT

AUTHENTIC VIETNAMESE CUISINE

LEMONGRASS & TERIYAKI CHICKEN PLATE

VEGAN AND VEGATERIAN NOODLE PLATE

FRESH SPRING ROLLS & BUBBLE TEA

ToGo: 733-8473

VIETNAMESE STYLE EGG ROLLS WITH LETTUCE WRAP

If you're craving fresh, authentic Vietnamese food for dinner tonight, pay a visit to Pho Sure on W. Ashby Place in San Antonio. Here we have some of these most delicious and authentic Vietnamese food in the entire San Antonio area. You will be amazed by all that our menu has to offer from appetizers, rolls, sandwichs and salads to traditional Vietnamese rice and noodle bolls, here we truly have it all! We don't just stop at delicious food either, we also have delicious drink as well, try one of our specialty coffees or bubble milk teas for a unique addition to your meal. Stop by our location and take your order to go or place an order for delivery with our online ordering system and enjoy your Vietnamese meal from the comfort of your own home!

Egg Rolls:
1 lb. ground meat – pork
½ lb. peeled shrimp
1 C. of lump crab meat
3 chopped garlic cloves
1 carrot, peeled and shredded
¼ cabbage, shredded
1 medium size jicama shredded
2 oz. dried vermicelli noodles
1 oz. dried black fungus/cloud ear mushrooms
2-3 large eggs
ground black pepper
2-3 tbsp. of fish sauce (depending on taste)
2 tbsp. oyster sauce (optional)
egg roll wrappers – 12 oz package (30-50 rice paper sheets, 10 inch diameter)
frying oil – vegetable, corn, canola, peanut

Sweet Fish Sauce:
2 garlic cloves chopped or smashed
1 fresh Thai Chili (or ¼ tsp of hot chili peppers flakes)
¼ C. fish sauce
⅔ C. water
2 tbsp. fresh lime/lemon juice
¼ C. sugar
2-4 tbsp. shredded carrots (or Vietnamese Relish)

Lettuce Wrap fixings (optional):
1 washed head of lettuce (crisphead, butterhead or red leaf)
1 cucumber julienned
1 bunch of cilantro

1. Soak vermicelli noodles and mushrooms in a bowl of warm water for 20 minutes.
2. In a food processor pulse grind shrimp, crab meat, garlic until roughly chopped. Add to mixture, drained vermicelli noodles and mushrooms, pulse grind briefly until all ingredients are integrated.
3. In a large mixing bowl, transfer ingredients from food processor and combine with ground meat, shredded vegetables. Add black pepper, fish sauce, oyster sauce, and 2 eggs. Use hands to mix ingredients together. If the mixture seems dry, add the other egg.
4. Wrapping the egg rolls with rice paper. Fill a shallow dish with 1 inch of warm water. Quickly dip rice paper in the water bath, making sure all parts of the paper is wet. Place wet rice paper on a clean dish towel/plate and let it soften. Once it is soft and pliable, peel it off the towel and place on to a plate. Lay 1 ½ tbsp of filling on the lower edge of the rice paper, near you, leaving 1 inch edge. Begin to fold egg roll like an envelop: first, fold over the lower 1 inch edge over the filing, then the left edge, then the right edge. Now roll the roll up to the top edge. Place the wrapped egg roll on a platter and keep on rolling!
5. Heat the oil in a large, deep frying pan over medium high heat. Tess the oil by dipping the tip of a wooden spoon or wooden chop stick – if it bubbles around the tip then the oil is ready. Place egg roll one at a time into hot oil, with the seam down (this will keep it from unraveling) and then quickly turn the egg roll to ensure the skin crisp up and does not stick to other egg rolls in the pan. Adjust heat so that the oil is bubbling gently and not too vigorously around the egg rolls. Each egg roll will take about 5 minutes to cook – golden brown spots and skin is super crispy. Shake the egg roll over the pan to help remove the excess oil. Place egg roll on layers of paper towels to drain.
6. Next, make the sweet fish sauce for dipping. Either finely chop garlic and pepper OR use a mortar and pestle to smash garlic and hot pepper. If you are using pepper flakes, no need to smash. Place the chopped or smashed garlic and pepper into a small bowl then add the rest of the ingredients for the dressing. Stir well until sugar dissolves. If the sauce is not quite sweet enough add a bit more sugar. If the sauce is too sweet and not tangy enough for your taste, squeeze in some lime/lemon juice to cut the sweetness.
7. Prepare the lettuce wrap fixings. Gently unwrap and separate the lettuce, one leaf at a time and arrange leaves on serving platter. On another small plate, arrange the julienned cucumber and the cilantro.
8. Serve egg rolls with the dipping sauce and the lettuce wrap fixings. How to eat – use lettuce as a wrap and place the egg roll in the middle with the cucumber, coriander, roll the lettuce up (like a burrito). Dip into sauce and enjoy.

PHO SURE (BIG KAHUNA'S)
741 W ASHBY PL, SAN ANTONIO, TX

"Good to eat, and wholesome to digest, as a worm to a toad, a toad to a snake, a snake to a pig, a pig to a man, and a man to a worm."
Ambrose Bierce

FANTAIL SHRIMP

Phoenix Cafe specializes in serving traditional and Americanized versions of Chinese cuisine. Phoenix Cafe first opened in 2001 by Ren and Lisa Wu. Originally from Guangzhou, China Ren has been learning the art of Chinese cuisine for several decades focusing on "southern" style of Cantonese cooking. The Wu family first moved to Houston, TX, but relocated to San Antonio in hopes of a new and successful restaurant and here we are now! A decade later and proudly serving San Antonio.

1 dozen jumbo shrimp

Marinade:
1 tbsp. finely minced fresh ginger
1 tbsp. finely minced garlic
2 tbsp. Asian sesame oil

Sesame Seed Batter:
1½ C. flour
1 tbsp. baking powder
½ tsp. salt, or to taste
1½ C. water
¼ C. sesame seeds
4 C. oil

1. Rinse, dry, shell, and devein the shrimp if necessary, but leave the tails on. Split the shrimp along the inner curve, but do not cut all the way through. Spread each shrimp out flat and tap with the broad of a cleaver or knife. (Cutting along the inner curve prevents the shrimp from curling out of shape during the cooking.)

2. Make the marinade by combining in a bowl the ginger, garlic, and oil. Season shrimp with the marinade, cover and chill 30 minutes.

3. Make the batter by measuring out the dry ingredients into a mixing bowl and then adding the liquid ones, singly and little by little, stirring until the mixture is a smooth, thick batter. Fold in the sesame seeds last. Place the batter by the shrimp near the stove.

4. Heat the wok or heavy, deep pot; then add and heat the oil until a drop of batter foams instantly, about 375 degrees F. Lower the heat a little. Then hold 1 shrimp by its tail and dip it into the batter to coat evenly; slip it into the hot oil. Repeat rapidly with the rest of the shrimp and deep-fry them for 3 minutes. Turn the shrimp constantly, with a gentle motion, after they're all in the oil. When they are golden brown, remove them with chopsticks, a skimmer, or a slotted spoon to paper towels to drain.

5. Arrange the shrimp on a serving platter and sprinkle a little roasted salt-pepper on top. The shrimp may be done 10 to 15 minutes in advance and kept hot and crisp in a 200 degree F oven. Or decrease the frying time by 30 to 45 seconds; then drain on paper towels. When ready to serve, refry until brown and crisp, about 30 seconds.

"We are all dietetic sinners; only a small percent of what we eat nourishes us; the balance goes to waste and loss of energy."
William Osler

GNOCCHI AL POMODORO

Piccolo's has long seemed like the quintessential red-sauce palace æ dark, dependable, but hardly inspiring. The service is good, the staff are knowledgeable about the food on offer, and the prices for food and drink are reasonable. Plus they have exceptionally good food.

Signature Tastes of SAN ANTONIO

Sauce:
3 tbsp. (60 ml.) olive oil
¼ tsp. (1 ml.) yellow asafoetida powder
3 ½ C. (875 ml.) tomatoes, blanched, peeled, and pureed
1 tsp. (5 ml.) salt
¼ tsp. (1 ml.) freshly ground black pepper
2 tbsp. (40 ml.) chopped fresh basil
grated parmesan cheese
2 tbsp. (40 ml.) chopped fresh parsley

Dumplings:
500 g. (17 ½ oz.) old potatoes
1½ C. (375 ml.) self-raising flour
½ tsp. (2 ml.) salt
¼ tsp. (1 ml.) nutmeg
1 tbsp. (20 ml.) milk

1. Heat the olive oil in a heavy 4-litre/quart saucepan over moderate heat until hot but not smoking. Sauté the asafoetida in the hot oil. Add the tomatoes, salt, pepper, and basil; stirring occasionally, simmer the sauce for about 30 minutes or until reduced somewhat. Remove from the heat, cover, and keep warm.
2. Meanwhile, peel and quarter the potatoes and boil them in a saucepan of slightly salted water until very tender. Drain well and push the potatoes through a fine sieve into a bowl. Add the sifted flour, salt, nutmeg, and milk. Mix well. Turn the mixture out onto a lightly floured surface. Knead for 2 minutes.
3. Take one-quarter of the mixture and form it into a roll on a floured surface. The roll should be 2.5 cm (1-inch) in diameter. Repeat with the remaining dough. Cut the rolls into 1.25 cm (½-inch) gnocchi lengths.
4. With two fingers, press each gnocchi against a cheese grater (medium holes) to roughen the surface on one side, at the same time making a dent in the other side where the fingers press. This gives the traditional gnocchi shape. Repeat with the remaining gnocchi.
5. Place one-quarter of the gnocchi into a large saucepan of boiling salted water over full heat. The gnocchi will go straight to the bottom of the pan and then start to float to the top. When the last dumpling rises to the top, boil for 1 minute; then remove them from the pan with a slotted spoon. Repeat with the remaining gnocchi in batches. Add the gnocchi to the prepared tomato sauce and simmer uncovered for 5 minutes over low heat. Place the gnocchi in a serving bowl and spoon over half the sauce. Serve the remaining sauce and grated parmesan cheese separately. Garnish with chopped parsley.

PICCOLO'S ITALIAN
5703 EVERS RD., SAN ANTONIO, TX

"If God had intended us to follow recipes, He wouldn't have given us grandmothers."
Linda Henley

POMPEII PIZZA

Welcome to Pompeii Italian Grill Restaurant... a place for an exquisite Italian cuisine in the heart of San Antonio, Texas. Voted as one of the best Italian restaurants in San Antonio, we are sure that you will have a great dining experience. At Pompeii Italian Grill, it's our goal to provide you with a great place for parties and informal get-together's, evenings out with the family or a delicious change of taste from fast-food lunches. All served with a smile. The entire staff at Pompeii Italian Grill takes pride in preparing great Italian food of the finest quality in a comfortable setting, and ensuring that the dining experience is as pleasant as possible.

Signature Tastes of SAN ANTONIO

POMPEII ITALIAN GRILL
16109 NACOGDOCHES RD., SAN ANTONIO, TX

1½ tsp. white sugar
1 C. warm water (100 degrees F/40 degrees c)
1½ tsp. active dry yeast
1 tbsp. olive oil
½ tsp. salt
2 C. all-purpose flour
8 oz. crushed tomatoes
1 tbsp. brown sugar (packed)
½ tsp. garlic powder
1 tsp. olive oil
½ tsp. salt
3 C. shredded mozzarella cheese (divided)
½ lb. italian sausage (bulk)
4 oz. pepperoni (sliced)
8 oz. fresh mushrooms (sliced)
½ green bell pepper (chopped)
½ red bell pepper (chopped)

1. Combine the white sugar and the warm water in a large bowl or in the work bowl of a stand mixer. Sprinkle the yeast over the warm sugar water, and let stand for 5 minutes until the yeast softens and begins to form a creamy foam. Stir 1 tablespoon olive oil into the yeast mixture.

2. Stir ½ teaspoon salt into the flour. Mix half of the flour mixture into the yeast water, and stir until no dry spots remain. Stir in the remaining flour, a ½ cup at a time, mixing well after each addition. When the dough has pulled together, turn it out onto a lightly floured surface and knead until smooth and elastic, about 8 minutes (or mix with dough hook in stand mixer).

3. Lightly oil a large bowl, place the dough in the bowl and turn to coat with oil. Cover with a light cloth, and let rise in a warm place until doubled in volume, about 1 hour.

4. Combine the crushed tomatoes, brown sugar, garlic powder, 1 teaspoon olive oil, and salt in small saucepan. Cover pan, and cook over low heat until tomatoes start to break down, about 30 minutes.

5. Preheat an oven to 450 degrees F (230 degrees C). Deflate the dough and turn it out onto a lightly floured surface. Cut the dough into 2 equal pieces. Roll one piece into a 12 inch thin circle. Roll the other half into a thicker, 9 inch circle.

6. Place the 12 inch dough round into an ungreased 9 inch springform pan. Sprinkle dough with 1 cup of cheese. Shape sausage into a 9 inch patty and place in pan on top of the cheese. Layer pepperoni, mushrooms, green pepper, red pepper, and remaining cheese on top of sausage patty. Top with the 9 inch dough round and pinch edges to seal. Cut several ½ inch vent holes in the top crust. Spread sauce evenly on the top crust, leaving a ½ inch border at the edges.

7. Bake pizza in the preheated oven until the crust is set, the cheese is melted, and the sausage is cooked through, 40 to 45 minutes. Let hot pizza rest for 15 minutes before cutting into wedges and serving.

"Rice is born in water and must die in wine."
Italian Proverb

231

ON THE RIVERWALK

Kielbasa Sausage

In America, it probably originated during the cattle drives of the 1800s, as chuck wagon cooks tried to tenderize inexpensive cuts of meat for the trail drivers. But the Chinese could lay claim to having a form of BBQ long before America was discovered. As well as the Romans and the Greeks. We'll never know who really invented it. But what we do know is that BBQ is a planet-wide phenomenon, cooked in various forms of meats, sauces and spices over a broad range of wood fires. That brings us to Q.

Signature Tastes of SAN ANTONIO

1½ lbs. polska kielbasa, smoked
1 tbsp. butter
3 tbsp. sugar
1 onion, sliced
3 C. sauerkraut, drained
3 tbsp. fresh parsley leaves, freshly chopped

1. Preheat grill. Preheat oven to 400 degrees F.

2. Cut kielbasa into 3-inch lengths and butterfly lengthwise. Place on hot groll and cook for 4 to 5 minutes on each side turning frequently, charring all sides. Remove from grill. transfer kielbasa to a baking sheet and place in oven to cook for another 5 to 6 minutes.

3. In a large skillet over medium-high heat, add butter and sugar. Allow sugar to cook to a golden brown color. Add onions and cook until caramelized. Stir in the sauerkraut and cook for 5 to 6 minutes until onions and sauerkraut are wilted and colored.

4. Remove kielbasa from oven and cut into 1-inch pieces. Add to pan of sauerkraut and onions. Toss together and cook for 1 minute. Transfer to a platter, garnish with parsley and serve with your favorite mustard dipping sauce.

Q ON THE RIVERWALK – HYATT REGENCY
123 LOSOYA ST., SAN ANTONIO, TX

"In general, mankind, since the improvement in cookery, eats twice as much as nature requires."
Benjamin Franklin

Delaware Classic

This place is great! They really do have the best hot dogs in town. They have authentic chicago style food and have got it all right, everything from the hot peppers to neon green relish had a taste straight from Chicago. If you're looking for a real hot dog you have got to try this place. This is one if my new favorite places and I will certainly be back!

3 red bell peppers
3 tbsp. extra virgin olive oil
1 tsp. sugar
¼ C. dry white wine
⅓ tsp. salt
¼ tsp. ground pepper
4 oz. genoa salami
4 oz. prosciutto
4 oz. thin ham slices
4 oz. provolone cheese
4 marinated mushrooms, sliced
8 Italian bread, slices

1. Starting with the red bell pepper first, remove seeds and core. Now cut red bell peppers into 1-inch-wide strips.

2. Heat a saucepan to medium temperature and when the pan is hot add oil and peppers.

3. Cover and cook 20 minutes. Every 2 minutes, you want to toss the peppers.

4. Sprinkle peppers with the sugar and add the wine. Continue to cook, covered, an additional 5 minutes.

5. You want the peppers are very tender and caramelized. Now add the salt and pepper.

6. Allow peppers to cool for 15 minutes before adding to sandwich.

7. On your bread slices, add 1-ounce each of salami, prosciutto, ham, provolone, mushrooms, and peppers.

R&B's TASTE OF CHICAGO
1308 AUSTIN HWY., SAN ANTONIO, TX

"A man may be a pessimistic determinist before lunch and an optimistic believer in the will's freedom after it."
Aldous Huxley

CHICKEN FRIED STEAK

Signature Tastes of SAN ANTONIO

Where better to get good country cooking than a little bit out in the country. The trip to Spring Branch is worth it for Richter's classic comfort food, think chicken fried steak, pork chops, mac 'n' cheese. The burgers with fried egg are a favorite of many patrons, and Richter's has all your favorite Southern sides to go with it.

2 lb. beef bottom round, trimmed of excess fat
2 tsp. kosher salt
1 tsp. freshly ground black pepper
1 C. all-purpose flour
3 whole eggs, beaten
¼ C. vegetable oil
2 C. chicken broth
½ C. whole milk
½ tsp. fresh thyme leaves

1. Preheat oven to 250 degrees F.
2. Cut the meat with the grain into ½-inch thick slices. Season each piece on both sides with the salt and pepper. Place the flour into a pie pan. Place the eggs into a separate pie pan. Dredge the meat on both sides in the flour. Tenderize the meat, using a needling device, until each slice is ¼-inch thick. Once tenderized, dredge the meat again in the flour, followed by the egg and finally in the flour again. Repeat with all the pieces of meat. Place the meat onto a plate and allow it to sit for 10 to 15 minutes before cooking.
3. Place enough of the vegetable oil to cover the bottom of a 12-inch slope-sided skillet and set over medium-high heat. Once the oil begins to shimmer, add the meat in batches, being careful not to overcrowd the pan. Cook each piece on both sides until golden brown, approximately 4 minutes per side. Remove the steaks to a wire rack set in a half sheet pan and place into the oven. Repeat until all of the meat is browned.
4. Add the remaining vegetable oil, or at least 1 tablespoon, to the pan. Whisk in 3 tablespoons of the flour left over from the dredging. Add the chicken broth and deglaze the pan. Whisk until the gravy comes to a boil and begins to thicken. Add the milk and thyme and whisk until the gravy coats the back of a spoon, approximately 5 to 10 minutes. Season to taste, with more salt and pepper, if needed. Serve the gravy over the steaks.

RICHTER'S ANTLER CAFE
1 SUN VALLEY DR., SPRING BRANCH, TX

"But when the time comes that a man has had his dinner, then the true man comes to the surface."
Mark Twain

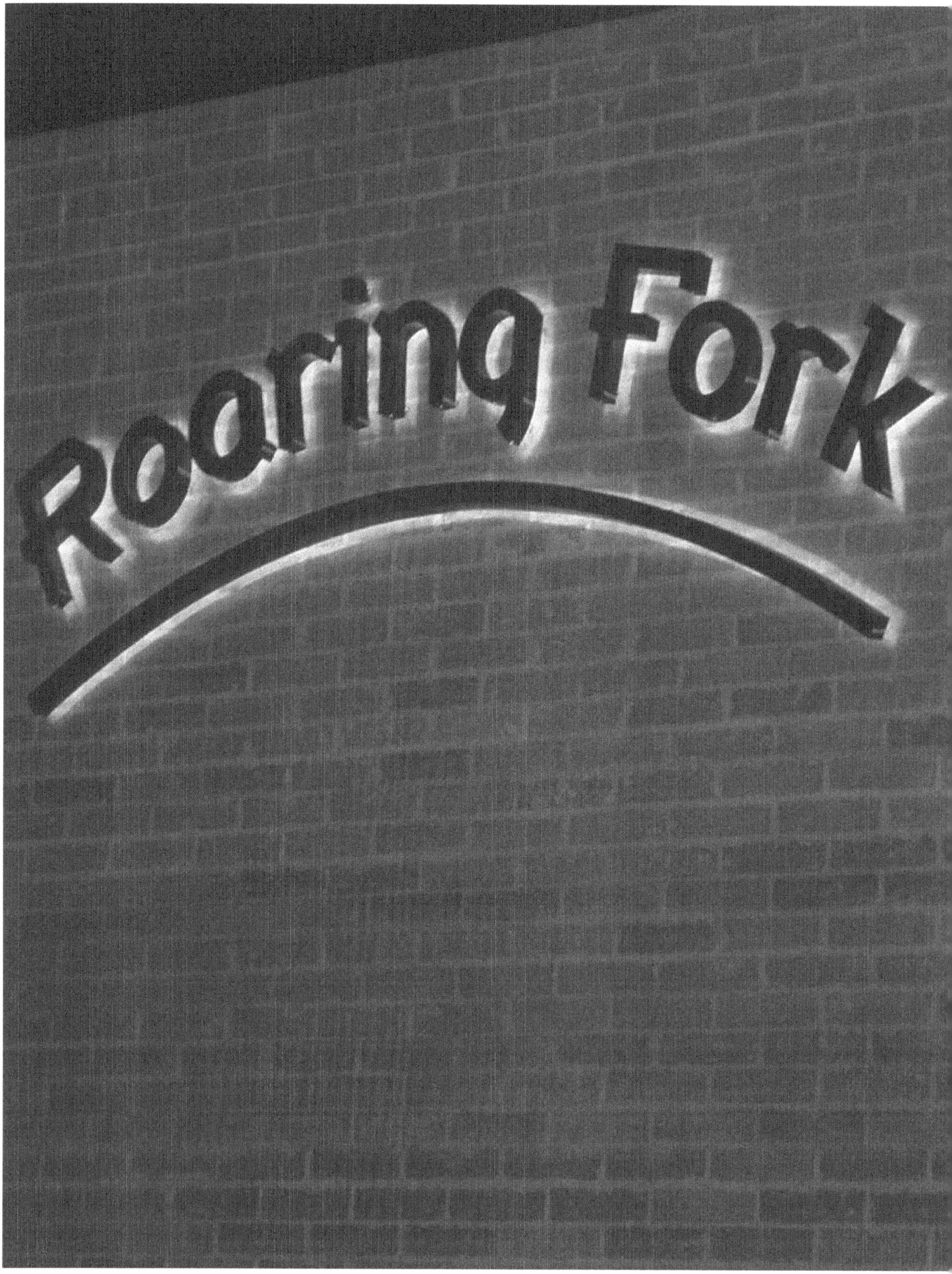
Roaring Fork

Spinach Chicken Waldorf Salad

Signature Tastes of SAN ANTONIO

7 oz. (1 breast) poached chicken breast
2 C. fat free chicken broth
1 medium apple, peeled and cut into small cubes
1 C. red seedless grapes, cut in half
½ C. celery, chopped
¼ C. light Hellman's mayonnaise
2 tbsp. fat free Greek yogurt
salt and pepper
2 tbsp. pecans or walnuts
6 C. mixed baby greens like spinach and arugula

1. Cover chicken breast in broth in a small pot, add water if it doesn't cover the chicken. Add salt and pepper, a piece of celery and it's leaves (you could add herbs like parsley, garlic, onion, or whatever you want) and bring to a boil.

2. Reduce to a simmer and cook 5 minutes. Remove from heat, cover tight and let it sit for 15-20 minutes or until thickest part of the breast registers 160 degrees.

3. Chicken will be cooked through. Let it cool and cut into small cubes.

4. Combine mayo, yogurt, salt, pepper and mix well. Add chicken, grapes, apples, celery, and let it chill in the refrigerator until you are ready to eat it. Mix in pecans right before serving.

5. Serve over baby greens.

1806 NW LOOP 1604, SAN ANTONIO, TX

ROARING FORK

"I eat so poorly during the stressful part of my day I need to have a vegetable orgy for dinner just to make up for it."
Carrie Latet

Causa con Pollo

We are a family business oriented to bring Latino American food with the specialty of Peruvian food to the city of San Antonio. We invite to taste the exquisites Latino American dishes. Our mission and goal is to introduce the flavor, history and overall Latin culture to our community.

ROCOTOS SABOR LATINO GRILL
10555 CULEBRA ROAD, SUITE 101, SAN ANTONIO, TX

3 lb. yellow potatoes (about 8)
3 yellow chiles, such as aji, seeds removed and chopped
1 -2 tbsp. vegetable oil
3 garlic cloves, minced
3 limes, juiced
2 chicken breasts, boneless and skinless
white wine (optional but recommended) ½ C. mayonnaise
1 tsp. yellow mustard
1 avocado, ripe, sliced
salt and pepper
cilantro
1 hard-boiled egg
black olives (for decoration)

1. Boil potatoes until soft, then mash thoroughly.
2. Sauté chopped chilies and minced garlic in a little vegetable oil until soft, being careful not to burn garlic or it will be bitter.
3. Add lime juice to blender, along with sautéed peppers and garlic. Blend thoroughly, then add salt and pepper to taste and blend again.
4. Pour lime juice mixture from blender into potatoes and mix thoroughly.
5. Poach chicken in water flavored with salt and pepper. For more flavor but nontraditional taste add a little white wine to poaching liquid.
6. Shred the chicken and mix with the mustard and mayonnaise.
7. Grease the inside of a cheesecake pan with removable sides.
8. Place a half of the potatoes on the bottom of pan, then the chicken, then the avocado and top with rest of potatoes.
9. Decorate with cilantro, sliced hard boiled eggs and black olives.
10. Cover with plastic wrap and chill for at least an hour.
11. Carefully remove sides of pan, then slice and serve.

"Chili represents your three stages of matter: solid, liquid, and eventually gas."
Roseanne

ROSEMARY GARLIC CHICKEN

Signature Taste of SAN ANTONIO

Pizza lovers have enjoyed Rome's cozy atmosphere and gourmet food for nearly two generations. Whether you want to dine-in, pick-up, or enjoy take out, one of our restaurant locations may be just what you want. And of course, if you want delivery or catering, just give us a call and we'll deliver it hot, fresh, and delicious.

¾ lb. small red-skinned potatoes, halved, or quartered if large
kosher salt
2 sprigs fresh rosemary, plus 1 tbsp. leaves
1 clove garlic, smashed
pinch of red pepper flakes
juice of 2 lemons (squeezed halves reserved)
2 tbsp. extra-virgin olive oil
4 skin-on, bone-in chicken breasts (6 to 8 oz. each)
10 oz. cremini mushrooms, halved

1. Preheat the oven to 450. Cover the potatoes with cold water in a saucepan and salt the water. Bring to a boil over medium-high heat and cook until tender, about 8 minutes; drain and set aside.

2. Pile the rosemary leaves, garlic, 2 teaspoons salt and the red pepper flakes on a cutting board, then mince and mash into a paste using a large knife. Transfer the paste to a bowl. Stir in the juice of 1 lemon and the olive oil. Add the chicken and turn to coat.

3. Heat a large cast-iron skillet over medium-high heat. Add the chicken, skin-side down, cover and cook until the skin browns, about 5 minutes. Turn the chicken; add the mushrooms and potatoes to the skillet and drizzle with the juice of the remaining lemon.

4. Add the rosemary sprigs and the squeezed lemon halves to the skillet; transfer to the oven and roast, uncovered, until the chicken is cooked through and the skin is crisp, 20 to 25 minutes.

5999 DE ZAVALA RD., SAN ANTONIO, TX

ROME'S PIZZA

"I'm trying to eat better. And, I do feel wise after drinking tea. After eating vegetables, I just feel hungry."
Carrie Latet

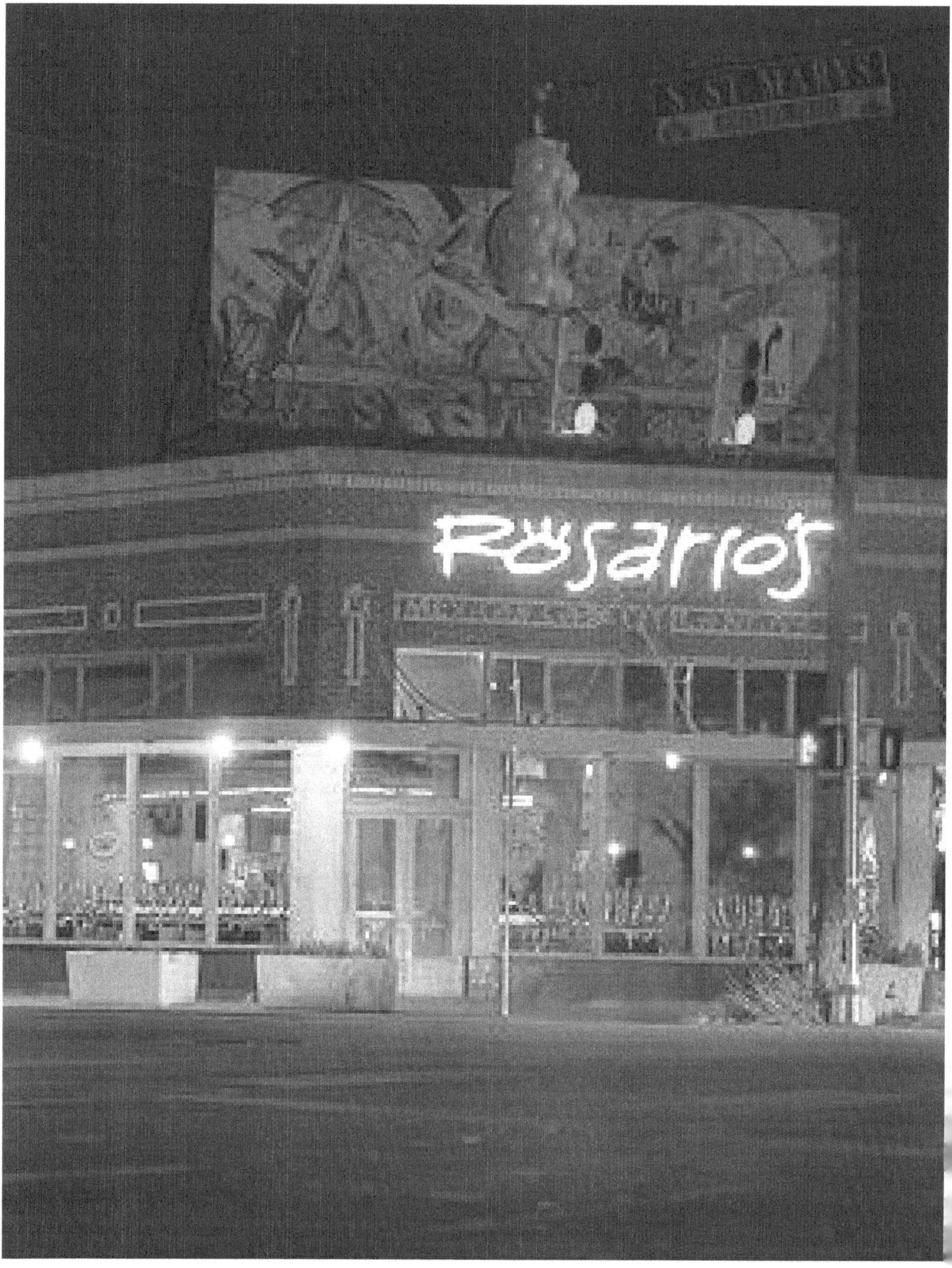
Rosario's

ANGELICA'S CEVICHE FINO

In May 1992, an enterprising and bold restaurateur named Lisa Wong rescued Rosario's from bankruptcy court and within one year transformed it into a favorite meeting place for the local arts crowd, visitors, neighborhood residents, politicos, celebrities and other luminaries. It also became the anchor business for the area, a revitalized urban neighborhood thriving with artists, musicians and small business owners.

1 lb. tilapia fillets
1½ C. freshly squeezed lime juice, divided
½ tbsp. dried oregano
3 to 4 serrano chiles, stemmed, seeded and cut into thin strips
1½ C. thinly sliced red onion
½ tsp. salt
½ tsp. seasoned salt, such as Lawry's
1 C. cubed jicama
3 tbsp. olive oil
¾ C. cilantro leaves

1. Place tilapia in a glass bowl, and add 1 cup of lime juice and the oregano. Refrigerate, and let marinate for about 3 hours.

2. In another bowl, combine remaining lime juice, chiles, onion, salt, seasoned salt, jicama, olive oil and cilantro.

3. Refrigerate, and let marinate for 1 to 2 hours. Drain excess juices from each of the marinated products, and combine the two, stirring to break up the fish.

4. Serve chilled.

ROSARIO'S MEXICAN CAFE Y CANTINA

910 S ALAMO ST., SAN ANTONIO, TX

"Food for all is a necessity. Food should not be a merchandise, to be bought and sold as jewels are bought and sold by those who have the money to buy. Food is a human necessity, like water and air, it should be available."
Pearl Buck

SHRIMP BROCCOLI IN GARLIC SAUCE

Royal Inn Oriental Cuisine is a Vietnamese restaurant that has food for pick up or delivery in the San Antonio, Texas area. It offers your standard lunch and dinner specials that come with soup, fried or white rice and Rangoon or egg roll. The food is really delicious and way above your basic Chinese restaurant. The Lo Mien is fantastic. They also have a more extensive menu if you choose not to go the lunch/dinner special route. Prices are very affordable. Service is really great. They also have take out and delivery.

Signature Tastes of SAN ANTONIO

Shrimp:
2 C. canola oil
1 lb. large shrimp, peeled and deveined
½ C. cornstarch

Garlic Sauce:
2 tbsp. brown sugar
¼ C. low-sodium soy sauce
1 tbsp. rice vinegar
1 C. vegetable broth
1½ tbsp. cornstarch
2 tbsp. canola oil
½ medium onion, sliced
3 tbsp. chopped garlic
1 tbsp. chopped ginger
½ red bell pepper, chopped
2 C. broccoli florets, blanched
1 (8-oz.) can water chestnuts, drained
4 C. cooked white rice, for serving

For the Shrimp:
1. Heat the oil until it reaches 360 degrees F in wok or large skillet over medium-high heat.
2. Dredge the raw shrimp in the cornstarch. Fry in batches, so as not to overcrowd the pan, until their exteriors crisp up, about 4 to 5 minutes. With a slotted spoon, remove the shrimp from the oil and put them onto a paper towel-lined plate to drain.

For the Sauce:
1. In a small bowl, whisk together the brown sugar, soy sauce, vinegar, vegetable broth and cornstarch. Set the bowl aside.
2. Heat the canola oil in a wok or large skillet over high heat. Add the onions, garlic and ginger and stir-fry for 30 seconds. Add the bell pepper and cook for another 30 seconds. Pour in the prepared sauce and cook until the sauce thickens.
3. Stir in the broccoli and water chestnuts and cook for 1 minute, then add the shrimp and fry for 1 minute more. Transfer the shrimp with garlic sauce to a serving bowl and serve hot with cooked rice.

ROYAL INN ORIENTAL CUISINE
5440 BABCOCK RD., SAN ANTONIO, TX

"Most of the food allergies die under garlic and onion."
Martin H. Fischer

EAT HERE

Ruthie's
OPEN SEVEN DAYS A WEEK
BREAKFAST SERVED ALL DAY
DAILY LUNCH SPECIALS
210.308-0253

MACHACADO

Ruthie's has wonderful tortillas, excellent sides, and great service! The service was fast, efficient, and the waiter was even enthusiastic about his job. He was happy to be there, and was willing to help. The sides were fantastic! The beans were obviously fresh, and delicious. The rice was seasoned perfectly and warm and fluffy. They were hand made, and still hot off the comal. Ruthie's has its own bakery right in the same parking lot, which was awesome. The place was clean, and well lit.

¼ to ½ C. of Machacado (Dried Shredded beef)
6 eggs
½ onion diced
1 tomato diced
¼ C. chopped cilantro (coriander)
½ of a Diced serrano pepper
1 clove of garlic (diced)
salt to taste (as machacado meat is generally salty, be careful with adding salt to this recipe. any additional salt should be added by the individual.)

1. Place the Onion in a skillet with some oil on medium heat and cook until tender.

2. Add the Tomato, Serrano and Garlic and cook for 3 minutes.

3. Add the Machacado and Eggs together and scramble until cooked.

4. Stir in the Cilantro.

5. Serve either as an egg scramble, or in tortillas as tacos.

11423 WEST AVE., SAN ANTONIO, TX

RUTHIE'S

"Food to a large extent is what holds a society together and eating is closely linked to deep spiritual experiences."
Peter Farb and George Armelagos

RED DRAGON ROLL

This hidden secret has some of the city's best Japanese food. The sushi is always fresh and tasty. They have the best seaweed salad I have ever tasted. The service is good too. Everyone is always very friendly.

6 sheets nori
3 C. sumeshi
6 oz. sashimi-grade tuna
1 small avocado
½ small cucumber
1 tbsp. Sriracha sauce
¼ C. tobiko
¼ C. fried onions
1 tbsp. black sesame seeds

1. Cook sushi rice.

2. Slice the tuna into 1 cm square sticks.

3. Cut the avocado in half, discarding the pit.

4. Use a large spoon to scoop the avocado out of the hard skin, being careful to keep the avocado half as whole as possible.

5. Slice the avocado into slices.

6. Slice the cucumber into long, thin sticks.

7. Roll the sushi inside-out, using some tuna, avocado, cucumber, and a thin line of Sriracha sauce as your fillings.

8. Sprinkle the tobiko, fried onions, and black sesame seeds on top. Enjoy!

19179 BLANCO RD., SAN ANTONIO, TX

SAKE CAFE

"Food is not about impressing people. It's about making them feel comfortable."
Ina Garte

FRIED ZUCCHINI

Having been in my share of live music venues, I feel comfortable saying Sam's Burger Joint has it all. Great sound, a perfectly sized music venue, nothing obstructing the view of the stage, top notch burgers, full bar and a fun staff to be around. Hope to see you at Sam's.

Signature Tastes of SAN ANTONIO

2 zucchini, quartered and sliced
1 onion, sliced into rings
½ C. all-purpose flour
½ C. cornmeal
½ tsp. salt
½ tsp. ground black pepper
¼ tsp. garlic powder
1 C. vegetable oil for frying

1. Place zucchini and onions in a medium bowl and mix together.

2. In a small bowl mix flour, cornmeal, salt, pepper and garlic powder.

3. Pour dry mixture over zucchini/onion mixture, cover bowl and shake well. Let mixture sit for about 30 minutes; a batter will form on the vegetables.

4. In a medium skillet heat oil over medium heat. When oil is hot add breaded vegetables and fry, turning to brown evenly.

SAM'S BURGER JOINT
330 E GRAYSON ST., SAN ANTONIO, TX

"The food that enters the mind must be watched as closely as the food that enters the body."
Patrick Buchanan

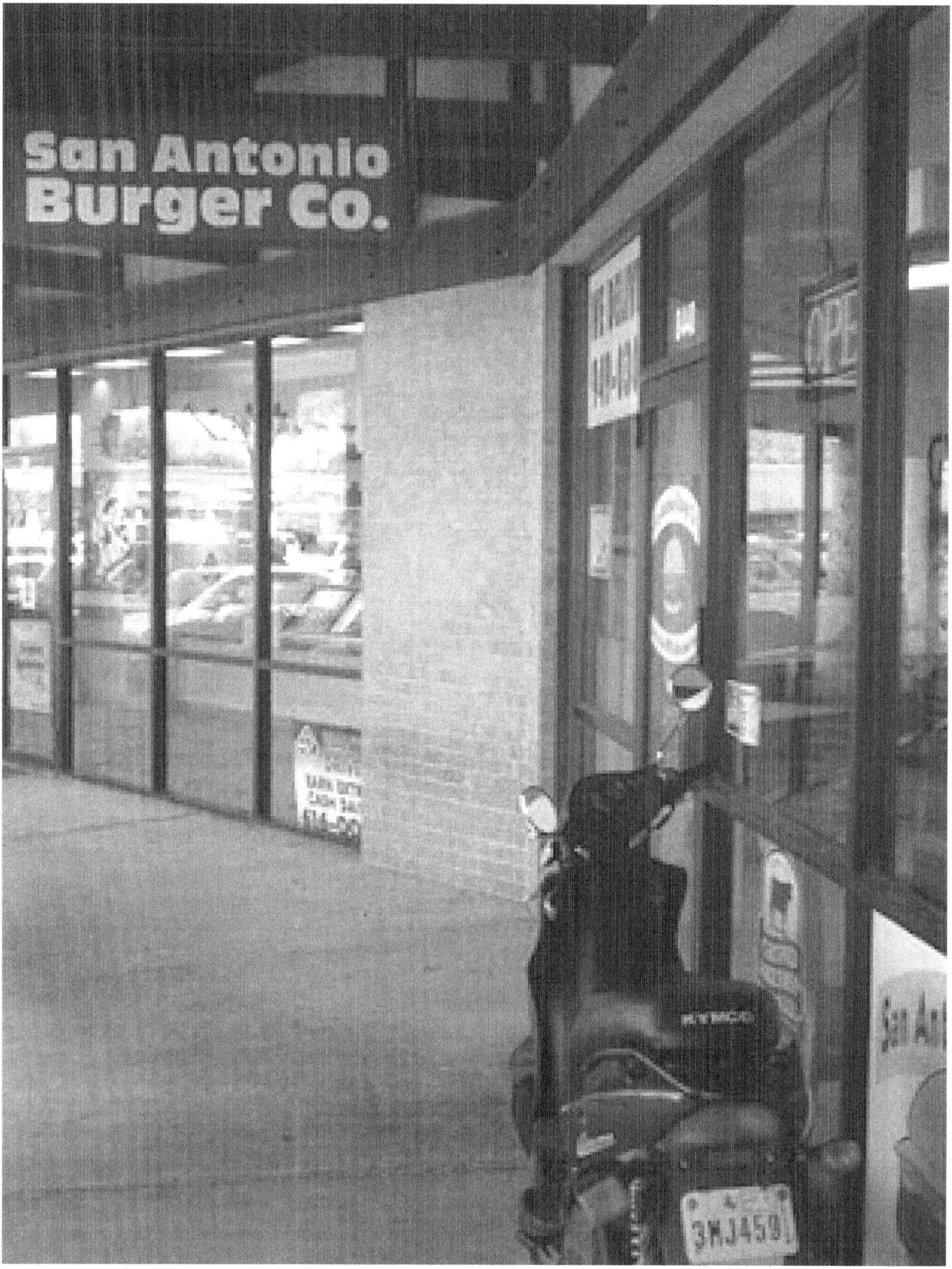
San Antonio
Burger Co.
3MJ459

PHILLY CHEESE STEAK

2 fresh Italian sandwich rolls or Kaiser buns, split in half crosswise
1 white onion, thinly sliced
½ large green bell pepper, thinly sliced
1 tsp. minced garlic
½ tsp. salt
¼ tsp. ground black pepper
½ lb. rib-eye steak, very very thinly shaved or sliced
⅓ lb. thinly sliced white American cheese, or Provolone cheese or 4 oz melted cheese whiz
ketchup, optional topping
Italian pickled peppers, accompaniment

1. Preheat the oven to 200 degrees F.

2. Heat a cast-iron skillet or griddle over medium-high heat. When hot add the oil, onions and bell peppers, and cook, stirring, until caramelized, about 6 minutes. Add the garlic, salt, and pepper, and cook, stirring, for 30 seconds. Push off to 1 side of the griddle.

3. Add the meat to the hot pan and cook, stirring and breaking up with the back of 2 metal spatulas, until almost no longer pink, about 2 minutes. Mix in the Sautéed vegetables. Top with cheese slices and melt. Spoon the cheesy meat mixture into the warm buns and serve immediately with condiments of choice or Put the meat in the bun and dip the spatula in the cheese whiz and then wipe the spatula down the inside of the bread.

SAN ANTONIO BURGER CO.
8440 FREDERICKSBURG ROAD, SAN ANTONIO, TX

"If there is anything we are serious about, it is neither religion nor learning, but food."
Lin Yutang

SPLIT PEA SOUP

Welcome to Schilo's Delicatessen, a San Antonio institution. Our authentic German Deli located in the heart of downtown San Antonio has been serving authentic German cuisine since 1917. Schilo's is one of the oldest continually operated restaurants in the State of Texas. Housed in an old mercantile exchange building dating back to the 1800's, Schilo's embodies that time in San Antonio when the majority of the citizens were of German decent.

1 lb. dry green split peas
2 qt. water
1 meaty ham bone
1 C. chopped onion
¼ tsp. garlic powder
¼ tsp. dried marjoram, crushed
¼ tsp. dried thyme, crushed
dash pepper
1 C. chopped celery
1 C. chopped carrot
½ tsp. salt, or to taste

1. In a large saucepan or Dutch oven, cover dried peas with 2 quarts of water. Bring split peas to a boil; boil gently for 2 minutes. Set aside to soak for 1 hour. Add ham bone, chopped onion, garlic powder, marjoram, thyme, and pepper. Bring split pea soup to a boil; cover, reduce heat, and simmer for 2 hours, stirring occasionally.

2. Remove meat from bone; dice and return to pea soup with chopped celery and carrot. Simmer split pea soup slowly for 45 minutes, stirring occasionally.

3. Taste split pea soup and add salt. Split pea soup serves 8.

SCHILO'S DELICATESSEN
424 E COMMERCE ST., SAN ANTONIO, TX

"Soup and fish explain half the emotions of human life."
Sydney Smith

Catfish & Shrimp

Pulled fresh straight from the ocean to you, we bring you delicious wild-caught fish and shrimp covered in crisp handmade breading that you can't get anywhere else. Taking original family recipes, from our family to yours, we make every side fresh on the spot daily. At Sea Island Shrimp House we are committed to using the freshest ingredients and spices to ensure every meal served is absolute perfection. Don't take our word for it, San Antonio agrees; voted "Best Seafood Restaurant" in the Express News' Reader's Choice Poll since it began 2001! Thank you San Antonio seafood lovers!

1 C. seasoned flour
1 tsp. cajun spice
1 8 oz. catfish fillet
½ C. celery; onions, green peppers
¼ C. diced tomatoes
3 large shrimp
¼ C. white wine; (optional)
1 oz. vegetable oil to cook with
1 tbsp. julienne scallions

1. Heat oil in skillet.

2. Dredge catfish in seasoned flour and pan fry.

3. Add shrimp and cook for one minute. Add cajun spice. Add celery, onions, peppers, tomatoes. Add white wine. Place catfish on plate and top with 3 shrimp. Pour sauce over and top with scallions.

Signature Tastes of SAN ANTONIO

SEA ISLAND SHRIMP HOUSE
11715 BANDERA RD., SAN ANTONIO, TX

"More die in the United States of too much food than of too little."
John Kenneth Galbraith

BELGIAN DARK CHOCOLATE TART

Signature Tastes of SAN ANTONIO

12 (3 in.) Tenderflake tart shells
⅓ C. whipping cream
4 oz. (125g) dark Belgian chocolate, chopped into small pieces
1 tbsp. brandy, rum or orange liquer
72 to 96 raspberries (about 3 C.)
2 tbsp. icing sugar, or to taste

1. Preheat the oven to 350 degrees F. Place the tart shells on a baking sheet. Prick each one a few times with a fork to help prevent them from puffing as they bake. Bake tarts until golden brown, about 15 to 18 minutes.
2. Cool tarts to room temperature. Carefully remove tarts from their foil liners and set on a platter.
3. Place whipping cream in a small pot and bring to a boil. Stir in chocolate and brandy, rum or orange liqueur. Mix just until chocolate is melted and well incorporated. Carefully place chocolate mixture into the tart shells, using a small spatula to ensure you get every last bit of it.
4. Cool tarts to room temperature. Tent tarts with plastic wrap and refrigerate until ready to serve. (Tarts can be made to this point a day before needed.)
5. When ready to serve, uncover and top each tart with 6 to 8 raspberries, depending on their size. Dust the tarts with icing sugar and serve.

To Serve Alongside:
1. Serve the tarts with rich coffee and, if desired a little of the orange liqueur you used in the chocolate filling.

SILO ELEVATED CUISINE
1133 AUSTIN HWY., SAN ANTONIO, TX

"It is illegal to give someone food in which has been found a dead mouse or weasel."
Ancient Irish law

CHICKEN VINDALOO

Signature Tastes of SAN ANTONIO

Since 1989, Simi's India Cuisine has served the highest quality Indian food in a clean and friendly environment. Owner, Amarjit Singh, works daily to make your dining experience pleasurable by personally overseeing all food preparation. Ambi's partner, Nancy, and the rest of the able and friendly staff work hard to ensure that your dining experience is the best it can be. If you have never been to Simi's before, Amarjit would like to personally invite you try his version of India. If you are a long time returning customer, he sends his thanks for your support over the years.

(3 lb.) chicken, skinned and chopped into 8 pieces (deboned chicken pieces are used at the restaurant, but you can keep the bones on if preferred)

Marinade:
1 C. plain yogurt
¼ C. white vinegar
6 cloves garlic, mashed
1 pc fresh ginger, size of a walnut (abt. 1½ tsp.), minced
2 tbsp. oil
2 onions, chopped fine
2 tomatoes, chopped fine

Dry Masala:
1 tsp. dried red pepper flakes, or to taste
¼ tsp. turmeric
¼ tsp. paprika

Vegetables:
1 large potato, peeled and cubed
1 tbsp. tomato paste
salt and pepper to taste

1. Prepare chicken and set aside.

2. Mix together the yogurt, vinegar, garlic and ginger. Then add the chicken pieces. Mix ingredients well, cover and refrigerate at least 4 hours, preferably overnight.

3. In a heavy skillet, heat the oil and saute onions until they are golden brown. Add tomatoes and dry masala, cook over high heat, stirring constantly, for 5 minutes. Add the chicken with its marinade. Simmer 20 minutes.

4. Add the cubed potato, tomato paste and about ½ cup water (more if you prefer more gravy). Cover and simmer for 10 minutes or until chicken and potatoes are tender.

5. Season generously with salt and pepper, and additional red pepper flakes if you prefer a hot dish.Broil the fish under the preheated broiler on the oven's center rack for 10 minutes; turn the fish and brush with reserved marinade. Continue cooking until the fish flakes easily with a fork, about 7 minutes more. Serve hot.

SIMI'S INDIA CUISINE
4535 FREDERICKSBURG RD., SAN ANTONIO, TX

"Food, like a loving touch or a glimpse of divine power, has that ability to comfort."
Norman Kolpas

259

BUTTERED POTATOES

Smokey Mo (Morris Melchor) and family opened their first location in Cedar park in 2000. Morris has been in the bbq business for about 50 years. He started in 1962 with Longhorn BBQ at the age of 12. (For only $1.32 per hour) A half century later he and his family have really created a great family restaurant with friendly staff and great barbecue.

Signature Tastes of SAN ANTONIO

salt
3½ lb. white or all-purpose potatoes, peeled and cut into large chunks
1 stick plus 2 tbsp. unsalted butter
1 C. milk
¼ C. crème fraîche

1. In a large pot of boiling salted water, cook the potatoes over moderate heat until tender, about 25 minutes. Drain well. Return the potatoes to the pot and cook over high heat for 1 minute to dry them out slightly. Pass the potatoes through a ricer and return them to the pot.

2. In a small saucepan, cook the butter over moderate heat until the milk solids turn dark golden, about 4 minutes. Add all but 2 tablespoons of the brown butter to the potatoes along with the milk and crème fraîche and stir well.

3. Season with salt and stir over moderate heat until hot. Drizzle the remaining brown butter over the potatoes and serve.

SMOKEY MO'S BAR-B-Q

22106 BULVERDE RD., SAN ANTONIO, TX

"Food... can look beautiful, taste exquisite, smell wonderful, make people feel good, bring them together, inspire romantic feelings.... At its most basic, it is fuel for a hungry machine."
Rosamond Richardson

Y'all come back
... or else!!

POTATO SALAD

Signature Tastes of SAN ANTONIO

Smokin Joe's of Texas is a family owned restaurant on the Northeast side of San Antonio. Joe has been Smoking BBQ in San Antonio, Texas for over 35 years and decided to open a BBQ joint in 2010. The word has spread quickly and we now have a steady flow of loyal customers each week. Smokin Joe's has not advertised but the food speaks for itself.

2 lb. small Yukon gold potatoes
2 large eggs
kosher salt
½ bunch sliced scallions, white and green parts
2 tbsp. drained capers
2 C. mayonnaise
¼ C. Dijon mustard
¼ C. finely chopped dill pickles with ¼ C. juice, about 2 pickles
½ small red onion, chopped
2 tbsp. chopped fresh flat-leaf parsley
½ bunch dill, chopped
½ lemon, juiced
freshly ground black pepper
extra-virgin olive oil, for drizzling

1. Put the potatoes and eggs into a big saucepan of cold salted water. Bring to a simmer. After 12 minutes remove the eggs with a slotted spoon and let cool.
2. Continue cooking the potatoes until a paring knife poked into them goes in without resistance, about 3 minutes longer. Drain the potatoes in a colander and let them cool.
3. Reserve some scallion greens and capers for garnish.
4. Meanwhile, stir together the mayonnaise, mustard, pickles and their juice, onion, remaining scallions and capers, parsley, and lemon juice in a bowl large enough to hold the potatoes. Peel the cool eggs and grate them into the bowl.
5. Stick a fork into the potatoes and lift them 1 at a time out of the colander. Break up the potatoes by hand into rough chunks, add them to the bowl and toss to coat with the dressing.
6. Season, to taste, with salt and pepper. Drizzle with a little olive oil before serving.

SMOKIN JOE'S OF TEXAS
114 N WEIDNER RD., SAN ANTONIO, TX

"Food: Part of the spiritual expression of the French, and I do not believe that they have ever heard of calories."
Beverley Baxter

263

Sorrento Ristorante e Pizzeria

Gino's Authentic New York-style

Pizza	Small	Medium	Large
Mozzarella	$8.70	$10.90	$12.00
Sausage	$9.80	$12.25	$13.75
Pepperoni	$9.80	$12.25	$13.75
Green Pepper	$9.80	$12.25	$13.75
Extra Cheese	$9.80	$12.25	$13.75
Onion	$9.80	$12.25	$13.75
Anchovy	$9.80	$12.25	$13.75
Jalapeno	$9.80	$12.25	$13.75
Meatball	$9.80	$12.25	$13.75
Mushroom	$9.80	$12.25	$13.75
Bacon	$9.80	$12.25	$13.75
Gino's Special (Includes ingredients above)	$17.80	$19.20	$21.25
Margherita (Basil, Tomato, Garlic)	$11.50	$13.40	$15.95

	Small	Medium	Large
Clam	$10.00	$12.80	$15.50
Fresh Tomato	$10.00	$12.80	$15.50
Broccoli	$10.00	$12.80	$15.50
Garlic	$10.00	$12.80	$15.50
Clams Casino (Clams, Bacon, Green Peppers)	$14.00	$18.00	$20.50
Eggplant	$10.00	$12.80	$15.50
Pineapple	$10.00	$12.80	$15.50
Ham	$10.00	$12.80	$15.50
Olive	$10.00	$12.80	$15.50
Vegetarian (mushrooms, peppers, olives, onions, broccoli & eggplant)	$17.00	$19.25	$22.25

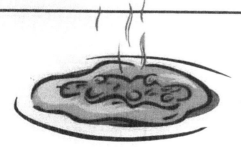

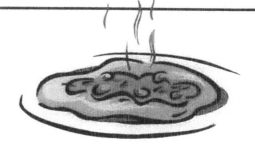

THERE WILL BE A $ 2.00 CHARGE FOR SPLIT DISHES

POLLO CACCIATORE

Signature Tastes of SAN ANTONIO

chicken thighs and drumsticks (abt. 2 lbs.), skinned and on the bone
1 large onion, cut into half-moon slices or however
kosher salt
freshly ground pepper
shopping list
few sprinkles of spices/dried herbs (cumin and chipotle powder; or garlic powder, basil, and oregano)
marinara sauce or diced tomatoes or salsa - about ½ to ¾ C.

Add any kind of veggie you want: peppers, carrots, mushrooms, broccoli, squash, just be careful with timing and add quicker cooking things only in the last hour or so (till they're done)

1. Hack up the onion and throw it in the crock pot. Sprinkle with S & P.

2. Pat the chicken dry after separating and skinning.

3. Season it to taste with S & P and spices/herbs.

4. Rest the chicken on the onions.

5. Spoon a little sauce over, no need to cover it all, or to stir it around.

6. Cook in crock pot on low for 4 to 6 hours or high for just a few, basically until you pick up a piece of chicken and you lose everything but the bone.

SORRENTO RISTORANTE AND PIZZA
5146 BROADWAY ST., SAN ANTONIO, TX

"Thy food is such As hath been belched on by infected lungs."
William Shakespeare

DEEP FRIED MUSHROOMS

Stone Werks is a San Antonio success story in upscale casual dining that offers a winning mix of fresh food, great drinks and a high energy atmosphere. Stone Werks offers a wide variety of signature American Rustic menu items prepared fresh every day, as well as Executive Chef daily specials at all three locations. Stone Werks features an extensive wine list, liquor selection, draft and specialty bottled beers and weekend live entertainment on some of the best patios in San Antonio.

1 C. all-purpose flour
1 tsp. garlic salt
1 egg
1 C. water
1 lb. button mushrooms, quartered
2 C. oil for frying, or as needed

1. In a medium bowl, stir together the flour and garlic salt. Mix in egg and water until smooth.

2. Heat the oil in a large deep skillet over medium-high heat. Test to see if oil is hot by frying a drop of batter. If it sizzles and floats to the top, the oil is ready.

3. Dip mushrooms into the batter and then place in the hot oil. Fry a few at a time so they are not crowded, until golden brown, 3 to 5 minutes. Remove from oil with a slotted spoon and drain on paper towels.

STONE WERKS BIG ROCK GRILLE
1201 N LOOP 1604 W, SAN ANTONIO, TX

"Food without wine is a corpse; wine without food is a ghost; united and well mitched they are as body and soul, living partners."
Andre Simon

MISOSHIRU

Explore the exotically familiar and the authentically creative as Sushi Zushi fuses Japanese traditions with modern tastes. Dedicated to purists, adventurers and first-timers alike, our masterful chefs select the freshest ingredients and combine them into extraordinary, hand-prepared artistry for the body and soul. Embark on a memorable dining experience, prepared to amaze. Satisfy your appetite and your curiosity as Sushi Zushi balances traditional Japanese roots with Latin American influences into an expansive menu far beyond the ordinary. We integrate local ingredients and age-old practices into modern, healthy and superior dining pleasure on every plate, every time. This harmony of culture and cuisine culminates in a complete sensory experience for our patrons.

Signature Tastes of SAN ANTONIO

4 C. dashi stock
¼ C. miso

Garnishes:
1 to 2 scallions, sliced into thin rounds
¼ lb. soft tofu, cut into small cubes
2 tbsp. wakame (dried seaweed), soaked in warm water and shredded

1. Bring the dashi to a simmer over medium heat.

2. Using the back of a spoon, rub the miso though a fine sieve into the simmering dashi. Bring soup back to a low simmer.

3. Place a small amount of garnish in each individual's bowl. Remove soup from heat, pour into bowls and serve immediately.

18720 STONE OAK PKWY., SAN ANTONIO, TX

SUSHI ZUSHI

"When we decode a cookbook, every one of us is a practicing chemist. Cooking is really the oldest, most basic application of physical and chemical forces to natural materials."
Arthur E. Grosser

GRILLED CHICKEN YAKITORI

At Sushihana, we offer both traditional Japanese cuisine and Asian Fusion dishes. For us, sushi and Japanese food are more than California rolls. Our creativity is highlighted in our sushi rolls and our Asian Fusion dishes. Sushihana Japanese Restaurant features superb Asian food and an excellent sushi bar earning us many regular guests within San Antonio. Rent our banquet room for your next business luncheon, private party, or wedding rehearsal dinner. We also cater special events.

2 chicken breasts
1 medium leek
1 tbsp. sugar
2 tbsp. sake
3 tbsp. mirin
3 tbsp. soy sauce
a good Teriyaki sauce can be substituted for the sauce ingredients listed here (except the Sake)
bamboo skewers (soaked in water to prevent burning)

1. Cut chicken breasts into bite-sized pieces.

2. Cut the leek into 1 inch lengths Skewer the chicken and leek pieces in alternating order.

3. Mix sugar, sake, mirin, and soy sauce in a bowl.

4. Grill the skewered chicken over hot coals, basting with teriyaki sauce until the chicken is cooked.

SUSHIHANA JAPANESE RESTAURANT
1810 NW MILITARY HWY., SAN ANTONIO, TX

"My mother was a good recreational cook, but what she basically believed about cooking was that if you worked hard and prospered, someone else would do it for you."
Nora Ephron

SHRIMP TACOS

Signature Tastes of SAN ANTONIO

Since 2005, we've been serving, simply, the best Tex-Mex food in San Antonio from what was once a Brake Check. No frills, no mariachi band and nothing out of a can. Just simple homemade goodness. From our breakfast tacos that come served on fresh, hand-made corn and flour tortillas to our made-to-order Tecate beer battered "Chopped & Dropped" fajitas, our food will leave you with a full tank and a smile on your face. Oh yeah, our margaritas are no joke either. So whether you're out on our patio enjoying the live music and a V6 margarita sampler, stopping by to pick up breakfast tacos on the way to the office or just enjoying a big, hot plate of chilaquiles on a Saturday morning, we hope you keep coming back for more.

2 C. shredded green cabbage
¼ C. shredded carrots
3 tbsp. sliced scallions
1 tbsp. finely chopped cilantro
½ C. ranch salad dressing
1 tbsp. fresh lime juice
1 C. canned black beans, rinsed and drained
12 corn tortillas (6 in.)
24 sea best breaded jumbo butterfly shrimp
1 C. shredded Monterey Jack cheese

1. In a small bowl, combine the cabbage, carrots, scallions and cilantro. Stir in the ranch dressing and lime juice; set aside.

2. In a small saucepan over medium heat, warm the black beans.

3. Heat corn tortillas; keep warm. Cook Sea Best Breaded Jumbo Butterfly Shrimp according to package directions until crispy and golden brown. Remove shrimp tails.

4. Top each warm tortilla with cabbage mixture and warm black beans. Add two fried butterfly shrimp and shredded Monterey Jack cheese. Fold in half.

8403 BROADWAY ST SAN ANTONIO, TX

TACO GARAGE

"Food is all those substances which, submitted to the action of the stomach, can be assimilated or changed into life by digestion, and can thus repair the losses which the human body suffers through the act of living."
Jean-Antheleme Brillat-Savarin

CALDO DE RES

Welcome to the home of the finest authentic Mexican food in the State of Texas. Torres Taco Haven, nestled in the historic and beautiful section of Southtown San Antonio, has been a staple of fine Mexican cuisine in the Alamo City area for decades.

2 lb. beef shank, with bone
1 tbsp. vegetable oil
2 tsp. salt
2 tsp. ground black pepper
1 onion, chopped
1 (14.5 oz.) can diced tomatoes
3 C. beef broth
4 C. water
2 medium carrot, coarsely chopped
¼ C. chopped fresh cilantro
1 potato, quartered (optional)
2 ears corn, husked and cut into thirds
2 chayotes, quartered (optional)
1 medium head cabbage, cored and cut into wedges
¼ C. sliced pickled jalapenos
¼ C. finely chopped onion
1 C. chopped fresh cilantro
2 limes, cut into wedges
4 radishes, quartered

1. Cut the meat from the beef bones into about ½ inch pieces, leaving some on the bones.

2. Heat a heavy soup pot over medium-high heat until very hot. Add the oil, tilting the pan to coat the bottom. Add the meat and bones, and season with salt and pepper. Cook and stir until thoroughly browned.

3. Add 1 onion, and cook until onion is also lightly browned. Stir in the tomatoes and broth. The liquid should cover the bones by ½ inch. If not, add enough water to compensate. Reduce heat to low, and simmer for 1 hour with the lid on loosely. If meat is not tender, continue cooking for another 10 minutes or so.

4. Pour in the water, and return to a simmer. Add the carrot and ¼ cup cilantro, and cook for 10 minutes, then stir in the potato, corn and chayote. Simmer until vegetables are tender. Push the cabbage wedges into the soup, and cook for about 10 more minutes.

5. Ladle soup into large bowls, including meat vegetables and bones. Garnish with jalapenos, minced onion, and additional cilantro. Squeeze lime juice over all, and serve with radishes.

TACO HAVEN — 1032 S PRESA ST., SAN ANTONIO, TX

"Nearly everyone wants as least one outstanding meal a day."
Duncan Hines

274

CHALUPA COMPUESTA

At Taco Taco Cafe, "choice" is what really sets us apart from those other Mexican restaurants. Our fans know that Taco Taco Cafe means more delicious choices for your Mexican food pleasure, you'll see why our food really does deserve to be considered the best. All the meals in Taco Taco Cafe are prepared with fresh and special ingredients. Everything is made in house.

2 C. lettuce; shredded
1 C. cheddar cheese; shredded
4 C. refried beans; to 6 C. guacamole
12 tostadas; (fried tortillas)
2 C. chili con carne; NO BEANS

1. Place tostadas on baking sheet; spread with refried beans and shredded cheese.

2. Place under broiler just until cheese melts.

3. Remove from oven; spread chili and shredded lettuce over tostadas and serve at once.

4. Serve with guacamole.

145 E HILDEBRAND AVE., SAN ANTONIO, TX

TACO TACO CAFE

"The quality of food is in inverse proportion to the altitude of the dining room, with airplanes the extreme example."
Bryan Miller

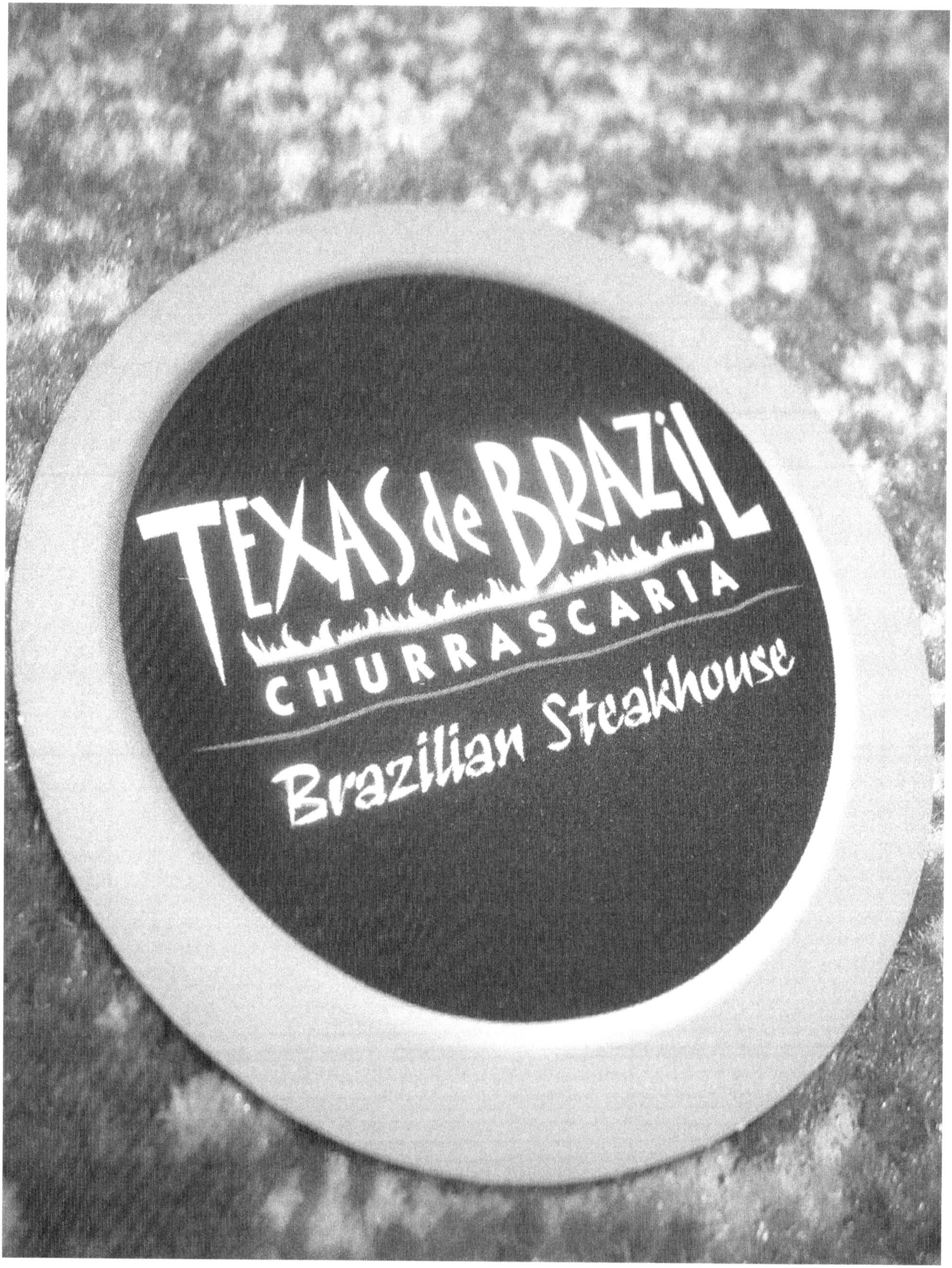
TEXAS de BRAZIL
CHURRASCARIA
Brazilian Steakhouse

Brazilian Papaya Cream

Texas de Brazil is an authentic Brazilian-American Churrascaria (steakhouse) that combines the cuisine of Southern Brazil with the generous spirit of Texas. Texas de Brazil is carving out a whole new experience in fine dining. The restaurant is an authentic Brazilian-American "Churrascaria" or steakhouse that combines the cuisines of Southern Brazil with the generous spirit of Texas.

2 scoops vanilla ice cream
1 fresh ripe papaya, peeled and cut into small dice, plus additional papaya for garnish
creme de cassis (same as cassis)

1. Using a blender, mix ice cream and papaya until well blended.

2. Pour creamy mixture into tall chilled dessert glasses.

3. Drizzle crème de cassis on top. Garnish with fresh papaya. Serve immediately.

313 E. Houston St., San Antonio, TX

Texas de Brazil

"Food for thought is no substitute for the real thing."
Walt Kelly

DRUNKEN NOODLE

Signature Tastes of SAN ANTONIO

8 oz. flat rice noodles
2 tbsp. kikoman soy sauce
1 tbsp. oyster sauce
1 tsp. brown sugar
1 tbsp. canola oil
1 C. diced extra firm tofu
2 tsp. minced garlic
1 sliced Thai chiles or thai chili paste just use very little the first time and then you'll know how much to increase or decrease it by the)
1½ C. sliced broccoli
½ C. thinly sliced red onion
1 C. bean sprouts
1 C. Thai basil (you can use regular basil leaves in its place if you can't find this ingredient but it will give it)

1. Soak noodles for 15 minutes in warm water. In a large pot of boiling water, cook rice noodles until just tender, about 1 minute; drain and set aside.

2. In a small bowl, combine the Kikoman sauce, oyster sauce and sugar and put it aside. Heat oil in a large skillet or wok over medium-high heat.

3. Add tofu and cook until its a golden colour which should take about 30 seconds to a minute and set this aside.

4. Add garlic and cook 10 seconds. Add chili, broccoli, onion and stir fry for 30 secs.

5. Add the soy sauce mixture, noodles, sprouts, basil and reserved tofu and stir-fry for 1 minute, or until hot. Serve in a serving platter.

5999 DE ZAVALA ROAD, SAN ANTONIO, TX

THAI BISTRO & SUSHI

"Food history is as important as a baroque church. Governments should recognize cultural heritage and protect traditional foods. A cheese is as worthy of preserving as a sixteenth-century building."
Carlo Petrini

Tom Yum Chicken

Signature Tastes of SAN ANTONIO

8 oz. chicken breast, cut into 1 ½ inch pcs. (with or without bone) or shrimp
4-5 kaffir lime leaves
2-3 pcs. galangal, slices
1½ C. straw mushroom, halved
4 tbsp. Thai fish sauce
3 C. water
1 stalk lemon grass, cut into 2" long pcs.
2 tbsp. lime juice
1 tbsp. Thai chili pepper, chopped

1. Bring water to boil in a medium-sized pot over high heat. Add kaffir lime leaves, galangal and lemon grass. Cook for 2 minutes.

2. Add straw mushrooms. Cook for a few minutes more. Add chicken. Do not stir. Cook for 5 minutes or less until the chicken is cooked through - do not over-cook.

3. Remove from heat. Season to taste with fish sauce, lime juice and chili peppers. Serve immediately with steamed jasmine rice.

11318 Perrin Beitel Rd., San Antonio, TX

Thai Cafe

"The history of government regulation of food safety is one of government watchdogs chasing the horse after it's out of the barn."
David A. Kessler

THAI CHILI ORIENTAL RESTAURANT

Authentic Healthy Thai Food

Thai chili Cuisine brings you healthy Thai cooking with 65 original family recipes.

Executive Chef **Chai**

4303 Thousand Oak Dr., SA 78217

Tel no. 210-656-8589

Thai Chili has really good lunch specials, $7.95 for soup, appetizer and entree or $7.95 for the lunch buffet (even better). I feel like a lot of the Thai restaurants in SA just throw the typical Thai spices together and call it Thai food but Thai chili is nothing like that. Not only are their dishes highly flavored (which is one of the characteristic of Thai) but comes in HUGE portions.

1⅓ C. coconut cream, reserve 2 tablespoons (30 ml.) for garnish
2¼ C. coconut milk
6 oz. (200 g) roast duck, thinly sliced
1.76 oz. (50 g) red curry paste
3 tbsp. Thai fish sauce
1 tbsp. (20 g) palm sugar
3 kaffir lime leaves: 2 torn into pieces, discarding the stem and 1 finely shredded (for garnish)
1 large eggplant, cut into ½ inch (1 cm) pieces
1½ C. (5 oz., 150 g) fresh pineapple, cut into bite-sized pieces (1 inch x 1.5 inch)
6 small cherry tomatoes (4 oz., 100 g)
10 seedless grapes (optional)
¾ C. (1 oz., 30 g) sweet basil leaves (reserve some for garnish)

1. Pour the coconut cream into a wok or sauce pan and simmer for 2 minutes, stirring constantly, until the coconut oil begins to separate out.

2. Add the curry paste, fish sauce, palm sugar and torn kaffir lime leaves. Simmer for 2 more minutes.

3. Add the duck and eggplant. Bring to a boil. Then add the coconut milk and simmer for 5 minutes.

4. Add the pineapple and cherry tomatoes and simmer for 2 minutes. Then add the grapes (if using) and sweet basil leaves. Turn off the heat and serve garnished with the remaining kaffir lime leaves, sweet basil and a few spoonfuls of thick coconut milk.

19141 STONE OAK PKWY. ST., SAN ANTONIO, TX

THAI CHILI

"Skilful and refined cookery has always been a feature of the most glorious epochs in history."
Lucien Tendret

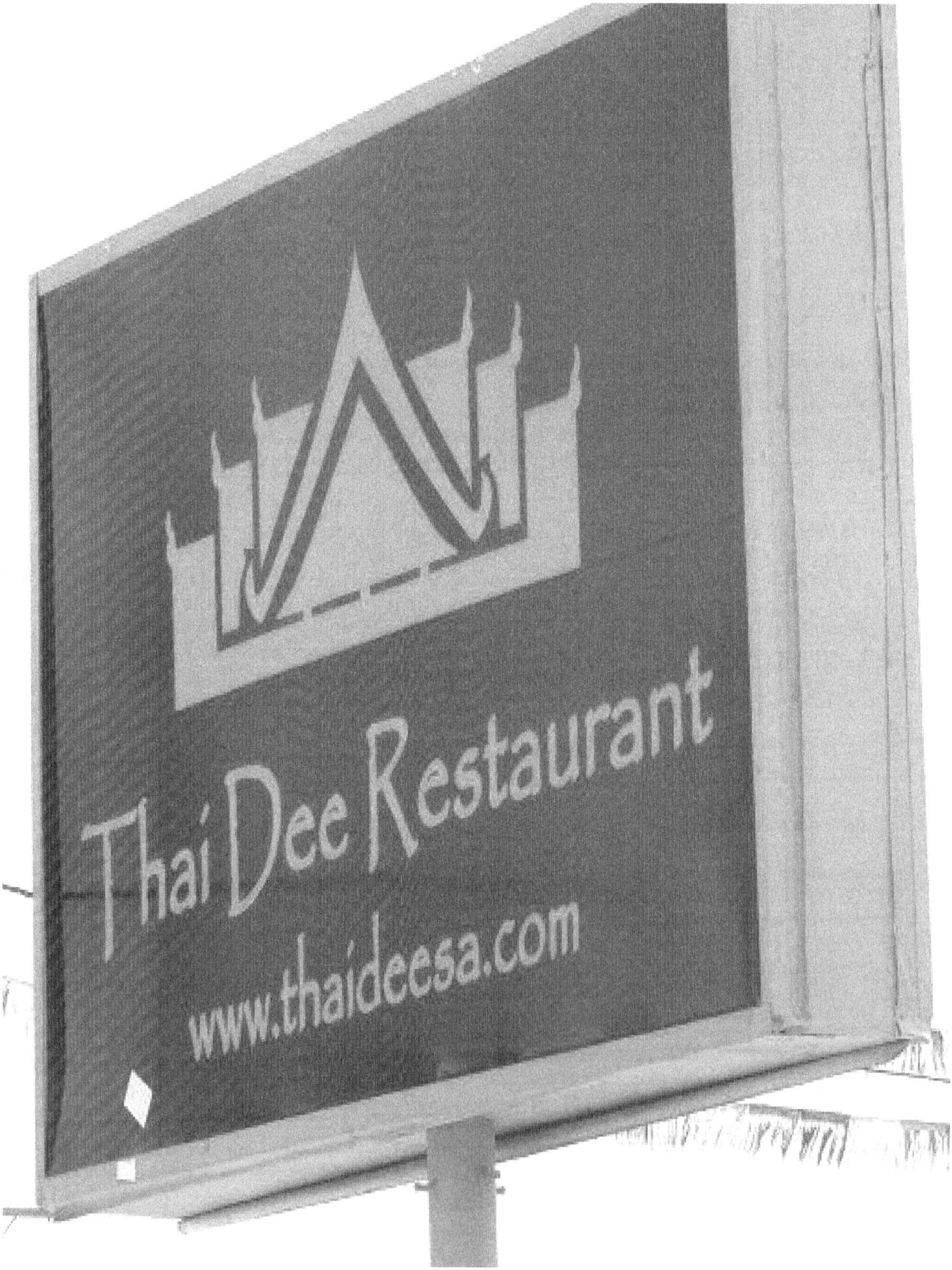
Thai Dee Restaurant
www.thaideesa.com

Tom Kha

Signature Tastes of SAN ANTONIO

Thai Dee Restaurant where everyone can experience authentic flavors from different regions of Thailand. Our menu will take you from the northern mountains to the southern sea. Our dishes include many natural herbs & spices that mother nature has to offer, which makes our meals delicious yet healthy! Thai cooking has a free-style attitude which ensures that we can accommodate your diet restrictions.

1 C. good quality Chinese chicken stock
1 C. coconut milk
½ a stalk fresh or frozen lemongrass
6 slices galangal - fresh
2 (hand-torn) Kaffir lime leaves
2-3 (big slices so you can avoid them easily) Thai bird's eye chillies (or Serrano chillies)
1 tbsp. fish sauce (The saltiness can vary a lot across brands, so start with less always.)
2 tbsp. lime juice
½ tsp. sugar
2 tbsp. coriander (cilantro for the Americans) leaves
50 gm (chopped) boneless chicken breast
4 (sliced) straw mushrooms (or regular button mushrooms)

1. For the lemongrass, use only the bottom white part (about 6 inches) and discard the woody grass part of it. With the flat side of a cleaver or a heavy object, pound and bruise the lemongrass so it releases the flavour. Cut into 2 inch segments. (Watch yourself with the cleaver, please. We only want to bruise the lemongrass, not your fingers.)

2. Put the stock into a pot and bring to a boil. Toss the galangal, lemongrass, sugar, and lime leaves in. Simmer for 5 minutes.

3. Add the coconut milk, chillies, fish sauce and simmer for another 5 minutes.

4. Finally, add the chicken and mushrooms and cook till the chicken is just cooked. The moment you see it turning all white on the outside, it's 90% done.

5. Turn off the heat, add lime juice and garnish with coriander leaves. Test for saltiness and sourness.

6. You should get the earthy flavour of galangal, noticeable amount of saltiness, sweetness from the coconut milk, and a fair bit of lime flavour, with a hint of chilli in the background. If required, adjust with more fish sauce (salt) and lemon juice (sour).

5307 Blanco Rd., San Antonio, TX

Thai Dee

"A good cook is the peculiar gift of the gods. He must be a perfect creature from the brain to the palate, from the palate to the finger's end."
Walter Savage Landor

285

SESAME CHICKEN

We, at Thai Hut, continue to pride ourselves in service and authentic Thai dishes. Our family was the first to establish a Thai Restaurant in the city of San Antonio, TX, back in 1982. Like many of you, we had a dream. A dream to own a business that would represent who we are at home and who we are culturally. The Thai culture is known for its hard work and service. Therefore we combined who we are and what you love to give you a taste of Thailand.

Signature Tastes of SAN ANTONIO

3 whole boneless chicken breasts

Marinade:
2 tbsp. light soy sauce
1 tbsp. cooking wine or dry sherry
a few drops of sesame oil
2 tbsp. flour
2 tbsp. cornstarch
2 tbsp. water
¼ tsp. baking powder
¼ tsp. baking soda
1 tsp. vegetable oil

Sauce for Sesame Chicken:
½ C. water
1 C. chicken broth
⅛ C. vinegar
¼ C. cornstarch
1 C. sugar
2 tbsp. dark soy sauce
2 tbsp. sesame oil
1 tsp. chili paste, or more if desired
1 clove garlic (minced)

Other:
2 tbsp. toasted sesame seeds (see recipe directions for link to how to toast)
3 ½ - 4 C. peanut oil for deep-frying

For Sesame Chicken:
1. Toast the sesame seeds and set aside.
2. Cut the chicken into 1-inch cubes. Mix the marinade ingredients and marinate the chicken for 20 minutes.

To prepare the sauce:
1. Mix together all of the sauce ingredients. Pour them into a small pot and bring to a boil, stirring continuously. Turn the heat down to low and keep warm while you are deep-frying the chicken.

To deep-fry the chicken:
1. Add the marinated chicken pieces a few at a time, and deep-fry until golden brown. Drain on paper towels. Repeat with the remainder of the chicken.
2. Just before you are finished deep-frying, bring the sauce back up to a boil.
3. Place the chicken on a large platter and pour the sauce over. Sprinkle with sesame seeds. Serve the Sesame Chicken with rice.

9902 POTRANCO RD. STE 101, SAN ANTONIO, TX

THAI HUT

"I won't eat anything that has intelligent life, but I'd gladly eat a network executive or a politician."
Marty Feldman

287

SHRIMP PARCEL

Signature Tastes of SAN ANTONIO

Thai Topaz, a San Antonio favorite, family-owned restaurant, was founded in 2005 by Somchai and JirapornNamarsa, my parents. Although Dad and Mom have different educational backgrounds, running a Thai restaurant brings out the best of their talents.

THAI TOPAZ - HEALTHY, FINE THAI CUISINE
9386 HUEBNER RD., STEIOL, SAN ANTONIO, TX

*1 tbsp. oil
2 cloves garlic, crushed
1 tbsp. grated fresh ginger
2 scallions, chopped
1 lb. raw shrimps, peeled and chopped
½ tsp. fish sauce
½ tsp. sugar
1 tbsp. lemon juice
2 tbsp. chopped fresh cilantro
6 large spring roll wrappers, cut into quarters
oil, for deep-frying
fresh chives, for serving
sweetchilli sauce, for serving*

1. Heat the oil in a skillet, add the garlic and ginger and cook over low heat for 2 minutes. Add the scallion and cook for 2 minutes. Increase the heat to high, add the shrimps and stir-fry for 2 minutes, or until the colour just changes. Be careful not to overcook the shrimps or they will become tough once deep-fried.

2. Add the fish sauce, sugar, lemon juice and cilantro to the pan. Toss with the shrimps for 1 minute. Remove from the heat; cool slightly.

3. Divide the cooled mixture into 24 portions. Place one portion in the centre of each piece of spring roll wrapper. Brush the edges with water and fold to form a parcel.

4. Fill a deep heavy-based pan one third full of oil. Heat the oil to 180°C (350°F). The oil is hot enough when a cube of bread dropped into the oil turns golden brown in 15 seconds. Deep-fry the parcels one at a time, holding them with tongs for the first few seconds to keep them intact. Cook until golden brown. Drain on crumpled paper towels. Tie with lengths of chives. Serve with sweet chilli sauce.

"An empty stomach is not a good political advisor."
Albert Einstein

TEX MEX EGGROLLS

For Eggrolls:
1 chicken breast fillet
1 tbsp. vegetable oil
2 tbsp. red bell peppers, minced
2 tbsp. green onions, minced
⅓ C. frozen corn
¼ C. canned black bean, rinsed and drained
2 tbsp. frozen spinach, thawed and drained
2 tbsp. jalapeno peppers, diced
½ tbsp. fresh parsley, minced
½ tsp. cumin
¼ tsp. salt
¾ C. monterey jack cheese, shredded
8 egg roll wraps

For Dip:
¼ C. fresh avocado, mashed (about half of an avocado)
¼ C. mayonnaise
¼ C. sour cream
1 ½ tsp. white vinegar
⅛ tsp. salt
⅛ tsp. dried parsley
⅛ tsp. paprika
⅛ tsp. garlic powder
1 tbsp. onion, finely chopped
1 dash pepper

1. Season chicken breast with salt and pepper (on both sides).
2. Grill for 4 to 5 minutes per side or until done.
3. In a skillet, heat 1 tablespoon of vegetable oil on medium-high heat.
4. Add the red pepper and onion and sauté for a few minutes, until tender.
5. Cut the cooked chicken into small cubes and add it to the pepper and onion mixture.
6. Add the corn, black beans, spinach, jalapeno peppers, parsley, cumin, and salt.
7. Cook 5- 10 minutes more, stirring frequently, until everything is heated throughout.
8. Remove pan from heat and add the cheese.
9. Stir until the cheese is mixed in well and melted.
10. Wrap about ten eggroll wrappers in a moist paper towel and microwave on high temperature for about fifteen seconds.
11. Spoon approximately two tablespoons of the chicken mixture into the center.
12. Roll it up like you would a burrito (ends in first, then around the middle), making sure its very tight.
13. If desired, place a toothpick in it to hold, then arrange on a plate.
14. Cover the plate with plastic wrap and freeze for at least 6 hours (or overnight).
15. Make the dip by combining all ingredients in a bowl.
16. Spoon into container and refrigerate until needed.
17. Preheat frying oil to 375 degrees.
18. Deep fry the eggrolls in the hot oil for 2-5 minutes, until golden brown.
19. Place on a warm plate lined with paper towels to drain.
20. Slice each eggroll diagonally and serve with dipping sauce.

"There has always been a food processor in the kitchen. But once upon a time she was usually called the missus or Mom."
Sue Berkman

PORTOBELLO AND SPINACH QUESADILLA

Signature Tastes of SAN ANTONIO

Welcome to The Cove! Restaurant, Beer Garden, Live Music venue and oh yeah, a laundromat and carwash. Don't let that throw you off, The Cove is all about having a good time and enjoying great food with friends and family and doing laundry or washing your car, if your in the mood. All of our meats (beef, bison, lamb and chicken) are grass fed and from Texas. No Antibiotics, No Hormones. All of our greens are organic - no pesticide residue. All of our oils are non-hydrogenated. We serve Boylan Sodas- no high fructose corn syrup.

1 lb. of spinach, washed
2 portobello mushroom caps, grilled or sauteed and sliced thinly
1 clove of garlic, minced
1 onion, sliced thin and caramelized
½ tbsp. extra virgin olive oil
4 (12 in.) flour tortillas
½ C. grated cheddar jack blend cheese, shredded
salsa, guacamole, sour cream, for serving

1. In a large skillet, heat the olive oil over medium heat. Sauté the garlic for 1 minute, and then add the spinach. Cook until the spinach is wilted and turn off the heat. Set aside.

2. Lay out 2 of the flour tortillas on a flat surface. Top with ½ cup of the cheese, spreading evenly over the tortillas. Divide the portobello mushrooms, the onions and the spinach among the tortillas. Top with remaining tortillas and press to seal.

3. Heat a large sauté pan over high heat. Add enough oil to coat the bottom of the pan and lower the heat to medium. Cook until golden brown on both sides, about 3 minutes per side. Repeat with the other quesadilla.

4. Let cool for 5 minutes. Slice into 8 or 10 pieces. Garnish with salsa and cilantro sprigs.

606 W CYPRESS ST., SAN ANTONIO, TX

THE COVE

"The quality of food is in inverse proportion to a dining room's altitude, especially atop bank and hotel buildings (airplanes are an extreme example)."
Bryan Miller

291

Con Salsa Fresca

Opening at 11 in the morning and closing at midnight (earlier in the winter), TFS offers 180 or so beers, many on tap. Limited to beer and wine sales, they also offer ciders, wines, sangria and wine-based "cocktails," that mimic rum punches, magaritas and others. Micheladas — cousin to the Bloody Mary, made with beer instead of vodka — are also a staple. TFS also has a food menu, consisting mainly of finger foods of interior Mexican cuisine: quesadillas, tacos, queso and more. On Sundays they offer a brunch menu with weekend Mexican specialties.

2 lb. plum tomatoes, ripe
1 white onion, large
3 jalapenos or 3 serrano peppers
2 tbsp. fresh cilantro (optional)
1 yellow sweet pepper (optional)
1 tbsp. lime juice
salt

1. Chop all veggies fine.

2. Add lime juice, cilantro, and salt, adjust to taste.

The Friendly Spot Ice House
943 S Alamo St., San Antonio, TX

"If you have formed the habit of checking on every new diet that comes along, you will find that, mercifully, they all blur together, leaving you with only one definite piece of information: french-fried potatoes are out."
Jean Kerr

CURRIED CAULIFLOWER SOUP

The food should be delicious, inexpensive, and a hell of a lot of fun to eat. The beer list should celebrate craft brewers and microbreweries. Our wine list ought to be comprised of varietally-correct, terroir-driven selections that are interesting and affordable. And we'll open it in the beautiful King William neighborhood, in a converted old Sunglo gas station (with a great big open patio). And, well, that's what we've done. We've built The Monterey as a place for our fellow food lovers, beer nerds, and wine geeks. And we hope you'll come join us at our sweet little addition to San Antonio.

1 tbsp. olive oil *1 medium brown onion, halved, chopped* *1 garlic clove, crushed* *80ml (⅓ C.) mild curry paste (Sharwood's brand)* *1.5kg cauliflower, trimmed, coarsely chopped* *1L (4 C.) vegetable stock* *500ml (2 C.) cold water* *250ml (1 C.) coconut cream* *2 tbsp. roughly chopped fresh continental parsley leaves* *salt* *6 pcs. warm naan bread, to serve*	**1.** Heat oil in a large saucepan over medium heat. Add onion and garlic and cook, stirring, for 3 minutes or until onion softens. Add curry paste and cook, stirring, for 1 minute or until fragrant. **2.** Add the cauliflower, stock and water and bring to the boil. Reduce heat to low and simmer, stirring occasionally, for 15 minutes or until the cauliflower is tender. Set aside for 5 minutes to cool. **3.** Transfer half the cauliflower mixture to a clean saucepan. Blend or process the remaining cauliflower mixture, in batches, until smooth. Add to saucepan with unblended cauliflower mixture. (To freeze, see below.) **4.** Add coconut cream and stir over medium heat for 5 minutes. Remove from heat, stir in parsley and season with salt. **5.** Ladle soup into bowls and serve with warm naan bread, if desired.

1127 S. St. Mary's, San Antonio, TX

THE MONTEREY

"He who receives his friends and gives no personal attention to the meal which is being prepared for them, is not worthy of having friends."
Jean-Anthelme Brillat-Savarin

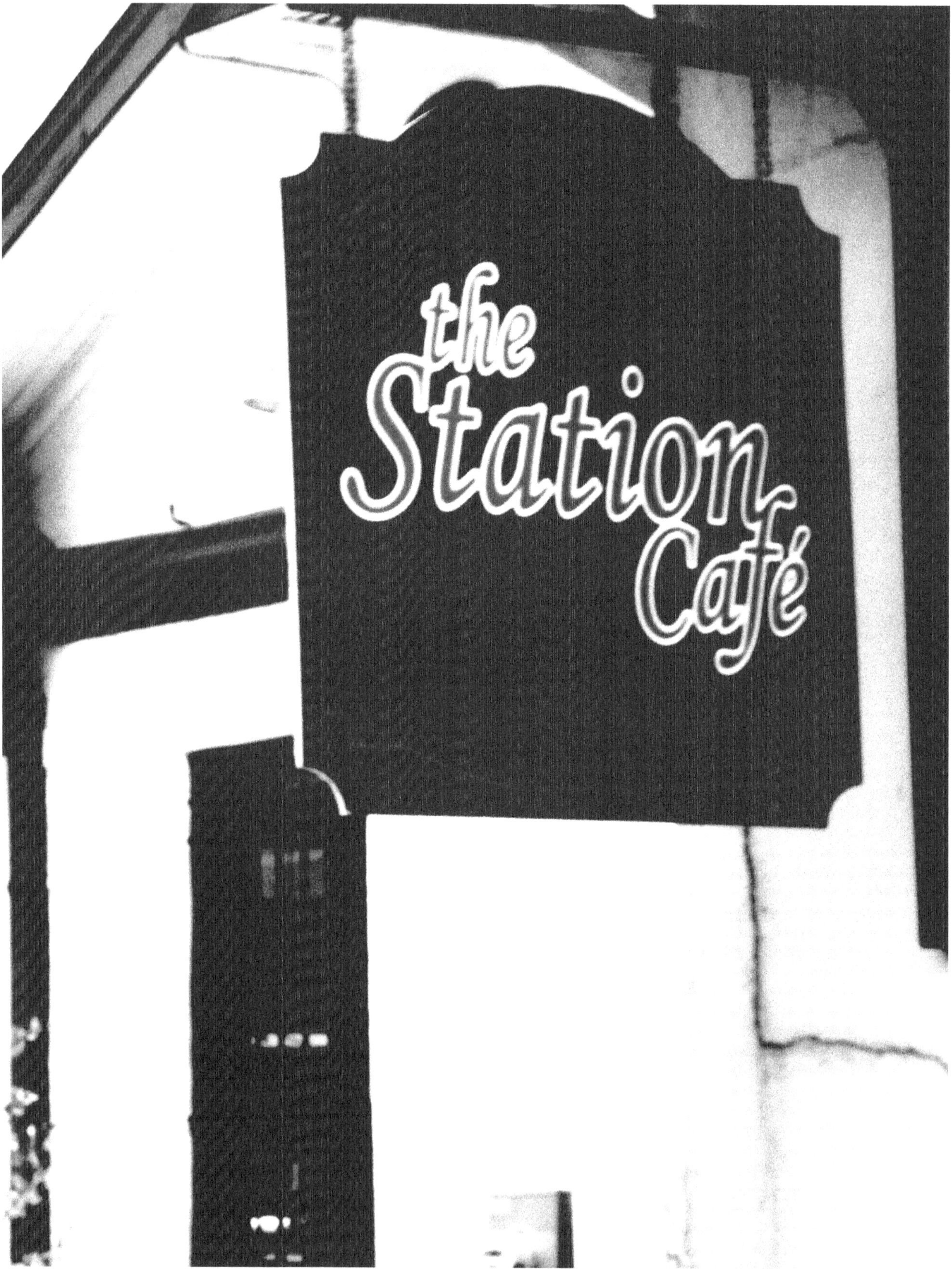
the
Station
Café

CHICKEN CHEDDAR CHIPOTLE

Signature Tastes of SAN ANTONIO

The Filling Station is making its second debut, this time as The Station Café, in the much larger space next door. But change is a tricky thing, and we wanted to see if The Station Café could live up to the legend established by The Filling Station. You can still expect a line at lunchtime, but now it stretches comfortably through the air-conditioned dining area. Whereas before customers had to grab and go, now the people-watching is paramount: elegant ladies, dating teens, K9 unit police, and a prominent Southtown gallerist all lunched side by side on a recent weekday. And a peek behind the curtain reveals a richly deserved workspace. Most importantly, the food is as great, or possibly better than ever.

Ingredients	Instructions
2 tsp. canola oil **1 onion (halved and thinly sliced)** **1 lb. chard (stems and leaves separated chopped see note)** **1 tomato (chopped)** **¼ C. chicken broth (water)** **¼-½ tsp. chipotle pepper (ground)** **¼ tsp. salt** **⅔ C. sharp cheddar cheese (shredded)**	**1.** Heat oil in a large skillet over medium heat. Add onion and chard stems and cook, stirring often, until softened, 3 to 5 minutes. Add tomato, broth (or water), chipotle to taste and salt; bring to a simmer. **2.** Add chard leaves and cook, covered, stirring once, until just tender, about 2 minutes. Scatter cheese evenly over the chard and cook, uncovered, until the cheese is melted, 1 to 2 minutes more. Serve immediately. **3.** After washing the chard for these recipes, allow some of the water to cling to the leaves. It helps steam the chard and prevents a dry finished dish.

THE STATION CAFÉ

108 KING WILLIAM ST., SAN ANTONIO, TX

"How can one make friends without exquisite dishes! It is mainly through the table that one governs!"
Jean-Jacques Regis de Cambaceres

HUEVOS RANCHEROS

Where locals eat, Tito's Restaurant is located in the Historic King William District. Fresh handmade flour and corn tortillas are served daily. Tito's specializes in grilled fajitas and an assortment of enchiladas. Open every day serving breakfast, lunch & dinner. Tito's has a full cantina along with the best Margaritas around.

Signature Tastes of SAN ANTONIO

TITO'S MEXICAN RESTAURANT AND CANTINA

955 S ALAMO ST., SAN ANTONIO, TX

olive oil
½ medium onion, chopped (about a half cup)
1 15-oz. can whole tomatoes, preferably fire-roasted, if you can get it (or 1 -2 large fresh vine-ripened tomatoes, when in season)
½ 6-oz. can diced green Anaheim chiles
chipotle chili powder, adobo sauce, or ground cumin to taste (optional)
4 corn tortillas
butter
4 fresh eggs
2 tbsp. fresh cilantro, chopped (optional)

1. Make the sauce first by softening the onions in a little olive oil in a large skillet on medium heat. Once translucent, add the tomatoes and the juice the tomatoes are packed in. Break up the tomatoes with your fingers as you put them in the pan. If you are using fresh tomatoes, chop them first, then add. Note that fresh tomatoes will take longer to cook as canned tomatoes are already cooked to begin with. Add chopped green chilies. Add additional chili to taste, either chipotle chili powder, adobo sauce, regular chili powder, or even ground cumin. Bring to a simmer, reduce heat to low, and let simmer while you do the rest of the cooking, stirring occasionally. Reduce to warm after it has been simmering for 10 minutes. Add salt to taste if needed.

2. Prepare the tortillas. Heat the oven to a warm 150°F, place serving plates in the oven to keep warm. Heat a teaspoon of olive oil in a large non-stick skillet on medium high, coating the pan with the oil. One by one (or more if your pan is big enough) heat the tortillas in the pan, a minute or two on each side, until they are heated through, softened, and pockets of air bubble up inside of them. Then remove them and stack them on one of the warming plates in the oven to keep warm while you continue cooking the rest of the tortillas and the eggs.

3. Fry the eggs. Using the same skillet as was used for the tortillas, add a little butter to the pan, about two teaspoons for 4 eggs. Heat the pan on medium high heat. Crack 4 eggs into the skillet and cook for 3 to 4 minutes for runny yolks, more for firmer eggs.

4. To serve, spoon a little of the sauce onto a warmed plate. Top with a tortilla, then a fried egg. Top with more sauce, sprinkle with cilantro if desired.

"It is a true saying that a man must eat a peck of salt with his friend before he knows him."
Miguel de Cervantes

BLUE CHEESEBURGER

They have some of the best fried pickles I've ever had. As for the burgers they could use a little seasoning and the buns toasted, but they were still pretty good. I also had the chili cheese tots and all I can say is the chili needs a lot of improvement. Still if you've never been there you should try it out.

Signature Tastes of SAN ANTONIO

2 oz. cream cheese
2 oz. crumbled blue cheese
⅛ tsp. onion powder
1 tsp. chopped fresh parsley
salt and pepper to taste
1 lb. ground beef (I use 85% lean)
salt and pepper
coarsely ground black pepper (optional)

1. In a small bowl, mash together cream cheese and blue cheese then stir in the onion powder and parsley. Taste and season with salt and pepper.

2. Divide ground beef into 8 equal pieces. I first divide it into four pieces then divide each piece again. Form the pieces into balls then sprinkle the balls lightly with salt and pepper, rolling them around a bit to make sure all sides are covered. Flatten each ball to form thin patties of equal size. I find it easiest to form the patties on a sheet of waxed paper.

3. To fill burgers, place a tablespoonful of cream cheese mixture in the center of each of four patties. Spread the filling out evenly to within half an inch of the edge of each patty. Place the remaining patties on top to form four filled burgers. Gently press the edges of each burger together to form a seal.

4. Sprinkle burgers liberally with coarsely ground black pepper (optional).

5. Prepare your grill and cook burgers until the internal temperature reaches 160 degrees (USDA recommendation) or until desired degree of doneness. Let rest for ten minutes. Enjoy!

TJ's BURGERS & MORE

263 LOOP 337 STE 900, NEW BRAUNFELS, TX

"And do as adversaries do in law, strive mightily, but eat and drink as friends."
William Shakespeare

301

We would like to welcome you to Tong's Thai, where we offer a unique fusion of new and exciting Thai and Chinese cuisine. We have selected the most popular traditional dishes from the northern region of Thailand (Chiang Mai), which have their own distinct flavors and added new ways to tantalize your senses. We're very proud to serve San Antonio authentic Asian dishes, prepared fresh each day, as well as creating more contemporary appealing entrees. Don't forget to try our famous spring rolls and our award winning seafood dishes, like Haw-Mok, which have made multiple appearances in the local media! Tong's Thai was the very first in town to serve the trendy "Bubble Teas". The bubble drink is a one of a kind drink, originating in Taiwan, which has quickly become an international phenomenon.

4 small bundles of cellophane noodles (mung bean noodles).
¼ C. dried chili peppers
½ C. roasted peanuts
1 C. of chicken broth
1 lb. of fresh peeled prawns
2 large fresh and juicy limes
3-4 tbsp. fish sauce
2 fresh Thai Chili peppers
½ of medium size red onion
2 stalks of green onion
½ bunch of cilantro
1 stalk of celery
lettuce (iceberg or romaine)

1. Soak 4 little bundles of mung bean noodles in cold water for at least 10 minutes. Drain and cut them into 4" long strips. Heat a small pan on low heat.
2. Add the chili peppers and toast them until they turn real dark. (turn your stove exhaust up to maximum so any smoke from roasting chilies don't overwhelm you)
3. Set the chilies aside in a bowl and then toast the roasted peanuts...just a bit to make sure they are nice and crunchy.
4. Bring 1 cup of chicken broth to a boil in a deep pan. Add fresh prawns (Make sure they are peeled. If you use the frozen ones you have to thaw them first).
5. Cook prawns in broth until they turn pink Add the mung bean noodles and so they don't stick together. When the noodles become transparent they are cooked. (It only takes only few minutes to cook them.)
6. Turn the heat off.
7. Put the cooked noodles and prawns into a large mixing bowl and set them aside. Next, slice up red onion, green onion and cilantro, Thai chili peppers and celery.
8. Pour lime juice dressing over the mixing bowl containing your noodles and prawns.
9. Toss it so it mixes well. (Taste to see if you want to add any more lime juice or fish sauce) Add the cut up vegetables to the mixing bowl and toss again
10. Garnish with roasted peanuts and roasted dried chili pepper. Serve on lettuce.

Dressing:
1. Squeeze 2 large fresh and juicy limes into a bowl.
2. Add about 3-4 tbsp fish sauce. Mix them together and set the dressing aside.

1146 Austin Hwy., San Antonio, TX

Tong's Thai

"If we do not permit the earth to produce beauty and joy, it will in the end not produce food either."
Joseph Wood Krutch

Italian "Sweet Tea"

Tuscan-inspired Italian fare features house-made fresh pasta, antipasti, salumi, signature cast-iron pizzas and simply prepared entrees. The wine list features each region in Italy and offers quartino and bottle service. Signature hand-crafted cocktails offer exciting blends from the bar. Open seven days a week.

2 oz. deep Eddy sweet tea vodka
2 oz. San Pellegrino sparkling mineral water juice from 1 whole lemon

1. Squeeze the Lemon over a tall rocks glass, add Deep Eddy's Sweet Tea Vodka and Pellegrino, stir.

2. Garnish with Lemon Husk and Enjoy! Cheers!

Signature Tastes of SAN ANTONIO

TRE TRATTORIA ALAMO HEIGHTS

4003 BROADWAY ST., SAN ANTONIO, TX

"So long as you have food in your mouth, you have solved all questions for the time being."
Franz Kafka

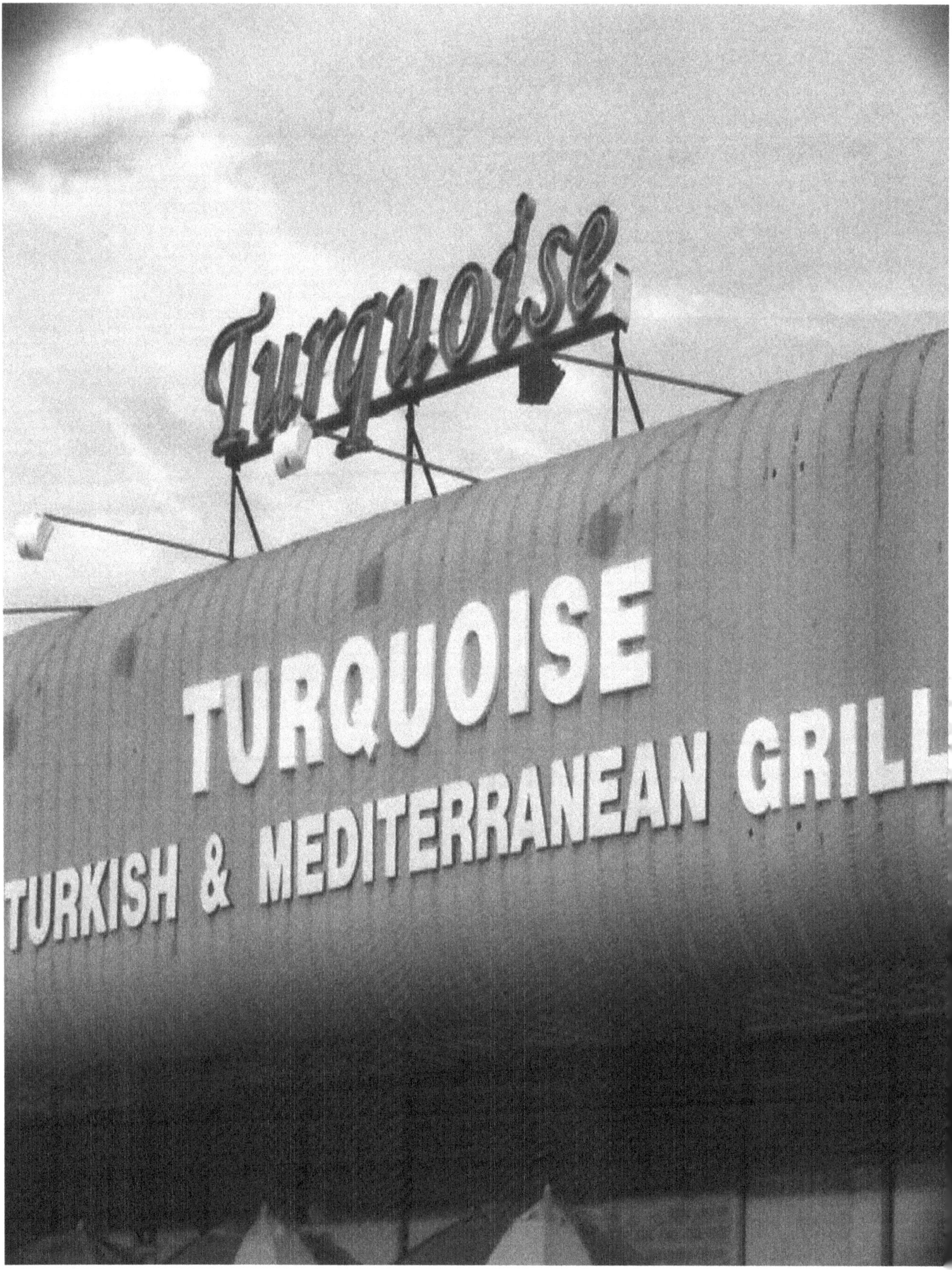
Turquoise
TURQUOISE
TURKISH & MEDITERRANEAN GRILL

"Turquoise Grill " comes from Old French for "Turkish." Like many Europeans at that time, the French believed that the turquoise stone came from Turkey. It did arrive in Europe from Turkey because of trade routes, but originated in Persia. The French called it the "pierre turquois," or "Turkish stone."

1 C. sugar, divided
3 whole eggs
3 egg yolks
2 c. milk, very warm
1½ tsp. vanilla extract

1. In a heavy saucepan over medium heat, melt ½ cup sugar, stirring constantly, until golden brown. Remove from heat; immediately pour about 1 tablespoon into each of 6 (6-ounce size) custard cups. Set aside.

2. In a bowl, combine eggs, egg yolks, and remaining sugar; blend well. Gradually stir in the heated milk, then stir in the vanilla. Pour into prepared custard cups. Set cups in a large baking pan, place on the oven rack, then add very hot water to the pan, up to within about ½-inch of top of custard cups. Bake custard at 350° for 45 to 50 minutes, or until a knife inserted in center comes out clean.

3. Remove cups from hot water right away. Cool for 5 to 10 minutes; gently and carefully loosen sides of custard with a narrow spatula then invert on serving plate. Drizzle and spoon any remaining caramel in cup over the custard.

3720 NORTHWEST INTERSTATE 410 LOOP FRONTAGE ROAD, SAN ANTONIO, TX

TURQUOISE GRILL

"We are indeed much more than what we eat, but what we eat can nevertheless help us to be much more than what we are."
Adelle Davis

POTATO, CORN AND POBLANO FLAUTAS

Vegeria Vegan Restaurant offers customers Tex-Mex and American cuisine minus the meat and cheese. These dishes are packed with flavor. Vegeria is nestled in a cute, little building next to the Taco Garage. Fred Anthony Garza was inspired by his late grandmother, Rosalie Rodriguez Garza. The food is delicious. The pastries and cupcakes are to die for. We also tried the Vegan Corn Potato and Poblano Flautas and demanded they tell us how to make them.

1 tsp. sea salt
2 tsp. black pepper
¾ C. onion (chopped)
5 garlic cloves
2 Poblano peppers (De-seeded, De-ribbed, and Cubed)
1.5 C. corn
3 C. cooked potatoes (Lightly Chopped)
3 tbsp. olive oil
10 whole wheat tortillas
3 avocados
vegan sour cream
toothpicks

1. Heat olive oil in pan. Add pepper, onions, garlic, and poblanos. Cook 4 min. Add corn. Cook 2 more min.

2. Add potatoes and turn off heat. Mash mixture and add salt. Spoon into tortillas. Roll into taquitos, pierce close with toothpick.

3. In a seperate Pan fry with just enough enough oil to cover the pan. Fry both sides until lightly brown.

4. Top with avocado, vegan sour cream.

5. Garnish with red cabbage.

VEGERIA VEGAN TEX-MEX & AMERICAN CUISINE
8407 BROADWAY ST., SAN ANTONIO, TX

Signature Taste of SAN ANTONIO

"I'm a sweet eater. I love lemon pie and sweet potato pie."
Claude Williams

FOCCACCIA SUPREME TURKEY, AVOCADO, SWISS, ALFALFA SPROUTS AND MAYO ON FOCCACCIA BREAD

Signature Tastes of SAN ANTONIO

W. D. Deli is a cafe and catering business in San Antonio, Texas, specializing in soups, salads, and sandwiches. Since 1990, our goal has been to provide our customers with delicious, fresh food in healthy portions at reasonable prices. We take a lot of pride in the fact that we have scores of regular customers who have been enjoying lunch at the deli pretty much since we opened the doors. Come by sometime soon. And if you're not already one of those regulars, let us try to win you over.

8 slices beef bacon (cooked till crisp)
100 ml. homemade mayonnaise
2 tsp. coriander (minced)
2 tsp. parsley (minced)
2 squares Focaccia bread (8 in. each)
10 slices turkey breast
1 tomato (sliced)
½ avocado (sliced)
2 C. Alfalfa sprouts

For Mayonnaise:
2 eggs
2 tsp. lemon juice
2 tsp. Dijon mustard
3 drops hot pepper sauce
1½ C. oil
salt (Optional)

For Focaccia Bread:
1 (1 lb.) loaf frozen bread dough
2 tsp. onion (finely chopped)
1 garlic clove (minced)
2 tsp. olive oil
1 tsp. Italian seasoning

For Sandwich:
1. Combine mayonnaise with cilantro and parsley.
2. Cut each focaccia in half, forming 4 (8x4 inch) rectangles.
3. Spread half the mayonnaise on top of two of the focaccia halves.
4. Layer half the turkey, tomato, bacon, avocado and alfalfa sprouts onto each.
5. On the remaining slices of focaccia spread remaining mayonnaise & close the sandwich. Cut diagonally.

For Mayonnaise:
1. Combine eggs, lemon juice, mustard and hot pepper sauce in a blender.
2. Blend for 5-10 seconds. With the blender still running add oil in very slow stream from the top.
3. Blend until smooth, scraping sides. Season to taste with salt.

For Focaccia:
1. Allow the bread dough to thaw overnight in the refrigerator.
2. Cut dough in half and roll out each half to make an 8" square.
3. If the dough pulls back, let it rest for 15-30 seconds and roll out again.
4. Place the dough in 2 greased 8" square baking pans.
5. Thoroughly pierce dough at 1" intervals with a fork.
6. Sauté onion and garlic in olive oil until browned.
7. Add seasoning and brush the mixture over the dough squares.
8. Let it rise for 10 min.
9. Bake it 400F for 15-18 minutes. Let it cool.

W.D. DELI & BAKERY
3123 BROADWAY ST., SAN ANTONIO, TX

"I don't normally cook, but if I did it probably would be beans, sausage, bacon and eggs. I never really get to eat that to be honest."
Wayne Rooney

POT STICKERS

Wildfish serves only the very best prime seafood and steaks. Our seafood comes from the "top of the catch" right off the docks featuring oysters shucked to order from our oyster bar and Foley seafood prepared to your liking. If you're a steak lover, USDA prime, center-cut steaks are broiled to perfection. From the moment that you walk into Wildfish, you are embraced with the warmth that our team displays with their sincerity, caring, and attentiveness. Wildfish is a restaurant where the atmosphere is exciting, the food is center stage, and the staff is dedicated to every detail.

Signature Tastes of SAN ANTONIO

2 C. cabbage, finely chopped
1 tsp. salt
½ lb. shrimp, peeled, deveined and finely chopped
1 lb. lean pork, ground
2 tbsp. light soy sauce
2 tbsp. rice wine, sherry or 2 tbsp. white wine
1 tbsp. green onion, chopped
1 tbsp. sesame oil
2 tsp. fresh ginger, chopped
2 garlic cloves, minced
64 wonton wrappers (usually 1 pkg)
¼ C. vegetable oil
1 C. chicken stock

Dipping Sauce:
2 tbsp. light soy sauce
1 tbsp. rice vinegar
1 tsp. fresh ginger, minced

1. Sprinkle salt over the shredded cabbage and let stand for 5 minutes, then squeeze out liquid. Squeeze out any liquid from the shrimp. Mix cabbage, shrimp, pork, soy, wine, onion, oil, ginger and garlic (filling can be mixed and refrigerated for up to 6 hours in advance).

2. On each wrapper (keep them covered with a damp cloth so they do no dry out) place about 2 tsp of the mix and seal the edges, use a bit of water on the edge, try to press out all the air and ensure they are tightly sealed (At this point you can freeze them individually on a cookie sheet and them place in a plastic bag.

3. They will keep for a month. Defrost in fridge before continuing).

4. In 2 large skillets heat 1 tbsp oil, fry 16 dumplings for 1 minute or until golden on one side add ¼ cup of stock into the pan, reduce heat to low, cover and cook, without turning for about 7 minutes or until the dumpling is translucent and most of the liquid has evaporated Uncover and on higher heat cook for another 5-7 minutes or until the bottoms are dark brown, drain put on a platter and keep warm.

5. Repeat for the remaining 32 dumplings.

6. Mix the dipping sauce and serve with warm or hot dumplings.

WILDFISH SEAFOOD GRILLE
1834 N LOOP 1604 W, SAN ANTONIO, TX

"One of the very nicest things about life is the way we must regularly stop whatever it is we are doing and devote our attention to eating.
Luciano Pavarotti and William Wright

311

Black-N-Bleu Burger

Signature Taste of SAN ANTONIO

Beginning as a stand-alone burger joint back in 1982 in Houston, Texas, Willie's is still the place people go when they're lookin' to kick back with family and friends and dig in to some down-home Texas fare. Whether you're in the mood for a big juicy Icehouse Burger, our giant hand breaded Chicken Fried Steak, finger lickin' Baby Back Ribs, or some tasty Southern Style Seafood, Willie's is where it's at! Willie's captures the feel of the traditional Texas Icehouse… from a trough packed with iced down Cold Beer, to a menu on a pool table, to the open garage doors on a cool spring day. Add to that some lively music, a sandbox for the kids, and the friendliest service in Texas, and it's plain to see why Willie's is the place for "Great Food and More Fun" for Texans of all ages. With establishments peppering the Lone Star state, Willie's Grill & Icehouse is proud to call itself a Texas original and we look forward to serving Texas families for years to come.

1 lb. 80% lean ground beef
½ (1 oz.) package essential everyday dry Onion Soup Mix
1 tbsp. essential everyday Worcestershire sauce
2 tbsp. freshly cracked black pepper
4 slices cheddar cheese
4 kaiser rolls
4 tbsp. essential everyday blue cheese dressing
lettuce, tomato slices, onion slices

Dipping Sauce:
2 tbsp. light soy sauce
1 tbsp. rice vinegar
1 tsp. fresh ginger, minced

1. In medium bowl, combine ground beef, onion soup mix and Worcestershire sauce; mix well. Form into 4 patties.

2. Place cracked pepper in a shallow dish. Press both sides of burgers into pepper.

3. Prepare grill to medium heat. Place burgers on a grill; grill, turning once, 7-14 minutes or until internal temperature reaches 160°F on an instant read thermometer. Top burgers with cheese slices just before removing from grill.

4. Place burgers on Kaiser rolls and top each burger with 1 tablespoon of blue cheese dressing and lettuce, tomato and onions, if desired.

WILLIE'S GRILL & ICEHOUSE
15801 SAN PEDRO AVE., SAN ANTONIO, TX

"Words do two major things: They provide food for the mind and create light for understanding and awareness."
Jim Rohn

Ahi Poke Bowl

Yard House is the creation of founder and entrepreneur Steele Platt, who came up with the concept shortly after relocating from Denver, Colorado to Southern California in the early 1990s. Platt, along with partners Harald Herrmann and CarlitoJocson, wanted to create a restaurant that would offer one of the largest selections of draft beers, a diverse menu of American fare, and play a heady selection of classic rock music on a state-of-the-art sound system. On December 7, 1996, the flagship Yard House opened along the Long Beach waterfront in Southern California.

2 large sashimi grade ahi tuna steaks (1 ½ lbs.)
1 shallot, sliced
½ C. chopped green onion
3 tbsp. soy sauce
1 tsp. sesame oil
1 tsp. chili garlic sauce
1 tbsp. sesame seeds

1. Pat the Ahi dry, then neatly cut it into small ½ inch cubes. Place in a bowl.Add the shallots, green onion, soy sauce, sesame oil, chili garlic sauce, and sesame seeds.

2. Gently toss. Serve immediately or cover and refrigerate.

Signature Tastes of SAN ANTONIO

15900 La Cantera Parkway, San Antonio, TX

YARD HOUSE

"The tour ends with a huge dinner at a simple restaurant. They eat green cabbage and sausages, and wash them all down with beer and schnapps."
Jens Finke

Youz Guyz restaurant accepts phone orders too. And we take Mastercard, Visa and Discover Card. Our cheese steaks cannot be compared to any other Restaurants. The cheese steaks prepared here have the right quantity of cheese that compliments the meat. We also prepare pizza steaks and Italian hoagies, Italian hot sausage with Peppers and Onions. The best thing about Youz Guyz restaurant is that we provide indoor and outdoor dining facility which is not found in most restaurants located in Texas. So, for that reason and more, If you want to taste the best cheese steaks, just visit Youz Guyz cheese steaks and indulge! Also, Try our Italian Water Ice and direct from Philly TastyKakes

2 tsp. red wine vinegar 1 tbsp. dried oregano 1 tbsp. olive oil 4 hoagie or sub rolls, split horizontally mayonnaise (optional) ¼ lb. prosciutto, thinly sliced ¼ lb. capicola, thinly sliced ¼ lb. mortadella, thinly sliced ¼ lb. sopressata salami, thinly sliced ¼ lb. provolone cheese, thinly sliced 1 large tomato, thinly sliced 1 small onion, thinly sliced ½ green bell pepper, thinly sliced hot pickled peppers (optional) 3 or 4 romaine leaves, shredded	**1.** Place the vinegar and oregano in a small bowl. Slowly whisk in the oil until emulsified. Remove some of the bread from the center of each half of roll. (This is not a necessary step, but it makes room for the meats and cheese.) **2.** Save for future bread crumbs. If desired, lightly spread each half of roll with mayonnaise. Top the bottom halves first with the meats, then the cheese in layers. Top with the tomatoes, onions, green peppers, hot peppers, then the lettuce. **3.** Drizzle with the dressing, as desired. Top with the other half of bun. Serve immediately. YUM!

316 PAT BOOKER RD., UNIVERSAL CITY, TX

YOUZ GUYZ

"I don't like food that's too carefully arranged; it makes me think that the chef is spending too much time arranging and not enough time cooking. If I wanted a picture I'd buy a painting."
Andy Rooney

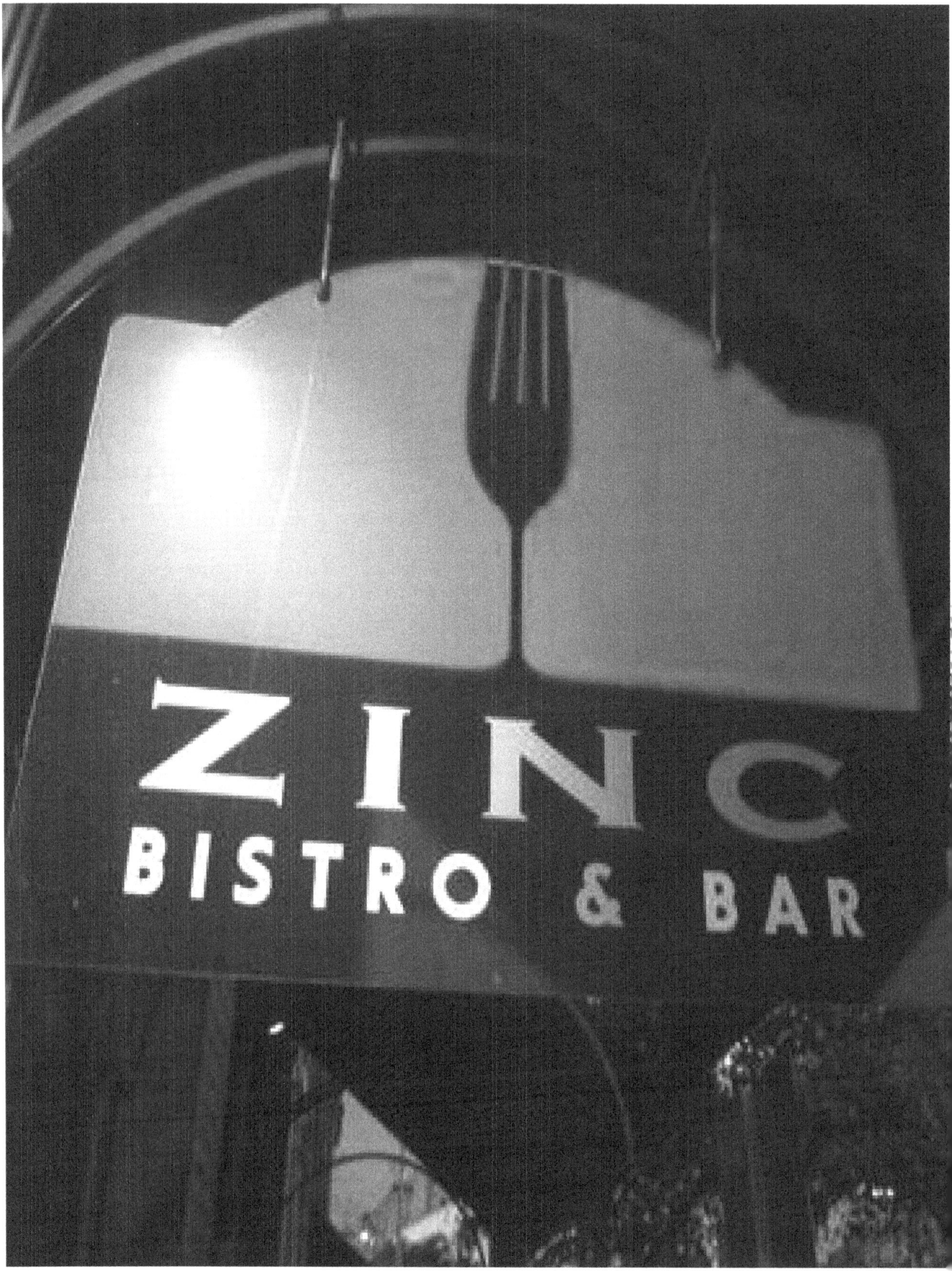
ZINC
BISTRO & BAR

PASTA PORTOFINO

Signature Tastes of SAN ANTONIO

Housed in an historic building more than a century old, Zinc takes its name from the metal popular for bar and table tops in France more than a century ago. Pronounced "zonc" in French, zinc soon became slang for a neighborhood bar. While we want to you think about Zinc for drinks, we don't recommend you get "zoncked" or in a "zonckered" state, terms derived from the French slang for a casual neighborhood spot - like Zinc.

2 tbsp. oil 4 green onions, chopped 1 C. sliced mushrooms (8) ½ lb. shrimp, fresh or frozen and thawed ½ lb. boneless chicken, cut in strips 1 C. snow peas ¼ C. dry white wine ½ C. whipping cream ½ tsp. salt ½ tsp. dried thyme ⅛ tsp. pepper 1 tomato, peeled, seeded and chopped 2 C. uncooked pasta (small shells or rotini) grated parmesan cheese	**1.** In a large frying pan, cook mushrooms and onions in oil over medium heat for 5 minutes. **2.** Add the shrimp and cook until it turns pink about 2-3 minutes. **3.** With a slotted spoon, remove the mixture from the pan and set aside. **4.** Cook the chicken in the same pan for 5 minutes add more oil if there's not enough. **5.** Add the snow peas and let cook 3-4 minutes. **6.** Put the shrimp mixture back into the pan. **7.** Add the wine to the pan and deglaze. **8.** Stir in the cream, salt, thyme, pepper and tomato. **9.** Let sauce simmer for 5 minutes for until it has slightly thickened. **10.** Cook pasta. **11.** Spoon sauce over pasta and top with lots of parmesan.

ZINC CHAMPAGNE & WINE BAR
207 NORTH PRESA STREET, SAN ANTONIO, TX

"Life is a combination of magic and pasta."
Federico Fellini

319

INDEX O' RECIPES

Signature Tastes of SAN ANTONIO

"I should have no objection to go over the same life from its beginning to the end: requesting only the advantage authors have, of correcting in a second edition the faults of the first."
Benjamin Franklin

Steven W. Siler is a firefighter-cum-chef serving in Bellingham, Washington. Long marinated in the epicurean heritage of the Deep South, Steven has spent over 20 years (dear God has it been that long?!) in the much-vaulted restaurant industry from BOH to FOH to chef. In addition, he has served as an editor and contributing writer for several food publications. When not trying to shove food down his fellow firefighters' gullets, he enjoys sailing and sampling the finest of scotches and

wines, and has an irrational love affair with opera. He swears one day he will relive the above picture on the Gulf Coast with a good Will.

The Signature Tastes series of cookbooks is the one of the first of a series of culinary celebrations from Smoke Alarm Media, based in the Pacific Northwest. Smoke Alarm Media is named for another series of unfortunate culinary accidents at an unnamed fire department, also in the Pacific Northwest. One of the founders was an active firefighter. Having been trained as a chef, he found himself in the position of cooking frequently at the fire station. Alas, his culinary skills were somewhat lacking in using the broiler and smoke would soon fill the kitchen and station. The incidents became so frequent that the 911 dispatch would call the station and ask if "Chef Smoke Alarm" would kindly refrain from cooking on his shift. Thus Smoke Alarm Media was born.

SMOKE ALARM MEDIA SERIES

| SIGNATURE TASTES | HIDDEN EATS | TABLE FACTS | BYGONE ERAS | ART OF CULINARY DIPLOMACY | VARSITY | SUBLIME NECTAR |

CPSIA information can be obtained at www.ICGtesting.com
Printed in the USA
LVOW021022011212

309622LV00006B/718/P